The *Imago Dei* as ꞯꞟ...

# Journal of Theological Interpretation Supplements

MURRAY RAE

University of Otago, New Zealand

Editor-in-Chief

1. Thomas Holsinger-Friesen, *Irenaeus and Genesis: A Study of Competition in Early Christian Hermeneutics*
2. Douglas S. Earl, *Reading Joshua as Christian Scripture*
3. Joshua N. Moon, *Jeremiah's New Covenant: An Augustinian Reading*
4. Csilla Saysell, *"According to the Law": Reading Ezra 9–10 as Christian Scripture*
5. Joshua Marshall Strahan, *The Limits of a Text: Luke 23:34a as a Case Study in Theological Interpretation*
6. Seth B. Tarrer, *Reading with the Faithful: Interpretation of True and False Prophecy in the Book of Jeremiah from Ancient Times to Modern*
7. Zoltán S. Schwáb, *Toward an Interpretation of the Book of Proverbs: Selfishness and Secularity Reconsidered*
8. Steven Joe Koskie, Jr., *Reading the Way to Heaven: A Wesleyan Theological Hermeneutic of Scripture*
9. Hubert James Keener, *A Canonical Exegesis of the Eighth Psalm: Yhwh's Maintenance of the Created Order through Divine Intervention*
10. Vincent K. H. Ooi, *Scripture and Its Readers: Readings of Israel's Story in Nehemiah 9, Ezekiel 20, and Acts 7*
11. Andrea D. Saner, *"Too Much to Grasp": Exodus 3:13–15 and the Reality of God*
12. Jonathan Douglas Hicks, *Trinity, Economy, and Scripture: Recovering Didymus the Blind*
13. Dru Johnson, *Knowledge by Ritual: A Biblical Prolegomenon to Sacramental Theology*
14. Ryan S. Peterson, *The* Imago Dei *as Human Identity: A Theological Interpretation*
15. Ron Haydon, *"Seventy Sevens Are Decreed": A Canonical Approach to Daniel 9:24–27*

# The *Imago Dei* as Human Identity

## A Theological Interpretation

RYAN S. PETERSON

Winona Lake, Indiana
EISENBRAUNS
2016

Printed in the United States of America

www.eisenbrauns.com

**Library of Congress Cataloging-in-Publication Data**

Names: Peterson, Ryan S.
Title: The Imago Dei as human identity : a theological interpretation / Ryan S.
   Peterson.
Description: Winona Lake, Indiana : Eisenbrauns, 2016. | Series: Journal
   of theological interpretation supplements ; 14 | Includes bibliographical
   references and index. | Description based on print version record and CIP
   data provided by publisher; resource not viewed.
Identifiers: LCCN 2015043624 (print) | LCCN 2015042031 (ebook) | ISBN
   9781575064345 (pdf) | ISBN 9781575064338 (pbk. : alk. paper)
Subjects: LCSH: Image of God. | Identity (Psychology)—Religious
   aspects—Christianity. | Identification (Religion) | Theological
   anthropology—Christianity.
Classification: LCC BT103 (print) | LCC BT103 .P47 2016 (ebook) | DDC
   233/.5—dc23
LC record available at http://lccn.loc.gov/2015043624

*For Christy,*

*imitator of God's mercy, comfort, patience, and justice*

# Table of Contents

# Acknowledgments

I am grateful to many people who, in various ways, aided the completion of this project. Specifically, many thanks are due to Michael Allen, Aaron James, and Adam Johnson for their friendship and theological camaraderie as I wrote and revised this book. My work has been energized by many joyful and fruitful conversations with each of them.

Special thanks are also due to my dissertation supervisor, Henri Blocher, second reader, Daniel Treier, and external examiner, Matthew Levering, for their wise advice and consistent encouragement when this thesis was first developed. Their generosity is greatly appreciated.

Throughout the course of my doctoral studies at Wheaton College, Timothy Larsen was a wonderful exemplar of Christian scholarship as I worked as his teaching assistant. John Walton has illustrated a compelling vision of the same, stretching all the way back to my undergraduate education. They have shaped my own conception of Christian academic work, and for this I am very grateful.

Thanks are also due to John Simons, my teaching assistant at Talbot School of Theology, who compiled the indexes.

I have many familial debts of gratitude also. I wish to thank my parents, Richard and Donna Peterson, for their continual encouragement and excitement regarding my academic work.

As I worked on this book, Christy and I have, with great joy, come to be parents of four wonderful children, Mercy, Comfort, Patience, and Justice. They deserve many thanks for their patience with my hours away working on this project and for the joy they have brought to Christy and me. I am filled with thanksgiving at all times for their presence in our life.

Most of all, I thank my wife, Christy, for her unwavering love shown in self-sacrificial support. I am proud to be her husband and thankful to have her as my wife. I love her dearly, and the book is dedicated to her.

Ultimately, whatever is good in this work belongs to the triune God. I hope it is a suitable offering of praise to God the Father, God the Son, and God the Holy Spirit and a service to the church.

Material previously published in "Genesis 1" in *Theological Commentary: Evangelical Perspectives* (ed. R. Michael Allen; New York: T&T Clark, 2011), 10-24, is used by permission of Bloomsbury Publishing Plc. and R. Michael Allen. I am grateful for these permissions.

# List of Abbreviations

| | |
|---|---|
| AB | Anchor Bible |
| ANF | Ante-Nicene Fathers |
| AOTC | Abingdon Old Testament Commentaries |
| ATR | *Anglican Theological Review* |
| AugStud | *Augustinian Studies* |
| BJRL | Bulletin of the John Rylands University Library of Manchester |
| BTCB | Brazos Theological Commentary on the Bible |
| ConBOT | Coniectanea Biblica: Old Testament Series |
| CC | Continental Commentaries |
| CCR | Cambridge Companions to Religion |
| CCT | Challenges in Contemporary Theology |
| CCTheo | Contours of Christian Theology |
| CGTC | Cambridge Greek Testament Commentary |
| CHANE | Culture and History of the Ancient Near East |
| CIT | Current Issues in Theology |
| CO | Christian Origins |
| CSCD | Cambridge Studies in Christian Doctrine |
| ESCT | Edinburgh Studies in Constructive Theology |
| FaithPhil | *Faith and Philosophy* |
| HTR | *Harvard Theological Review* |
| IBC | Interpretation: A Bible Commentary for Teaching and Preaching |
| ICC | International Critical Commentary |
| IJST | *International Journal of Systematic Theology* |
| JECS | *Journal of Early Christian Studies* |
| JETS | *Journal of the Evangelical Theological Society* |
| JR | *Journal of Religion* |
| JSOTSup | Journal for the Study of the Old Testament: Supplement Series |
| JTI | *Journal of Theological Interpretation* |
| JTS | *Journal of Theological Studies* |
| LCC | Library of Christian Classics, Philadelphia, 1953– |

| | |
|---|---|
| LCL | Loeb Classical Library |
| LTT | Library of Theological Translations |
| LW | *Luther's Works* |
| MBT | Münsterisch Beiträge zur Theologie |
| ModTheo | *Modern Theology* |
| MLBS | Mercer Library of Biblical Studies |
| NCBC | New Cambridge Bible Commentary |
| NICNT | New International Commentary on the New Testament |
| NIGTC | New International Greek Testament Commentary |
| NIVAC | NIV Application Commentary |
| NPNF[2] | Nicene and Post-Nicene Fathers, Series 2 |
| NSBT | New Studies in Biblical Theology |
| NTL | New Testament Library |
| NZST | *Neue Zeitschrift für Systematische und Theologie* |
| OBT | Overtures to Biblical Theology |
| OHRT | Oxford Handbooks in Religion and Theology |
| OTL | Old Testament Library |
| OTM | Oxford Theological Monographs |
| OTS | Old Testament Studies |
| PL | Patrologia latina [Patrologiae cursus completes: Series latina]. Edited by J.-P. Migne. 217 vols. Paris, 1844–1864 |
| PNTC | Pillar New Testament Commentary |
| ProEccl | *Pro Ecclesia* |
| PTM | Princeton Theological Monograph Series |
| RECM | Routledge Early Church Monographs |
| SacD | Sacra Doctrina: Christian Theology for a Postmodern Age |
| SD | Studies in Dogmatics |
| SJT | *Scottish Journal of Theology* |
| SMRT | Studies in Medieval and Reformation Thought |
| SNTM | Society for New Testament Monograph Series |
| SST | T & T Clark Studies in Systematic Theology |
| ST | Studies and Texts |
| SVTQ | *St. Vladimir's Theological Quarterly* |
| Tg. Onq. | *Targum Onqelos* |
| TH | Théologie historique |

| | |
|---|---|
| *TheorSoc* | *Theory and Society* |
| *Thomist* | *The Thomist: A Speculative Quarterly Review* |
| TS | *Theological Studies* |
| TJ | *Trinity Journal* |
| TW | Theologische Wissenschaft |
| *TynBul* | *Tyndale Bulletin* |
| UCOP | University of Cambridge Oriental Publications |
| WBC | Word Biblical Commentary |
| WSA | Works of Saint Augustine |
| *WTJ* | *Westminster Theological Journal* |

# Chapter 1

# Seeking a Theology of the *Imago Dei*

The *imago Dei* is humanity's identity, and this identity is basic to all human existence. God created humanity to establish an earthly image of God in the world. Humanity is thereby bound to God and God's purposes for creation. The material content of humanity's identity—what it means to image God in the world—is revealed through God's creational and covenantal action. Understanding the meaning of the *imago Dei*, therefore, demands that we have knowledge of God's identity and character. We must know who God is and what God is like.

The catholic Christian tradition has relied upon the OT and NT Scriptures to provide a coherent account of God's triune identity since the Scriptures reveal and interpret God's creational and covenantal acts. The divine economy bears witness to God's particular interest in humanity and to humanity's dependence upon God for its identity, being, and *telos*. God's interest in the realization of human identity culminates in the incarnation. Jesus Christ, being fully divine and fully human, is God's image in the world, revealing the identity and character of God. Rather than bringing a new intention into existence, Jesus Christ brings to fruition God's permanent intention for humanity. Jesus Christ also establishes the conditions for others to join him in the fulfillment of their human identity. Others join Jesus Christ in the realization of human identity by coming into union with Jesus Christ by the power of the Holy Spirit. Insofar as people are conformed to Jesus Christ through knowing, loving, and walking with God, we serve as earthly images of God, proclaiming the reality and character of God in the world.

To understate the matter, not everyone agrees that the *imago Dei* should be interpreted as I have just sketched it. There is agreement among scholars that Genesis 1 indicates that human existence is somehow modeled after God. However, there are many ways this modeling has been construed. The image has been taken to refer to the human soul (since God is spiritual), the human mind (since God is rational), the human body (since ancient Near Eastern people thought that the gods had physical forms), human dominion (since God rules all things), human relations (since God, being triune, is eternally relational), human virtue (since God is good), and human existence (since God is). The general strategy has been to look for some particular human attribute that matches analogously a divine attribute.

Because several analogies can potentially connect God's life with human life, theologians have often turned to a second comparative approach to determine which of these possibilities correlates best to the meaning of the image of God. This second comparison is between humans and animals. How does humanity compare to other earthly creatures? What is unique about us? If a unique human attribute can be determined, then there may be good reason to think that this unique attribute is the image of God.

These two comparative strategies have led theologians to define the image of God in terms of one human attribute over against others, such that the link between God and humanity is located in only one aspect of human nature. Generally, the comparison of God with humans has yielded the conclusion that the image of God is something spiritual (since God is spirit) and the comparison of humans with animals has yielded the conclusion that the image of God is rationality (since animals are irrational). However, Genesis 1:26-28 does not appear to limit the *imago Dei* to one aspect of humanity. Rather, in Genesis 1:26, God determines that an image of God will be created and the human creature, as a whole, is the result. We are told three things about the human creature: (1) Humanity is made in the image of God; (2) Humanity is intended to rule over other earthly creatures; (3) Humanity is made male and female. There is no suggestion in the text that leads us to separate humans into "spiritual" and "animal" parts or to limit the image of God to one human attribute. What if we forsake these kinds of comparative approaches? Is there another way forward?

One holistic suggestion has been to define the image of God as human dominion over creation. For example, J. Richard Middleton offers an interpretation of the image of God that involves the whole human person in representative rule over creation. Middleton rightly observes that it is appropriate for humans to rule the other earthly creatures because humans are God's creaturely image. God is the Ruler of all things, so God's earthly image is an earthly ruler. Middleton concludes that "[h]uman vocation is modeled on the nature and actions of the God portrayed in Genesis 1."[1] So, human rule should also be representational: human rule should look like divine rule. Humans are made in the image of a generous God and ought to replicate God's generosity analogously within creation.[2]

Middleton's broader argument is persuasive when it comes to detailed exegesis of Genesis 1 as a whole. However, Christian readers who look for coherence across the biblical canon often find this interpretation wanting due to its inability to explain the New Testament texts that refer to the image. Referring to seven New Testament texts that bind together the image of God and salvific

---

[1] J. Richard Middleton, *The Liberating Image: The* Imago Dei *in Genesis 1* (Grand Rapids: Brazos, 2005), 60.

[2] Ibid., 235-297.

renewal, Middleton himself states, "These texts speak of the church's (ethical) imitation of or (eschatological) conformity to Christ."[3] Because these texts do not speak of creation but recreation, Middleton takes them to be referring to something other than the meaning of the image of God in Genesis 1. But what if there is a deeper theological connection between the ethical imitation of Christ described in the New Testament and the claim in Genesis that humanity is made in God's image? Is there a way of interpreting the image of God that accommodates both Genesis 1 and these New Testament texts?

I believe such an interpretation is possible. This book provides the exegetical and theological resources needed to support the thesis that the *imago Dei* is best understood as human identity.[4] The meaning of "identity" will be explored more fully in chapter 3, but I will briefly indicate its usefulness here. Charles Taylor, in *Sources of the Self*, observes that there is an "essential link between identity and a kind of orientation. To know who you are is to be oriented in moral space, a space in which questions arise about what is good or bad, what is worth doing and what not, what has meaning and importance for you and what is trivial or secondary."[5] Taylor inquires, "Why this link between identity and orientation?"[6] He notes the following connection:

> [T]o be able to answer for oneself is to know where one stands. . . . And that is why we naturally tend to talk of our fundamental orientation in terms of who we are. To lose this orientation, or not to have found it, is not to know who one is. And this orientation, once attained, defines where you answer from, hence your identity.[7]

My claim is that every human person's identity is determined by the reality described in Genesis 1:26-28: a human knows who she is and how she is oriented within creation when she recognizes that she is made in God's image. Of course, each person has many secondary and tertiary aspects to her identity that give shape to the particularities of her life and its distinction from another person's life.[8] But everyone's "fundamental orientation" is established in the fact that they are made by God to represent God in the world. This reality provides the context for understanding the Christological fulfillment of

---

[3] Ibid., 17.

[4] The burden of my argument in this book is to show that interpreting the *imago Dei* as human identity is both exegetically and theologically compelling. An extensive exploration of the Christological fulfillment of humanity's divinely determined identity will have to be taken up in another context.

[5] Charles Taylor, *Sources of the Self: The Making of the Modern Identity* (Cambridge, Mass.: Harvard University Press, 1989), 28.

[6] Ibid., 28.

[7] Ibid., 29. I only wish to draw upon Taylor's description of the link between identity and orientation here. My use of the term "identity" differs from his.

[8] In the literature on human identity, there is debate about whether a person has multiple aspects of one identity or multiple identities. It is not necessary to enter this debate here so long as it is understood that by referring to the *imago Dei* I am referring to what is most fundamental to every human's existence.

human identity and the ethical implications of the *imago Dei* as they are described in both the OT and NT.

Genesis 1 teaches the reader how to identify properly God and God's creatures. אֱלֹהִים, God, is the Creator and Lord of the heavens and the earth. Every creature owes to God its existence, its particular place in creation, and its *telos*. God is the Creator and Lord of time and the rhythms of life, water and weather, land and agricultural production, the mobile creatures in the heavens, the sky, the seas, and on the land. Humanity is singled out as a land creature made for a particular purpose—to be God's image on the earth.

God's people are intended to interpret the world accordingly—to worship God alone, to live within the rhythms of life and time as God has established them, to trust God to provide through weather and agriculture, to interpret the sun, moon, and stars as creatures under authority so that the days, seasons, and years of creation are understood as God's determination, to discern the appropriate locations and contexts in which the mobile creatures of the sky, seas, and land should thrive and flourish, and to identify themselves as creatures set apart for the particular task of representing God on the earth. "Human identity" indicates our place within creation before God.

Interpreting the image of God as human identity resolves four tensions that exist in contemporary theological studies of this topic. First, the identity interpretation can accommodate the best exegetical insights on the meaning of Genesis 1 in OT studies. Often, explicitly constructive theological interpretations of the image of God are seen as exegetically problematic by OT scholars. Second, for interpreters with theological interests, the identity interpretation enables a canonical reading of the image of God that incorporates the entirety of the Scriptures. I am unsatisfied with a reading of the image of God that puts the OT and NT texts at odds. I will show how these are coherent. Third, the identity interpretation can accommodate the best insights about the image of God from the Christian tradition. Often, the various interpretations found in the tradition are pitted against each other as opposing views. I want to reclaim a number of important insights from the Christian tradition, showing how they are cooperative with the identity interpretation. Fourth, I suggest that the identity interpretation provides a compelling basis for addressing ethical questions, especially in those cases where other views of the image of God seem to run into conceptual difficulties. Much of the interest in the *imago Dei* has related to ethics, and certain interpretations that attach the *imago Dei* to a particular capacity seem to imply that human beings who do not share that capacity are not made in God's image. I suggest that the identity interpretation provides the conceptual framework needed to show how all humans are made in God's image, even though some humans are unable to exercise capacities that are directed toward the realization of the *imago Dei*.

In what follows, therefore, I will offer a theological interpretation of Gen 1:26–28 wherein I show what it means for the *imago Dei* to be human identity, a dogmatic account of the coherence of this interpretation, and an explanation of the reasons this interpretation is compelling from a canonical perspective.

This first chapter will provide: first, an initial analysis of some of the important recent treatments of this topic; second, a rationale for this study in the context of current biblical and theological scholarship; third, an explanation of the theological method that will be used; fourth, a brief outline of the following five chapters.

# 1. The Contours of Recent Interpretations

There is a long and well-known history of reflection on the meaning of the *imago Dei*. There is no need to recount that history here, but it is important to summarize a number of recent interpretations that provide the immediate context for my argument.[9]

Two important articles published in the *Tyndale Bulletin* serve as indicators of the need for this project: David Clines's 1967 Old Testament Lecture, "The Image of God in Man" and Gerald Bray's 1991 article, "The Significance of God's Image in Man."[10] Both of these articles include well-researched analyses of the biblical texts that mention the image of God, Clines for the OT texts and Bray for the NT texts. Both also include research into relevant backgrounds, Clines interacting with ancient Near Eastern literature and Bray with intertestamental Judaism. Nevertheless, the ultimate conclusions offered by Clines and Bray are odd in light of their detailed exegesis. The discontinuity between the implications of careful biblical research and the final conclusions drawn by these scholars leads one to ask whether a fuller theological synthesis of the biblical material is required. To demonstrate the force of this question, it is helpful to engage Clines's and Bray's essays here.

## 1.1. David J. A. Clines

The method of interpretation employed by Clines in his 1967 lecture is important. Clines works from the assumption that the historical method of modern OT studies should be used to correct pre-modern, dogmatic treatments of the *imago Dei*. Clines's criterion for demonstrating any success in this endeavor involves understanding what the human author of Genesis 1 intended when he wrote the text in question.[11] Philosophical and religious reflections

---

[9] For the history of interpretation, see, e.g., Karl Barth, *Church Dogmatics* III/1 (ed. G. W. Bromiley and T. F. Torrance, trans. J. W. Edwards, O. Bussey and Harold Knight; Edinburgh: T & T Clark, 1958), 183–196; David J. A. Clines, "The Image of God in Man," *TynBul* 19 (1968), 53–103; Stanley Grenz, *The Social God and the Relational Self: A Trinitarian Theology of the Imago Dei* (Louisville: Westminster John Knox, 2001), 141–222; Gunnlaugur A. Jónsson, *The Image of God: Genesis 1:26-28 in a Century of Old Testament Research* (trans. Lorraine Svendsen, rev. Michael Cheney; ConBOT 26; Stockholm, Sweden: Almqvist and Wiksell, 1988).

[10] David J. A. Clines, "The Image of God in Man," *TynBul* 19 (1968), 53–103; Gerald Bray, "The Significance of God's Image in Man," *TynBul* 42 (1991): 195–225.

[11] Clines, "The Image of God in Man," 54.

are deemed unhelpful, as are biblical indications of any likenesses between humans and God from outside of Genesis 1.

Clines's rationale appears to be that philosophy, religion, and even subsequent biblical reflection hinders the exegete in his task, especially in the case of the *imago Dei* since the history of interpretation shows an insistent impulse to import foreign anthropologies that misconstrue the meaning of the text.[12] Clines speaks of Genesis 1 as divine revelation, but the biblical text exists as divine revelation just as, and only as, the author of Genesis 1 could have understood its meaning. There is no room for what Kevin Vanhoozer, appropriating Clifford Geertz, has called "thick" description, namely, that the human author's intention must continue to have an important role in biblical interpretation but that the concurrent divine authorship of the biblical text entails that theological interpretations must be allowed to function at levels that transcend the human author's intentions.[13] Clines seeks to locate the meaning of Genesis 1 solely in the intention of its *human* author.

Regarding Clines's conclusions, his initial observation is quite simple: "One essential meaning of the statement that man was created 'in the image of God' is plain: it is that man is in some way and in some degree like God."[14] Clines then seeks to determine in what way and to what degree this is the case. He dismisses the traditional interpretation of the image, which "locates the image in some spiritual quality or faculty of the human person," because it overlooks the biblical view that a human being is a unity rather than a collection of disparate parts.[15] Clines considers the strengths of Gunkel's interpretation that the body is the image of God, but rejects Gunkel's argument that behind Gen 1:26–28 was an ancient Israelite belief in a physical deity. On the basis of his analysis of the ancient Near Eastern backgrounds, Clines concludes that humanity is God's "visible corporeal representative of the invisible, bodiless God."[16] The term "representative" is important here, because humanity is not a physical representation of God. Nor should the image be understood on-

---

[12] A pair of quotes from Karl Barth are used by several authors in support of this conclusion: "We might easily discuss which of these and the many other similar explanations is the finest or deepest or most serious. What we cannot discuss is which of them is the true explanation of Gen 1:26f" (*CD* III/1, 193); "Is it not astonishing that again and again expositors have ignored the definitive explanation given by the text itself, and instead of reflecting on it pursued all kinds of arbitrarily invented interpretations of the *imago Dei*?" (*CD* III/1, 195). As Nathan MacDonald has recently pointed out, Barth is misinterpreted if on the basis of these statements one concludes that he supports the methodology of modern OT scholarship ("The *Imago Dei* and Election: Reading Genesis 1:26–28 and Old Testament Scholarship with Karl Barth," *IJST* 10 [2008]: 303–27).

[13] Kevin Vanhoozer, *Is There a Meaning in this Text?: The Bible, the Reader, and the Morality of Literary Knowledge* (Grand Rapids: Zondervan, 1998), 201–80; Clifford Geertz, *The Interpretation of Cultures* (Scranton, Penn.: Basic, 1977), esp. 3–32.

[14] Clines, "The Image of God in Man," 53.

[15] Clines cites Eichrodt in support, *Theology of the Old Testament*, 2:529 n. 1.

[16] Ibid., 101.

tologically, but rather existentially: "It comes to expression not in the nature of man so much as in his activity and function."[17] In particular, the function of humanity as a whole, as well as individual humans, is to represent "God's lordship to the lower orders of creation."[18]

Clines's conclusion to this point is thoroughly consistent with his method, and this interpretation is popular today among OT scholars. What is odd, however, is the lecture's final section. In the end, Clines cannot resist providing a reading of the NT references to the *imago Dei*. In the NT, Clines finds that the image of God is Christ, the last Adam. The recapitulation of humanity in Christ is the establishment of a new humanity with an eschatological hope. "The protological doctrine of the image, which retains its existential implications, has become transformed in the New Testament into an eschatological doctrine itself with existential implications."[19] The image of God is fulfilled in Christ and realized in other humans through obedience to Christ. "Man is God's representative on earth; Christ in a *sensus plenior* is God's 'one' representative on earth and the community of believers becomes the dwelling-place of God on earth."[20] The reason these claims are odd is not that they are unfounded—quite the contrary. They are odd because Clines has definitively left behind his interpretive methodology at this point without acknowledging the implications this should have for his reading of the OT. Surprisingly, in the end, Clines's interpretation finds agreement with Martin Luther about the existential and eschatological understanding of the *imago Dei* when interpreted canonically.[21] Yet, throughout the essay Clines uses Luther's interpretation as a foil.[22] Moreover, Clines interprets the NT as suggesting a progressive realization of the image of God in humans through Christ. Rather than the image of God being settled in Genesis 1, then, the image of God is only fully realized in and through Christ. Clines's earlier conclusions appear to be contradicted by his NT interpretation. Only when Genesis 1 is separated from the rest of the canon do Clines's OT arguments find their place.

In the process of drawing his conclusions, Clines fails to consider three important questions: First, is it possible that the NT authors' use of the *imago Dei* with reference to Christ is fitting because they were faithfully interpreting Genesis 1—without restricting themselves to the thought of the original human author of the text? If so, then why does Clines cling so tightly to his methodology when interpreting Genesis 1? If not, then how can Clines accept the NT use of the text? Second, if Christ is God's true representative on earth, then it appears that there has been a significant change in the meaning of the

---

[17] Ibid., 101.

[18] Ibid.

[19] Ibid., 103.

[20] Ibid.

[21] Martin Luther's interpretation of the image of God will be considered in chapter 6.

[22] Clines does not always name Luther directly, but he regularly refers to the view that the image has been lost after humanity's fall into sin.

*imago Dei* from its use in Genesis 1 to its use in the NT texts at least with respect to what what it means to be God's representative. Is this change a development of Genesis 1 or a contradiction of it? Third, are there any links or developments in the theology of the OT that bridge the horizons of Genesis 1 and the NT? Partly because these questions go unanswered, Clines's otherwise helpful article is unsatisfying. While these questions are often overlooked in studies of the *imago Dei*, they appear to be crucial to discovering what the implications of the *imago Dei* may be, and whether the OT and NT definitions of the *imago Dei* are compatible.

### 1.2. Gerald Bray

Bray calls into question Clines's methodological separation of Genesis 1 from the rest of the canon. He also seeks to correct Clines's "radical repudiation of theological tradition" and his generous acceptance of ancient Near Eastern influences.[23] In place of Clines's approach, Bray intentionally focuses his energy on the NT texts and their implications. This canonical approach is intended to yield a "new reconstruction of the doctrine."[24] Bray also considers the contribution of intertestamental Judaism.

Bray begins his argument by summarizing the current state of exegesis. He dismisses the physical interpretation since the philological evidence demonstrates the possibility that צֶלֶם, image, should be understood metaphorically, and there are theological reasons to doubt the physical view. The view that humanity is set up as a sign of God's dominion is likewise bypassed because "it would mean that every single human being was an image representing the rule of God. While this is not completely impossible, it hardly sits well with the concept of a Chosen People who were called to fulfil the Law of God in a special way and therefore it is most improbable that it could be the work of P."[25] Bray recognizes that there is a relationship between the image and human dominion, although he understands it as an attribute of the image rather than constitutive of its essence. Bray's reference to P as a basis for his rejection of the dominion view is vitiated by his doubts about P's very existence as the author of Genesis 1! There is no further rationale given for why every human being could not be thought of as a representative of God's rule.

Much like Clines with the ancient Near Eastern material, Bray surveys the intertestamental material. Unlike Clines, however, Bray finds these extra-biblical documents to be the source of much unhelpful speculation—speculation that would lead the early church astray in their interpretations of the image of God. Bray sees the interpretations offered by the intertestamental literature as significant but ultimately unfounded, because these interpretations, and the early church interpretations following them, fall prey to the misguided assumption that Adam had moral awareness and was immortal.

---

[23] Bray, "The Significance of God's Image in Man," 195.
[24] Ibid., 195.
[25] Ibid., 197.

Since Bray finds neither of these qualities in Genesis 1–2, he argues along Irenaean lines that "the image was originally designed to progress from glory to
glory, as man got progressively nearer to God."[26] On the basis of his analysis of
the NT texts, he concludes that the image "is some permanent and unchanging
resemblance to God in man, whereas the *doxa* comes and goes according to
man's obedience to God's commands."[27] Bray whittles the relevant passages
down to 1 Cor 11:7 and Jas 3:9, and since both of these passages have to do with
relationships on Bray's reading, he presses further and suggests that the image
of God is that which makes a human a person capable of having relationships,
"the thing which defines man as a 'who', not as a 'what'."[28] Bray contrasts his
view with Barth's, asserting that relationships are a consequence of the image
rather than essential to it.[29] To summarize Bray's conclusions, then, dominion
and relationship are consequences of human personhood, and the physical
body is incidental to understanding the image. The *imago Dei* is an ontological
reality that makes human creatures to be persons; that humans are persons
also makes them responsible before God for their behavior. So, for Bray, the
image of God is the basis for the particular relationship that humans have with
God—a personal, accountable relationship.

Understanding the *imago Dei* as an ontological reality that is permanent
and unchanging, as Bray describes it, however, seems to contradict his claim
that the *imago Dei* was meant to progress from glory to glory as humanity pro-
gressed in nearness to God. It may be the case that Bray intends to include two
distinct aspects of human experience in his interpretation: first, that humans
experience the world as persons who remain identical to themselves throughout their lifetime; second, that persons develop over time. The first claim, in
this case, would be about one's personal identity and the ontological basis of it.
The second claim would be a claim about personal transformation that occurs
over the period of one's life. Even if this were his intention, Bray does not explain how these two aspects of human experience are related to one another.
Furthermore, Bray's conclusion seems to be quite separate from Genesis 1 and
the NT references he seeks to interpret. Personhood as the meaning of the
*imago Dei* arrives seemingly out of nowhere. Bray himself notes that the "Christian understanding of the person is built out of many elements, of which the
image of God is only one."[30] Why, then, should the image of God be interpreted
*as* personhood?

Clines's and Bray's articles are helpful for framing the current discussion
for four reasons. First, Clines's conclusion based upon Genesis 1 alone is

---

[26] Ibid., 208.

[27] Ibid., 220.

[28] Ibid., 222.

[29] Bray misrepresents Barth's view here. Barth's interpretation is Christological rather
than merely expressive of human relationships. Barth's interpretation will be addressed in chapter 2.

[30] Ibid., 222.

representative of the thrust of modern OT research on the *imago Dei*. Second, Bray's conclusion that the *imago Dei* should be understood as human person-hood has become popular among systematic theologians. Third, in both arti-cles lexical evidence carries a great part of the exegetical burden, a methodol-ogy that is common in biblical studies of the image. Fourth, at the end of both articles, the authors ultimately supplant the conclusions drawn on the basis of the lexical evidence in favor of conclusions they find more theologically con-vincing. This suggests that a different manner of theological reading may be required to arrive at an understanding of the *imago Dei* that is simultaneously theologically satisfying, exegetically faithful, and canonically formed. It is im-portant now to analyze four additional recent contributions to interpretation of the *imago Dei* in order to situate my argument on this point more fully.

### 1.3. Colin Gunton

Like Bray, Colin Gunton argues for an understanding of the *imago Dei* as personhood, but does so on the basis of the divine intra-Trinitarian relations. Gunton sees the strengths of the functional interpretation but concludes, "Such a theology is, however, too literalistic and too restricted, especially in light of the New Testament re-orienting of the doctrine to Christ."[31] Gunton also considers Barth's relational interpretation, but critiques it on the basis of a perceived binitarian tendency to understand the divine Father-Son relation to be reflected in the human male-female one. Moreover, Gunton argues that Barth neglected the importance of humanity for non-human creation and its relation to God. Moving beyond Barth, then, Gunton argues that the image of God should be understood as human personhood constituted by human rela-tions with God, other human persons, and non-human creation. "If God is a communion of persons inseparably related, then surely Barth is thus far cor-rect in saying that it is in our relatedness to others that our being human ex-ists."[32] Identifying the human person in relation as the *imago Dei*, Gunton ar-gues, relativizes the problematic dualisms in theological anthropology, such as the spiritual/physical or mind/body dualisms. Gunton emphasizes the need for particularity and community through a conception of otherness and rela-tion. The freedom to be other and yet to stand in intimate communion is a created metaphor of God's intra-Trinitarian life. Furthermore, this being-in-relation "is not a static possession, but comes to be realized in the various rela-tionships in which human life is set."[33] The paradigmatic pattern is the life of Christ: "Imaging is therefore a triune act: the Son images the Father as through the Spirit he realizes a particular pattern of life on earth."[34]

---

[31] Colin Gunton, *The Promise of Trinitarian Theology* (Edinburgh: T&T Clark, 1991), 115.

[32] Ibid., 116.

[33] Ibid., 119.

[34] Colin Gunton, *Christ and Creation: The Didsbury Lectures, 1990* (Carlisle: Paternoster, 1992), 101.

The strengths of Gunton's argument are threefold. First, Gunton identifies the whole human person as the *imago Dei*, thereby avoiding the pitfalls of identifying one aspect of humanity as the image to the neglect of the others. Second, Gunton's interpretation is theological in that he looks to God *in se* as the guide for his constructive understanding of the image. Third, not only does his concept of personhood hold together the important categories of otherness and relation, but it also holds together identity and transformation. Gunton does not develop this aspect of his view at length, but he acknowledges its promise for theological anthropology. The relationship between identity and transformation is important for my argument in chapters 3 and 4.

The first weakness of Gunton's interpretation is that it is exegetically problematic. Gunton explicitly modifies Barth's relational interpretation, but he does not consider the exegetical questions that have been raised against Barth's view.[35] Second, the concept of persons in relation, as Gunton develops it, may be based on an illegitimate analogy between the intra-Trinitarian relations of the divine Persons and created relations between human persons.[36] Third, it is not clear that defining human being as ontologically constituted by relations is cogent.[37]

### 1.4. Francis Watson

In his 1994 monograph *Text, Church and World*, Francis Watson followed a relational interpretation of the *imago Dei* similar to Gunton's. He was heavily influenced by Alistair McFadyen's *Call to Personhood* in the formulation of his view and its implications.[38] But in 1997, in *Text and Truth*, Watson is able to say, "Although I accepted this view in *Text, Church and World* . . . , I am no longer convinced of either its exegetical basis or its theological value."[39] In *Text and Truth*, then, he provides a detailed Christological interpretation of the *imago Dei*. He attempts to justify and draw out the implications of a pivotal claim: "In Jesus as the image of God we learn what it is to be human."[40] Jesus Christ is the divine and human image of God. In the incarnation, God the Son brings

---

[35] MacDonald, "The *Imago Dei* and Election," 306.

[36] For a helpful argument against this identification, see Oliver Crisp, "Problems with Perichoresis," *TynBul* 56 (2005): 119–40.

[37] See Richard Fermer, "The Limits of Trinitarian Theology as a Methodological Paradigm," *NZST* 41 (1999): 158–86; and Harriet Harris, "Should We Say that Personhood is Relational?" *SJT* 51 (1998): 214–34.

[38] Francis Watson, *Text, Church and World: Biblical Interpretation in Theological Perspective* (Grand Rapids: Eerdmans, 1994), 107–8, 149–51). See Alistair McFadyen, *The Call to Personhood: A Christian Theory of the Individual in Social Relationships* (Cambridge University Press, 1990).

[39] Francis Watson, *Text and Truth: Redefining Biblical Theology* (Grand Rapids: Eerdmans, 1997), 304 n. 26. He counters Jürgen Moltmann's interpretation specifically; see Moltmann *God in Creation: An Ecological Doctrine of Creation* (London: SCM, 1985), 223. My interpretation has gone through a similar transformation.

[40] Watson, *Text and Truth*, 288. This claim is repeated throughout Watson's study.

humanity into God, and it is this action which gives humanity its unique identity. Human identity as the image of God, in fact, must be understood to be constituted by Jesus, and only then applied to humanity in general. "If [Jesus] is indeed the paradigmatic case of the human likeness to God, then the notion of an original universal creation of humankind in the image of God must be understood to be retrospectively constituted."[41] Because of Jesus all humans are made in the image of God. It is worth quoting Watson at length:

> We are like God in the sense that we are like the human Jesus, whose person and actions are identified with the person and actions of God. . . . God has determined us to be 'conformed to the image of his Son, in order that he might be the firstborn among many brothers and sisters' (Rom. 8.29), and this 'conformation' is not a magical process but, negatively, a refusal to be 'conformed to this world', and, positively, a being 'transformed by the renewal of the mind so that you may discern what is the will of God, what is good and acceptable and perfect' (Rom. 12.2). In this way, a being and an action occur within the world in which the perfect likeness of Jesus' being and action to God's being and action is partially and fragmentarily reproduced. As this occurs, we are conformed to the image of God's Son and participate directly in the image of God that is uniquely his.[42]

Watson's claim is fascinating. Jesus is the image of God and humans image God to the extent that they participate in the actions that "partially and fragmentarily" reproduce Jesus's being and action in the world. Watson's interpretation moves the conversation further in a number of helpful ways. Rather than retreading the lexical and philological path toward an understanding of the *imago Dei*, Watson develops a theological interpretation that is situated within a larger dogmatic matrix, and he appropriately subordinates anthropology to Christology. Moreover, Watson's argument is supported by careful exegesis. This is especially evident in his analysis of the view that humanity's existence as male and female is constitutive of the *imago Dei*.[43]

While Watson's interpretation is helpful in its move toward a more robust biblical theology of the *imago Dei*, there are two areas of ambiguity in Watson's account. First, Watson claims that "Conformation to the image of God's Son is the goal of human creation in the image of God, and human creation in the image of God is the ontological presupposition of conformation to the image of God's Son."[44] A question must be asked: If conformity to Jesus's being and action, however partial, is the very definition of the image of God and explanation of how all humans share in it, then how can we understand this claim that conformation to the image of God's Son is the *telos* of the *imago Dei*? In this

[41] Ibid., 291.
[42] Ibid., 292.
[43] Ibid., 299.
[44] Ibid., 292–93.

case, the existence of the *imago Dei* must already be presupposed. In other words, how should we understand Watson's claim that while the goal of Christlikeness presupposes the reality that humans are made in God's image, what it means to be made in God's image is the partial manifestation of the goal? Second, in what sense does Watson understand the image of God to be ontological? These questions are not criticisms of the overall trajectory of Watson's interpretation. In fact, the argument sustained in the following chapters is complementary to Watson's interpretation. I attempt to bring analytic clarity to our doctrinal claims about the *imago Dei* so that biblical interpreters have the necessary resources available for making the kinds of claims Watson is interested in making.

### 1.5. J. Richard Middleton

In 2005, two important interpretations of the *imago Dei* were published: J. Richard Middleton's *The Liberating Image* and Ian McFarland's *The Divine Image*. Middleton's exegetical account was limited to Genesis 1, the ancient Near Eastern backgrounds of the text, and the theological implications that follow from a careful study of Genesis 1 in its social context. Middleton is conscious of his methodological presuppositions and interpretative location, and this self-awareness is one of the features that set his treatment apart from others. "My reading of the Genesis text is . . . undeniably a *construal*, ineradicably influenced by my preunderstandings and prejudices."[45] Yet, "One's original understandings and prejudices are often changed by encounter with the text and also by listening to other traditions of interpretation."[46] Middleton develops these reflections as follows:

> I approach the interpretive task with a 'robust . . . sense of self,' bringing my interests and questions (theological and otherwise) to the text of Genesis 1 that I might engage it fully, from where I stand. . . . Yet my willingness to put contemporary theological questions to the text is not meant to overwhelm it. On the contrary, I bring myself to the text *precisely to listen to what it is saying.* . . . Opening oneself up to the voice of a text over time will inevitably result in the suggestion of new questions and avenues for research, as the text increasingly has its own say.[47]

Middleton's specific goal is "to make Old Testament scholarship on the creation of humanity in God's image accessible as a resource for theological reflection on the meaning and significance of the *imago Dei* in Genesis 1."[48]

---

[45] Middleton, *The Liberating Image*, 36–37 (emphasis original).

[46] Ibid., 38.

[47] Ibid., 41.

[48] Ibid., 10. Commenting further on the problem he sought to correct, Middleton states, "What is problematic is that most contemporary proposals of either substantialistic or relational interpretations—which tend to be found in the writings of systematic theolo-

Following OT scholarship, then, Middleton takes the royal-functional interpre-tation: "On this reading, the *imago Dei* designates the royal office or calling of human beings as God's representatives and agents in the world, granted au-thorized power to share in God's rule or administration of the earth's re-sources and creatures."[49]

While weighted toward OT scholarship, Middleton's is the best interdisci-plinary interpretation to date. He succeeds in drawing upon the full range of contemporary OT scholarship on the *imago Dei* and expressing the theological implications that follow from this research. Because of this, the present study will engage his arguments throughout. Nevertheless, it is important to note two methodological limitations of his study. First, it is not clear that one can come to a satisfactory theological interpretation of the *imago Dei* on the basis of Genesis 1 and its backgrounds alone. Below, I argue that the authors of the biblical canon intentionally extend the implications of the *imago Dei* beyond those explicitly mentioned in Genesis 1. Second, while Middleton draws on relevant OT scholarship to arrive at a functional interpretation, he is not suffi-ciently critical of the artificial interpretive limits imposed by contemporary OT studies. It is as though Middleton is so concerned about democratizing the availability of the biblical studies scholarship on Genesis 1 that he myopically lets this goal determine his perspective, to the undue exclusion of dogmatic insights. All studies must have limits, but these particular limits may skew the constructive possibilities from the outset. I will draw upon Middleton's exeget-ical work. But I believe that his work needs to be situated in a broader canoni-cal and theological context.

### 1.6 Ian McFarland

In the same year as Middleton's exceptional book, Ian McFarland offered a very different interpretation of the *imago Dei*.[50] Rather than seeking to discern what it is about humanity that is made in God's image, McFarland reverses the direction of inquiry: "An image conveys knowledge of the thing imaged."[51] The *imago Dei* does not deliver knowledge about humanity; rather, it delivers knowledge of God. The pertinent questions, then, are how we know about God from the image and what we know about God from the image.

McFarland's answers to both questions are Christological. Specifically, God is made known in Jesus since Jesus is the true and concrete image of God. However, in light of God's transcendence and infinity, the manner in which God is known by human creatures through Jesus is not immediately clear since God cannot be circumscribed even by Jesus's human life. In order to move for-

---

gians—simply ignore the massive literature in Old Testament scholarship on the *imago Dei* that developed in the past century" (24).

[49] Ibid., 27.

[50] Ian McFarland, *The Divine Image: Envisioning the Invisible God* (Minneapolis: Fortress, 2005).

[51] Ibid., 11.

ward, McFarland pursues answers to two questions: the epistemological question of how an infinite God may be known by finite human creatures and the Christological question of how the life of Jesus is delimited. Because of the incarnation, divine destiny is joined to human destiny. Through divine action, human creatures are made the body of Christ. The church, as the body of Christ, is simultaneously identified with and distinct from Jesus, who is the head of the body.[52] One may have a third-person encounter with Jesus through his body so that Jesus is discovered and known through those in the church. It is useful to quote McFarland's important argument at length:

> As it happens, the particular form of [Jesus's] human life implicates the totality of other human lives. Because the image of God takes specifically human shape as a life with and for other human beings, its contours are fully resolved only in the destiny of humankind as a whole. It follows, paradoxically, that the historical person of Jesus does not exhaust the divine image, *precisely insofar as he defines it*. As members of (*mele*, 1 Cor. 12:27) or participants in (*metochoi*, Heb. 3:14) Christ, we are the means of his glorification (John 17:10) even as he is the source of ours (John 17:22). Jesus' priority as source and center of this glory dictates that ontologically this relationship is one of absolute dependence of humankind on Christ; epistemologically, however, it is one of mutual definition, though even here Jesus' role as the source of human glory dictates that the interdependence is decidedly asymmetric.[53]

McFarland proceeds to outline the "protocols of discernment" that would enable the church to discover the face of Jesus in the face of others. For McFarland, the *imago Dei* is defined through reference to Christ and his body, the NT church. The *imago Dei* is introduced in the OT, however, and it appears to say something about all humans. McFarland does not offer a sufficient explanation for how one's interpretation of the *imago Dei* should be connected to Genesis 1 or to Israel. Furthermore, it appears that McFarland collapses knowledge of God into knowledge of humanity, or at least he does not distinguish adequately between the two. McFarland gives priority to Christ as the source of the church's identity, yet affirms that an encounter with Christ's body is in reality an encounter with Christ. Elsewhere, McFarland has emphasized the importance of maintaining the ontological distinction between God and humanity.[54] However, the protocols for discerning the image of God through encounters with other humans, as outlined in *The Divine Image*, do not as persuasively explain how this distinction is maintained epistemologically. The interpretation described in the following chapters could aid an argument like McFarland's by connecting the OT and NT uses of the image of God in a doctrinally

---

[52] Ibid., 55.

[53] Ibid., 60–61 (emphasis original).

[54] Ian McFarland, "The Body of Christ: Rethinking a Classic Ecclesiological Model," *IJST* 7 (2005): 225–45.

coherent way and by providing the resources necessary for explaining how individuals in the church, and outside of it, are made in God's image.

## 2. The Conceptual Context for the Argument

Three interpretive trends can be identified at this point. First, according to some views the content of the image of God is found only and completely in Genesis 1, while according to other views the image of God is interpreted as purely Christological, with hardly any reference to Genesis 1 at all. In either case, for the most part, interpretation is limited to a small part of only one of the Testaments. Moreover, these interpretations of the *imago Dei* come to non-complementary conclusions based upon which Testament and which particular texts they incorporate. Sometimes, and more often in the case of those whose interpretation is restricted to Genesis 1:26–28, a view may depend upon which part of a verse it incorporates.[55] While the success of my objection to this approach will ultimately depend upon the success of the alternative I offer, it is important to note that the *imago Dei* is central to the creation narrative *and* NT Christology. Because of this, interpretations that limit their scope to either the OT or NT are reductionistic.

The second problem is the reverse of the first; nearly every major Christian theologian has found the concept of the *imago Dei* to be central to theological anthropology, redemption, and sanctification. When understood in relation to these doctrines, biblical scholars often argue that the exegesis of those texts which refer to the *imago Dei* is loose at best. The phrase "image of God" is used very rarely in Scripture, and allusions to it are also sparse. Many take this to show that dogmatic interpretations of the image of God are overblown. If the *imago Dei* ought to be used as a significant theme for Christian dogmatics, then an account of the theological interpretation of the *imago Dei* is needed, an account which demonstrates how theological interpretations are interpretations *of Scripture*.

The third problem is that the dominant theological interpretations of the *imago Dei* do not account for the fullness of what it means to image God in the world. Rather, they seem to describe conditions for the possibility of imaging God. Most of the aforementioned views seek to answer the following questions: What aspect of humanity was the author of Genesis 1 referring to by calling humanity the *imago Dei*? Or, what is it about humanity that warrants the attribution *imago Dei*? In answer to these questions we could offer any of the dominant interpretations: soul; rationality; physical shape and posture; form of relationships. From a theological perspective, however, the only answer that can be given to this question is "Nothing!" As will be developed in greater detail in chapter three, that the answer is "nothing" does not imply

---

[55] E.g., compare again Barth's relational and Christological view to the functional view most dominant in English and German OT scholarship.

that human ontology and function are arbitrary. The shape of human existence is determined by God's free decision to create a representative of God on the earth. Insofar as God wishes this contingent creature to participate analogically in God's attributes and activities, however, humanity needs to exist in a form appropriately designed to realize God's intention. Therefore, human ontology and function are determined by and for God's free decision.

Humanity is not a thing with attributes that God subsequently identified as his image. This would imply that humanity *qua* humanity preceded God's creative act. This creature's identity would, in this case, merely be a naming—God naming humanity what it was already.[56] On the contrary, God's creation of humanity established the very existence and being of humanity as it is, with all its abilities and attributes, for the purpose of establishing an image of himself on earth. The question that must be asked, if one is to understand the *imago Dei*, is: What does it mean for God to create a being with the *imago Dei* as its identity? When this question is answered, then one is able to understand why humans are spiritual, rational, physical, and relational, and why humans have the particular set of relationships we do. In other words, the abilities and attributes of human existence are subordinate to human identity. I will argue that God determined to create an image of God on the earth, and that humanity is the result of that determination. Therefore, God created humanity with the particular abilities and attributes necessary in order to be that image, in order to fulfill humanity's particular identity in the created order.

## 3. Major Conceptual Interests

In the past two decades there has been an effort by theologians to develop a dogmatic account of the *imago Dei* that is faithful to the biblical texts concerning the image, the relevant backgrounds for interpretation, and the theological tradition. It has been difficult, however, to hold these three interpretative poles together. My study is a proposal for interpreting the *imago Dei* in a manner that accomplishes this. I have seven conceptual interests in particular: (1) to provide a coherent explanation of how the *imago Dei* is a permanent descriptor of particular human persons without neglecting the connection between the image of God and personal transformation; (2) to explain, as clearly as possible in this context, just what the relationship between the *imago Dei* and personal transformation is; (3) to explain the manner in which the *imago*

---

[56] Francis Watson's language in *Text, Church and World* comes dangerously close to suggesting this kind of scenario: "We speak with those who are similar enough to ourselves to speak back to us; we do not speak to rocks, earthworms or vegetables. God, likewise, seeks in the created order a being similar enough to himself (created in his image, that is, in his likeness) to be able to speak back to him, to answer his Thou with a reciprocal Thou" (150). All hints of such language are eliminated in his more careful treatment in *Text and Truth*.

*Dei* refers to the whole human person, spiritual and physical; (4) to explain how the ontological "parts" of humanity, including rationality and physicality, relate to the *imago Dei*; (5) to investigate the dogmatic links between the image of God and other dogmatic *loci*: creation, revelation, Christology, Trinity, and covenant; (6) to relate the exegetical conclusions of this study to the key insights from the Christian theological tradition; (7) to offer an interpretation of the *imago Dei* that funds Christian ethical reflection. While these interests provide a wide scope for this study, I hope that they can be brought together by the theological interpretation of the *imago Dei* offered here so that these are no longer considered disparate topics. Through this investigation, I hope to move beyond some of the obstacles currently hindering the integration of the *imago Dei* into OT and dogmatic theologies.[57]

Before outlining the argument, it is necessary to explain briefly my approach to biblical interpretation and the method I will use to draw upon the catholic theological tradition for the development of my argument.

## 4. Theological Interpretation of Scripture

This study is intended as a contribution to the project of theological interpretation of Scripture.[58] As R. Michael Allen has argued, "Such interpretation assumes the trustworthiness of Scripture and attempts to engage critically with traditional readings of the Scriptures and the culture by the church in centuries past."[59] Reflection on the *imago Dei* is primarily a matter of biblical interpretation. Biblical interpretation mutually informs and is informed by dogmatic theology. Therefore, I will regularly draw upon the dogmatic tradition to shape my interpretation of the *imago Dei*. Specifically, I will enter into dialogue with the theologies and biblical interpretations of Irenaeus, Athanasius, Augustine, Thomas Aquinas, Martin Luther, and Karl Barth.

It is important to note that this is not an extended study of the theologies of the figures mentioned above. Rather, the purpose of this study is to demonstrate the advantages of a particular interpretation of the *imago Dei*, one that I find to be most convincing as an interpretation of the biblical texts, most theologically faithful to the Christian tradition, and most dogmatically coherent and illuminating. These voices from the catholic and Protestant theological traditions will serve as teachers informing the shape of my inquiry into theo-

---

[57] Of course, any one of these themes warrants a complete study in itself.

[58] See Kevin Vanhoozer, ed., *Dictionary for Theological Interpretation of the Bible* (Grand Rapids: Baker, 2005); two series of biblical commentaries, Brazos Theological Commentary on the Bible and Two Horizons Commentary; *JTI*; and Daniel Treier's introduction *Introducing Theological Interpretation of Scripture: Recovering a Christian Practice* (Grand Rapids: Baker Academic, 2008).

[59] R. Michael Allen, *The Christ's Faith: A Dogmatic Account* (SST 2; London: T&T Clark, 2009), 34.

logical anthropology and as conversation partners as I develop my constructive argument. The rationale for referring specifically to these figures rather than others is three-fold: first, each of these theologians has significantly influenced the tradition of interpretation of the *imago Dei*; second, each has situated interpretation of the *imago Dei* into a broader theological account of the gospel; third, each, in his own way, has illuminated a distinct aspect or question regarding the *imago Dei* that will be addressed in this study. My hope is that conversing with each of these theologians at relevant points in my argument will magnify the strengths of their interpretations. That said, I am not fully satisfied with any one of their portrayals of the *imago Dei*. If I can demonstrate that the strengths of their interpretations can be maintained while simultaneously avoiding the weaknesses of their portrayals, then I will be on firm ground in offering my interpretive alternative.

I will also draw regularly upon the findings of modern biblical scholars. However, the methods offered in the contemporary biblical studies guild will only be used in an *ad hoc* manner and will be critically engaged just as classic theological interpretations are. The goal is to benefit from the full range of exegetical discussions available without excluding any one of them in particular due to methodology. Various methods can help illumine the immediate context, the human author's likely concerns, the canonical development, etc., though each method—if isolated from a canonical-ecclesial framework—can also lead the reader astray.

I join the growing number of Christian theologians who argue that the Scriptures need to be read theologically and canonically.[60] However, the method for accomplishing such a reading varies dramatically.[61] The problem for interpretative clarity is compounded by the fact that the theological interpretation of Scripture heralded by theologians often authorizes a multiplicity of proper interpretations of the biblical text with the rule of faith as the final arbiter between proper and improper readings.[62] As noted above, Vanhoozer argues that the concurrent divine and human authorship of the biblical text

---

[60] See, e.g., the following: Watson, *Text and Truth*; Stephen Fowl, *Engaging Scripture: A Model for Theological Interpretation* (Oxford: Blackwell, 1998); Ellen F. Davis and Richard B. Hays, eds., *The Art of Reading Scripture* (Grand Rapids: Eerdmans, 2003). This movement is primarily noticed in Protestant scholarship written in the English-speaking world. It is not universal.

[61] See, e.g., A. K. M. Adam, Stephen Fowl, Kevin Vanhoozer, and Francis Watson, *Reading Scripture with the Church: Toward a Hermeneutic for Theological Interpretation* (Grand Rapids: Baker Academic, 2006). For summaries of the differences see Treier's *Introducing Theological Interpretation of Scripture* and Vanhoozer's "Introduction" in *Dictionary for Theological Interpretation of the Bible*, 21–23.

[62] Davis and Hays, *Art of Reading*. An important question in this debate is whether there are various proper meanings of a particular text or various proper appropriations of meaning.

entails that the Bible warrants "thick" theological interpretation.[63] I will attempt to offer just such a "thick" interpretation of the biblical material, guided by the canonical message of the book of Genesis for Israel and for the church.[64] My reading, therefore, is meant to participate primarily in the longstanding ecclesial tradition of reading Scripture for and in the church.

At various places in the argument, large sections of biblical material must be discussed. There will not be space to address each passage with the technical detail of a monograph in OT or NT studies. Nevertheless, the biblical material must be handled carefully and comprehensively. If my comments upon Scripture provoke others with expertise in these areas to further my findings, then this aspect of my book will have been successful.

## 5. Outline of the Argument

My argument unfolds in four parts: first, I demonstrate that identity (rather than substance, function, or relationship) is the concern of Gen 1:26–30; second, I show that understanding the image as human identity resolves a number of concerns that have been raised throughout the theological tradition regarding the permanent ontological reality of the image and its relation to the biblical indication that the image undergoes progressive development and transformation; third, I demonstrate that interpreting the image of God in Gen 1 as human identity makes it possible to clarify the meaning of the other canonical references to the image of God; fourth, I show that this identity interpretation accommodates several important interpretive insights from diverse streams of thought within the Christian theological tradition.

Chapter two consists of a careful consideration of the various kinds of interpretation offered in the theological literature. Rather roughly, these can be grouped into the broad categories of substantialistic, functional, and relational interpretations.[65] There is broad agreement in OT studies that the functional view is the most careful reading of Genesis 1 and the relevant backgrounds.[66]

---

[63] Vanhoozer, *Is There a Meaning in this Text?*, esp. 281–366; see also Stephen Fowl, "The Role of Authorial Intention in the Theological Interpretation of Scripture," in *Between Two Horizons: Spanning New Testament Studies and Systematic Theology* (ed. Joel Green and Max Turner; Grand Rapids: Eerdmans, 2000), 71–87.

[64] Each book will be considered in its present form since this study is focused upon the theological interpretation of the *imago Dei* in Israel and the church after the books in question are known to have been complete.

[65] The term "substantialistic" is taken from Middleton (*The Liberating Image*, 20 n. 19), who follows Douglas Hall, *Imaging God: Dominion as Stewardship* (Grand Rapids: Eerdmans, 1986), 89.

[66] This is the case, at least, in English, German, and Scandanavian studies. See Jónsson, *The Image of God*, for a thorough recounting of OT interpretations in these languages from the late nineteenth century to 1988.

Theologians prefer relational interpretations.[67] As will be demonstrated, none of these interpretations is entirely satisfactory in light of the full range of exegetical, canonical, and theological concerns that press in on the interpreter.

In chapter three, I argue that the *imago Dei* is best understood as human identity. As David Kelsey has noted, however, the notion of "identity" is ambiguous and has been used variously in theological literature.[68] Therefore, I draw upon conceptions of identity provided by Paul Ricoeur, Hans Frei, Robert Jenson, Kevin Vanhoozer, and Richard Bauckham in order to shape my account of identity and biblical interpretation. I then offer a close theological reading of Gen 1:26–30 that demonstrates that identity is the category required for understanding the meaning of the image of God in that text. In the end, I conclude that humanity is given an identity in Genesis 1 that shifts attention away from humanity to God. If we are to understand humanity, we are taught first to ask what God is like. The paradigm provided in Genesis 1 is one in which God reveals himself (i.e., as Ruler) and then bids humanity to participate in analogical imitation (i.e., of God's rule) as God's representative in the world.[69] One further inquiry will belong to chapter three. If substance, function, and relations are not the definition of the image of God, then how does the *imago Dei* relate conceptually to these categories? I will argue that substance and relations are conditions of possibility for being the image of God and realizing humanity's God-given identity. The function of ruling the earth is a partial realization of humanity's identity. Further realization of human identity is dependent upon further divine revelation through God's covenantal relationship with humanity.

Chapter four addresses the nature of this divine revelation and its implications for human identity. First, I argue that human identity is revealed by God progressively. Second, I argue that human identity is partly fulfilled through imitation of God. Two objections are addressed: (1) that the language of the *imago Dei* does not continue to be used in other contexts in which God's people are called to imitate him (e.g., Lev 11:45); (2) that imitation of God is not an

---

[67] See David Kelsey, "The Human Creature," in *The Oxford Handbook of Systematic Theology* (ed. John Webster, Kathryn Tanner, and Iain Torrance; OHRT; Oxford University Press, 2007), 129.

[68] Ibid., 129 and 137.

[69] Two early objections to the argument will also be addressed. These are: (1) that identity is merely another comparative term used to determine the way that humanity is different from the rest of creation and (2) that the *imago Dei* and personhood are identical to one another. The first of these objections is problematic because, as Gunton has noted, comparative approaches are not properly rooted in theology. See Gunton, *The Promise of Trinitarian Theology*, 115–16. The second objection depends too greatly on a method of correlation that assumes that what it means for humanity to be personal is the same thing as what it means for God to be personal. See Gunton, *The Promise of Trinitarian Theology*, 116–20. Gunton falls into this trap. I will argue that human personhood is a logical consequence of God's determination to make humans in his image but that the *imago Dei* is logically prior to human personhood.

appropriate category for understanding OT ethics. In reply to the first objection, I argue that not only is a relationship between God and humanity established in Genesis 1 but also a paradigm meant to guide the interpretation of that relationship; therefore, other examples of God inviting humanity to imitate him in position (e.g., as judge) or practice (e.g., as servant) should be interpreted according to the established canonical paradigm. To the second, I demonstrate that analogical divine imitation is an expectation of several OT texts even though there are also other ethical motivations present in the OT.

In chapter five, I argue that interpreting the *imago Dei* as human identity accommodates the full range of canonical references to the image of God. Moreover, the identity interpretation provides the conceptual tools necessary for clarifying exegesis. I offer theological readings of several OT and NT texts in order to demonstrate just how the identity interpretation can illuminate a canonical interpretation of the image of God.

Chapter six consists of analyses of the interpretations of the *imago Dei* offered by Irenaeus of Lyons, Athanasius of Alexandria, Augustine of Hippo, and Martin Luther. I argue that the identity interpretation can affirm and accommodate the most significant insights of the tradition of theological reflection on the *imago Dei*. Most often in the scholarly literature on the *imago Dei*, the interpretations of these great theologians are used as examples of poor biblical exegesis. Contrary to this, I argue that there is great value in following key aspects of their theological interpretations. Moreover, I demonstrate that the identity interpretation can accommodate these key theological insights of the Christian tradition while modifying those areas of the tradition that need adjustment.

# Chapter 2

# Image as Substance, Function, or Relationship?

In this chapter, I will evaluate substantialistic, functional, and relational interpretations of the *imago Dei* in detail. This part of the study is important for two reasons. First, although I have already registered my initial dissatisfaction with certain forms of these interpretations in the first chapter, they deserve more careful attention, especially in their classic formulations. Accordingly, I will focus on the interpretations provided by Thomas Aquinas and Karl Barth as representatives of the substantialistic and relational interpretations, respectively. Although the functional interpretation is not considered here in a classic formulation, its dominance in contemporary biblical studies requires engagement, for which I will have J. Richard Middleton's recent monograph in view since it is the most theologically astute defense of the functional interpretation to date. Second, analysis of the aforementioned interpretations will bring to light a variety of problems and questions that I will be addressing when I put forward an alternative reading of the *imago Dei* in the third chapter.

The question of the divine image is intricately connected to the broader question of the relation between God and creation. The orthodox Christian tradition is unanimous that God is ontologically distinct from creation. Yet, in treatments of the *imago Dei* it has been difficult for interpreters to describe just how humans are like God without assuming some kind of ontological kinship. Before proceeding to the material content mentioned above, therefore, it is necessary to trace the shape of the relation between God and creation in Christian theology.

## 1. God and Creation

Three theological propositions provide the fundamental pillars of the Christian understanding of God's relation to creation: (1) God is the Creator of all things that have come into being;[1] (2) God transcends creation; (3) God is actively involved in and with creation. How it is that these three claims are true has been the subject of much debate. Of particular interest for this study is the coherence of (2) and (3). Kathryn Tanner has provided a detailed account of the problem and its sources in Greek thought.[2] She argues that "God's involvement with the world is unproblematic when God does not transcend the world; the greater the transcendence, however, the greater the difficulty in understanding that involvement. . . . God's transcendence and involvement with the world vary inversely in this way only when God's transcendence is defined contrastively."[3] A non-contrastive understanding of God's transcendence, however, provides a way of conceiving of God's relation to the world in which (2) and (3) are complementary rather than competitive. Tanner argues that transcendence, in Christian theology, exceeds "all oppositional contrasts characteristic of the relations among finite creatures—including that of presence and absence."[4] If God's activity is in competition with creation, then God is merely one active agent among many. However, if God thoroughly transcends creation, then God's transcendence allows for God's immanent presence to all creation.

William Placher likewise addresses the nature of the relationship between divine transcendence and divine action in his important book, *The Domestication of Transcendence*.[5] In response to Langdon Gilkey's claim that the biblical

---

[1] Genesis 1; John 1:3; 1 Cor 8:6; so the first article of the Apostles' Creed, "*credo in deum patrem omnipotentem, creatorem cæli et terræ*," and the Nicene-Constantinopolitan Creed, "Πιστεύομεν εἰσ ἕνα Θεὸν πατέρα παντοκράτορα ποιητὴν οὐρανοῦ καὶ γῆς ὁρατῶν τε πάντων καὶ ἀοράτων."
The nature of this proposition as confession was discussed by Thomas Aquinas, who argues that God's creation of the world is believed by faith alone on the basis of revelation, since it cannot be demonstrated by reason (Thomas Aquinas, *Summa Theologiae*, 1a.46.2). Barth elaborates on the same point, "Our first emphasis is on this final point that the doctrine of creation no less than the whole remaining content of Christian confession is an article of faith, i.e., the rendering of a knowledge which no man has procured for himself or ever will; which is neither native to him nor accessible by way of observation and logical thinking; for which he has no organ and no ability; which he can in fact achieve only in faith; but which is actually consummated in faith, i.e., in the reception of and response to the divine witness, so that he is made to be strong in his weakness, to see in his blindness, and to hear in his deafness by the One who, according to the Easter story, goes through closed doors. It is a faith and doctrine of this kind which is expressed when in and with the whole of Christendom we confess that God is the Creator of heaven and earth" (CD III/1, 3–4).
[2] Kathryn Tanner, *God and Creation in Christian Theology* (Minneapolis: Fortress, 2005), 37–48.
[3] Ibid., 45.
[4] Ibid., 56.
[5] William Placher, *The Domestication of Transcendence: How Modern Thinking About God Went Wrong* (Louisville: Westminster John Knox, 1996).

accounts of divine action are not to be interpreted literally because such interpretation would imply that God occasionally interferes in the causal continuum of space and time, Placher argues that God "is an agent in *all* the world's events."[6] Placher's argument depends upon an understanding of divine transcendence similar to Tanner's. The apparent causal continuum known through scientific research is contingent upon God's continual action; it does not have its own independent existence. Placher argues that "Divine action is not an interruption in or a violation of the normal course of things, but precisely *is* the normal course of things."[7] Understood as God's active providence over all creation, then, God's agency does not conflict with scientific descriptions of physical causation.

But Placher is aware that many of the biblical accounts of divine action concern direct divine intervention in the physical world. This means that God not only acts to sustain the world in the normal course of things, but God also acts directly in history. The differences between God's activity in the normal course of things and his mighty acts in history, however, are not explained in Scripture. Placher concludes:

> The texts as we have them assume that God is at work in all of this history and do not reflect on the different modes of divine action they report in different periods. If one were trying to extract a "biblical point of view" from these texts, therefore, it would have to be something like, "God works in history—sometimes more dramatically and sometimes through the more ordinary behavior of natural forces and human actors—and the differences do not much matter."[8]

Because Scripture does not address the matter, it is impossible to explain exactly how the distinct modes of divine action differ from one another. At this point, two observations are in order. First, it is significant that Tanner and Placher have supported a radical understanding of God's transcendence over creation *as a means of* simultaneously supporting God's immanent action in the created world. Second, while there are different modes of divine action present in various biblical texts, the consistent testimony of Scripture is that God is an active agent in all history.[9] Further engagement with Placher's argument is necessary due to its bearing on my own constructive argument, but it must wait until chapter 3.

There is an objection that can be addressed here since it helpfully provides a theological context for the material discussion of the *imago Dei*. A radical understanding of God's transcendence gives rise to a radical understanding

---

[6] Ibid., 190 (emphasis original).

[7] Ibid., 190 (emphasis original).

[8] Ibid., 192.

[9] For a discussion of various degrees of divine presence and/or absence, see Terence Fretheim, *The Suffering of God: An Old Testament Perspective* (OBT 14; Minneapolis: Fortress, 1984), 60–78.

of *creatio ex nihilo*.[10] Creation is in no sense an emanation from God. Rather, there is an "absolute qualitative distinction between creator and creation."[11] This being the case, a further implication may be drawn. Since God is not working with an already existing set of materials, then God is radically free to create what he creates. In other words, it is not the case that God is fettered by the concrete reality of the world so that he has to work within its bounds. Rather, God establishes the boundaries of the earth and governs it in sovereignty and freedom. So, it is not as though God was working with concepts such as "human," "monkey," "unicorn," and the like and chose to create the best possible world out of these building blocks. The building blocks themselves are God's creation.[12] As Colin Gunton asserts, "That is the point of the teaching that creation is 'out of nothing': a creative act in the purest sense of the word, in which God brought it about that, when there was 'once' nothing but God, there is now God and a world other than he."[13] If it is the case that God is completely free to create what he wills and there are no preexisting materials limiting, and so structuring, God's options for creation, then does it not follow that God's creation of this particular creation is merely arbitrary?

In response to the charge of arbitrariness, Gunton argues that creation is purposive in two senses: first, "that it derives from the love of God, not simply his will"; second, "that it exists for a purpose."[14] So also Stephen Long reasons,

---

[10] As John Webster notes, "*creatio ex nihilo* is an unreservedly radical conception" ("Trinity and Creation," *IJST* 12 [2010]: 13).

[11] Colin Gunton, *The Triune Creator: A Historical and Systematic Study* (ESCT; Grand Rapids: Eerdmans, 1998), 83. It is interesting that Gunton uses the term "absolute" here since "infinite" is more often used of the qualitative distinction between God and creation. The semantic ranges of the terms overlap, but they are not identical. Rather, both of the terms illuminate aspects of it by referring to the distinction in different ways. Analogical language depends upon an appropriate understanding of the difference between God and creation (God's transcendence), and the relationship between God and creation (God's economy). Oliver O'Donovan's analysis is helpful: "The only pure teleological relation, unqualified by any generic equivalence, is that between the creature and its Creator; only there is there an ordering-to in which there is no element of ordering-alongside" (*Resurrection and Moral Order: An Outline for Evangelical Ethics* [2d ed.; Grand Rapids: Eerdmans, 1994], 33).

[12] See O'Donovan, *Resurrection and Moral Order*, 39: "It is not acceptable to think of God as being under a necessity to create the world as it is, not even a necessity arising from within his own being. For although we may perhaps dare to speak, by way of analogy and hesitantly, of a divine love that 'had' to express itself in creation, as soon as we go beyond that to suggest that it had to create this world and not some other one, we say in effect that the 'creation' is not a creation at all, but an emanation, a reflection of the inner law of God's being, sharing its necessity and thus, in some sense, sharing its divinity." Even using the language that God's love "had" to be expressed in creation is too daring for my taste.

[13] Gunton, *The Triune Creator*, 83.

[14] Ibid., 9.

> Moral theology assumes the doctrines of creation and salvation,
> which are grounded both in the procession of that love which is the
> 'gift' of the Holy Spirit and in the procession of the image, which is
> the Son. Although creation is purely gratuitous and non-necessary,
> it is not arbitrary. It has a purpose which is both disclosed by and
> accomplished in the incarnation of the Son, 'the Image' of God.[15]

Surely it is true *that* creation is a consequence of the love of God. But, following Placher, it is not possible to say *how* it is a consequence of God's love.
Moreover, the fact that creation has a purpose does not, by itself, constitute a
defeater to the objection about arbitrariness. The divine purpose for creation
pushes the objection back to the level of purpose. One may ask if the purpose
of creation is merely arbitrary. The answer at this point is that an *account of*
God's purpose for creation—and not an explanation of why or how God decided on this purpose—is the only answer allowed for by the gospel since
knowledge of this purpose is an article of faith. Thus, the responses provided
by Gunton and Long are correct even though they do not reflect on their
method explicitly in the passages quoted. The charge of arbitrariness cannot
be answered on its own terms.

There is a suitable answer to the charge of arbitrariness on theological
terms, however. It is that the use of the language of arbitrariness in this context is a category mistake.[16] When a human person is presented with a range of
options with no criteria, apart from personal opinion, by which to judge which
option is best, and nevertheless the person chooses one of the options, we call
the decision arbitrary. God is not in this kind of position, however. God does
not choose from a range of options provided for him. Nor are God's decisions a
matter of "personal opinion"; saying as much would be a backward projection
of human experience onto God and a violation of theology's language of transcendence. One may inquire into whether God's decisions are fitting or unfitting on the basis of God's self-revelation. But we cannot describe God's decision to make this particular creation as arbitrary because this is a false and
misleading use of the term "arbitrary." The linguistic rules that lead us to call

---

[15] D. Stephen Long, "Moral Theology," in *The Oxford Handbook of Systematic Theology* (ed. John Webster, Kathryn Tanner, and Iain Torrance; OHRT; Oxford University Press, 2007), 461.

[16] *Contra* O'Donovan who asserts, "Christianity is committed, in the first place, to a view of divine providence which expects it to act 'arbitrarily'. We should not be dismayed by this term, meaning simply that God exercises *arbitrium*, the right of decision in matters where there is no reason for him to do one thing rather than another" (*Resurrection and Moral Order*, 42). O'Donovan comes closer a few lines later with reference to God's deci-sion that one person die and another be born, "It is pointless to say 'It isn't fair'—and that not because God truculently exempts himself from the canons of fair behavior, but because such canons are inappropriate to judge the nature of such events" (*Resurrection and Moral Order*, 42).

something arbitrary simply do not apply to God.[17] At this point we run up against the limits of human signification since there is no analogy appropriate to this divine action—humans make nothing *ex nihilo*. If the charge of arbitrariness is not a problem for a radical understanding of *creatio ex nihilo*, then we can follow Gunton's description of the doctrine of creation. This radical conception of *creatio ex nihilo* is enabled by a radical, non-contrastive, understanding of divine transcendence, which is the basis for God's immanent presence to all creation.

## 2. Divine Essence and Human Substance: Maintaining the Distinction

Tanner and Placher, in the studies referenced above, find Thomas Aquinas to be a faithful guide in describing the relationship between the transcendent God and his *ex nihilo* creation. Thomas is acutely aware of the linguistic and conceptual limits entailed by a radical understanding of transcendence. Moreover, Thomas's account of how theological language refers to the transcendent God is instructive, as David Burrell has shown.[18] Because Thomas offers a sophisticated understanding of God's transcendence, including the theological language appropriate to it, and a substantialistic interpretation of the image of God as rationality, I will assess Thomas's interpretation here as a means of engaging with the substantialistic interpretation more broadly.[19]

The primary non-exegetical criticism of the substantialistic interpretation, as mentioned in chapter one, is that the human soul is not ontologically nearer to the divine essence than the physical body. It is not as though the human soul emanated from God while the physical body was created. Rather, God created the human soul and the body *ex nihilo*. Thomas affirms this; nevertheless, he still argues that the *imago Dei* is the existence of a rational soul in the human nature.[20] "Our being, or 'is', belongs to the image of God in us in that it is peculiar to us apart from the animals; for it belongs to us precisely as *human* beings, in so far as we have minds."[21] The immediate challenge, then, entails an investigation into why Thomas was convinced that the human mind

---

[17] I owe thanks here to Aaron B. James, who provided insightful input on this point.

[18] See, e.g., David Burrell, *Exercises in Religious Understanding* (Notre Dame: University of Notre Dame Press, 1974), 80–137.

[19] Specifically, I will interact with Thomas's account in the *Summa Theologiae*. For a magisterial study of the development of Thomas's interpretation of the *imago Dei* prior to and within the *Summa Theologiae*, see D. Juvenal Merriell, *To the Image of the Trinity: A Study in the Development of Aquinas' Teaching* (ST 96; Toronto: Pontifical Institute of Medieval Studies, 1990).

[20] See Thomas Aquinas, *Summa Theologiae*, 1a.90.2–4.

[21] Thomas Aquinas, *Summa Theologiae*, 1a.93.7, ad.1. The term translated as "being, or 'is'" is *esse*.

constitutes the image of God while the human body merely exhibits traces of the Creator.

Thomas argues that the soul subsists as part of the human nature like a hand subsists as part of the body.[22] The soul has its own operations; for example, the mind knows.[23] Since only things that subsist can have operations, the soul subsists. The body also has its own operation—sensation.[24] This implies, of course, that the body subsists as part of the human nature also. So, soul and body can be distinguished, but both are required to complete human nature.[25]

In order to focus on the meaning of the image, Thomas makes the apparently plain observation that the image of God refers to a likeness that humanity has to God. Developing the point, he argues that the image of God cannot merely refer to any likeness; rather, it must refer to a likeness in kind, which is discovered by attending to the *ultima differentia*.[26] His analysis is as follows:

> Now it is plain that you look for likeness in kind in terms of the ultimate divergence. But things are likened to God, first and most generally in so far as they are; secondly in so far as they are alive; thirdly and lastly in so far as they have discernment and intelligence. It is these latter, as Augustine says, which are *so close in likeness to God that there is nothing closer in all creation*. Thus it is clear that only intelligent creatures are properly speaking after God's image.[27]

This leads Thomas to question whether angels are God's image more perfectly than humans, to which he answers yes. From a biblical perspective, here is a sign that something in Thomas's interpretation has gone awry, since Scripture never connects the image of God to angels.[28]

In the end, Thomas is aware of the major objections to his position: (1) that the whole human creature is referred to as the image of God and not only the mind; (2) that the clarification in Gen 1:27 that God made humanity male and female leads one to think that the image refers to more than the mind; (3) that the term "image" refers to the shape of a thing, and therefore it must include the body.[29] Nevertheless, Thomas presses forward with his thesis unabated. His primary rationale for passing by these objections is comparative.

---

[22] Ibid., 1a.75.2, ad.1.

[23] Ibid., 1a.75.2, reply.

[24] Ibid., 1a.75.4, reply.

[25] See Robert Pasnau, *Thomas Aquinas on Human Nature: A Philosophical Study of Summa Theologiae 1a 75–89* (Cambridge University Press, 2002), esp. parts 1–2 for analysis of the relationship between body and soul.

[26] Thomas Aquinas, *Summa Theologiae*, 1a.93.2, reply.

[27] Ibid., 1a.93.2, reply. The quotation of Augustine comes from his *Eighty-three Different Questions* 51. PL 40:32.

[28] See Herman Bavinck, *Reformed Dogmatics* vol. 2: *God and Creation* (ed. John Bolt; trans. John Vriend; Grand Rapids: Baker Academic, 2004), 460–63; G. C. Berkouwer, *Man: The Image of God* (SD; Grand Rapids: Eerdmans, 1962), 85–87; Blocher, *In the Beginning*, 83.

[29] Thomas Aquinas, *Summa Theologiae*, 1a.93.6.

Rational creatures imitate God more completely by imitating God's being, living, and understanding, whereas other creatures lack understanding. Understanding is the additional component (constituent part), so understanding be the key to humanity's existence as the image. While Thomas identifies the image of God with human understanding, he does not take human understanding to be merely a static possession. In individual humans,

> God's image can be considered in man at three stages: the first stage is man's natural aptitude for understanding and loving God, an aptitude which consists in the very nature of the mind, which is common to all men. The next stage is where a man is actually and dispositively knowing and loving God, but still imperfectly; and here we have the image by conformity of grace. The third stage is where a man is actually knowing and loving God perfectly; and this is the image by likeness of glory.[30]

When situated in Thomas's eschatology, wherein the *visio dei* takes a prominent role, Thomas's interpretation finds its fulfillment.

## 2.1. An Ontological Objection?

Matthew Levering has recently written a defense of Thomas's interpretation of the image of God.[31] Levering properly situates Thomas's interpretation of the *imago Dei* in humanity alongside Thomas's Christological explication of "Image" as a personal name for the Son in question 35 of the *prima pars*. Here Thomas makes a fine distinction between "image" understood in two ways: "That is called an image in a literal sense which originates as the likeness of another; that in whose likeness something originates is strictly speaking an exemplar and an image only in an imprecise sense."[32] We should understand Image in reference to the Son in the first sense—as a personal name. The Son is the Image of the Father. The second sense of image, the imprecise attribution of the term when referring to an exemplar, is used in reference to the Trinity after which humanity is fashioned.

In particular, it is the human mind that is fashioned after the image of the Trinity. But the human mind is an imperfect image of God. Thomas had already discussed how the Son is the perfect Image generated by the Father through the Father's spiritual (intellective) understanding of himself.[33] The Father and the Image are identical except in the distinction established by this relation—the Father generates the Image, and the Image is generated by the Father. This intra-Trinitarian relation is the distinction between the Father

---

[30] Ibid., 1a.93.5, reply.

[31] Matthew Levering, "The *Imago Dei* in David Novak and Thomas Aquinas: A Jewish-Christian Dialogue," *Thomist* 72 (2008): 259–311.

[32] Thomas Aquinas, *Summa Theologiae*, 1a.35.1, ad.1.

[33] Ibid., 1a.27.1, ad.2.

and the Son in God. The Father and the Son do not differ in essence; rather, the Son is identical to the Father since the Father understands himself perfectly.[34]

In summary, then, the perfect Image is the Son whose nature is identical to the Father. Since the original (God) "infinitely surpasses the thing modelled on it" (humanity), the image of God in humanity is unequal to that which is imaged. God's image "is in man as in an alien nature (*aliena natura*)."[35] This distinction is important for the way Thomas understands the limits of the image of God in humanity.

One of Levering's primary concerns is to show that Thomas's interpretation of the image of God does not "undermine divine transcendence by claiming for humans an area of substantial identity with God."[36] Ultimately, Levering responds to this objection through reference to Thomas's understanding of the relationship between God and creation. God surpasses humanity infinitely.[37] This implies that "no attribute can be predicated univocally of God and human beings."[38] Therefore, the image of God in humanity must be an analogous likeness to God. Moreover, the likeness humanity has with God is from God; therefore, humanity's existence in the *imago Dei* comes through participation in God and not from itself. The theological context for this participation, and thus for the *imago Dei*, then, is God's understanding and love of himself. The divine processions of the Son and the Holy Spirit are the result of God's self-understanding and love. For this reason, the *imago Dei* is rooted in knowing and loving God. For humans, knowing and loving God is made possible by the mind.[39]

Levering's reconstruction of Thomas's doctrine of the image of God, drawn out of various passages from across the *prima pars*, provides ample evidence that Thomas's substantialistic interpretation does not fall prey to any ontological unification or blending of God and humanity. Humanity does not share God's essence, even in the spiritual part of human nature. Rather, for Thomas, the human mind is an imperfect image of the Trinity in that its understanding and loving are analogous to God's own eternal understanding and

---

[34] The human mind cannot boast the same identification of itself with its intellective images.

[35] Thomas Aquinas, *Summa Theologiae*, 1a.93.1, ad.2.

[36] Levering, "The *Imago Dei* in David Novak and Thomas Aquinas," 290.

[37] Thomas Aquinas, *Summa Theologiae*, 1a.93.1, ad.2.

[38] Levering, "The *Imago Dei* in David Novak and Thomas Aquinas," 304.

[39] Ibid., 304. Elsewhere, Levering demonstrates that, for Thomas, one cannot study the mind in order to come to know the Trinity. Rather, "once Christians have learned of the divine Image from revelation, the analogy can show that believers need not affirm a divine Image in a polytheistic manner." This is an enlightening explanation of how Thomas uses the human mind in his reflections on the Trinity throughout the *prima pars* (288).

loving. The clearest natural indication that the human image consists of rationality is that rationality is unique among earthly creatures.[40]

So, the ontological objection to Thomas's interpretation has no teeth. Even if some substantialistic interpretations undermine divine transcendence, Thomas's does not. It must be concluded, therefore, that the substantialistic interpretation *per se* is not diminished by this objection either.

### 2.2. Exegetical, Methodological, and Theological Objections

However, three other objections that may be raised against Thomas's interpretation will be considered here. First the exegetical: there is no evidence in Genesis 1 or its surrounding context to suggest that the image of God is primarily defined as the human mind. In fact, as my exegesis of Gen 1:26–30 in chapter 3 demonstrates, there are important indicators in this biblical text concerning the meaning of the image, and rationality is not central to its meaning even if rationality is central to human life. The human mind and its functions are certainly included as aspects of human existence, but they are not explicitly related to the meaning of the image of God in the OT. In the NT, there is possibly some support in Paul's letters. By coordinating Col 3:10, "which is being renewed in knowledge according to the image of its Creator" with Eph 4:22–24, "You were taught . . . to be renewed in the spirit of your minds, and to clothe yourselves with the new self, created according to the likeness of God in true righteousness and holiness," Thomas points out that Paul can be interpreted as having connected the image and likeness of God to the mind.[41] The connection of these Pauline comments to his interpretation of Genesis 1 seems compelling. But it is not at all clear that Paul's teaching assumes the mind to be the definition of the image. Rather, he makes clear that one's mind has to be renewed in order for one to clothe oneself with true righteousness and holiness. This teaching is similar to Rom 12:2, "Do not be conformed to this world, but be transformed by the renewing of your minds, so that you may discern what the will of God is—what is good and acceptable and perfect." Paul's claim is that the mind must be thoroughly renewed in order for humans to reflect the image and likeness of God. This text does not define the image of God as the mind, however. Since none of the other relevant NT texts connect image of God specifically to the mind, the biblical basis for Thomas's interpretation is dubious.

More problematic than this, Gen 1:26–30 appears to contradict an important component of Thomas's interpretation. Simply put, 'adam is said to be made in God's image. Humankind is in view. This implies that Genesis 1 refers not merely to a subsistent part of human nature, but to humankind as a whole. The manner in which this is the case will be discussed in the exegetical section in chapter 3, but it suffices here to point out that Genesis 1 refers to human-

---

[40] I intend "natural," here, to refer to the distinction Thomas draws between reason and revelation.

[41] Thomas Aquinas, *Summa Theologiae*, 1a.93.6, *sed contra*.

kind holistically. Thomas notes this himself as an objection to his position. While I do not think he convincingly avoids this exegetical problem, I do believe that Thomas's prioritization of understanding is important for a broader theological anthropology. I am hopeful that my interpretation of the *imago Dei* can accommodate Thomas's broader anthropological interests.

Second, a methodological objection: the phrase "image of God" should not be interpreted by comparing humanity to other creatures, identifying the differences, and positing the differences as the definition of the image.[42] But Thomas does just this. In the face of the various objections of which he is aware, Thomas continuously reminds the reader that humans are unique among earthly creatures in that humans are rational. This uniqueness is taken to be the definition of the image. The fundamental problem with this approach is that the image of God refers us to God for its meaning, not to creatures.[43] Humankind is unique among creatures, but so is every other kind of creature; every kind has its unique features that makes it the kind that it is. For the sake of argument, let us assume that there are many unique features distinguishing humankind from other kinds but that only some of these features are, in fact, the image of God. On the basis of this method, it would be impossible to know which features constitute the image. Initially, one would be led to include all of the differences in a definition of the image even though this would be wrong. If one decided to choose which differences constituted the image out of the pool of observed differences, they would have to project which of these is most suited to God's nature. But this would merely be a guess, based on the hope that they had observed the proper differences in the first place and that their knowledge of the divine nature was clear enough so as to pick out the appropriate manner of creaturely likeness to God.

However, perhaps Thomas is merely pointing out that his theological interpretation of the image of God is corroborated by the uniqueness of humankind among earthly creatures. The Trinity is the exemplar upon which humanity is modeled, and comparison to other creatures bears this out clearly. I believe it is likely that this is what Thomas is doing. Nevertheless, we must be cautious. The human mind, and its rational operations, should not be elevated to the center of human existence in a contrastive sense. Understanding does not, by itself, constitute human existence. According to Thomas, a human being is composed of body and soul.[44] This is demonstrated by the following test: "any given thing is identified with what carries out the operations of that thing."[45] The soul carries out the spiritual operations of a human being (e.g., memory and emotion) while the body carries out the physical operation of sensation. Because both the body and soul are necessary for a human being to

---

[42] For discussion of the comparative method see Gunton, *The Promise of Trinitarian Theology*, 104–6.

[43] See McFarland, *The Divine Image*, 11–14.

[44] Thomas Aquinas, *Summa Theologiae*, 1a.75.4.

[45] Ibid., 1a.75.4; see Robert Pasnau, *Thomas Aquinas on Human Nature*, 46.

carry out the operations appropriate to its nature, then neither the body nor the soul is, strictly speaking, the human nature or the human being. The context in Genesis 1 is very concrete and physical, and the consequence of the image, dominion over the earth, is a holistic enterprise.

Thomas puts the objection this way in 1a.93.6, citing 1 Cor 11:7: "For the Apostle says, 'the man is the image of God.' But man does not consist solely of mind. So being in God's image does not refer solely to mind."[46] In his reply, Thomas argues that all creation exhibits a trace of its creator, but only rational creatures are stamped with God's image. In human beings, therefore, the image is found in the mind whereas all other parts exhibit merely a trace of God. Thomas's direct response to the objection is that "Man is not called God's image because he is image by definition, but because God's image is stamped on him as regards his mind. . . . So we do not have to verify God's image of any and every part of man."[47] But this is merely an assertion. The rationale for Thomas's answer is two-fold.

First, by the word "image" Thomas means to indicate the kind of being that is closest in likeness to the divine nature. If every kind of earthly creature was ranked according to its likeness to God, then humanity would rank as the closest likeness of all. Thomas follows Augustine here. Humankind is closest to God because God gave it an intelligent mind (*mentem intellectualem*).[48]

Second, Thomas argues that the image of God is an image of the divine nature and an image of the Trinity.

> [T]he divine persons are distinguished from one another in a way that suits the divine nature. So being in God's image in the sense of imitating the divine nature does not exclude being in God's image in the sense of representing the three persons; indeed one follows on the other. Thus we must say that God's image is in man with reference to both the divine nature and the Trinity of persons; for after all, that is what God actually is, one nature and three persons.[49]

But this explanation appears to be far from the meaning of Genesis 1 or the NT references to the image of God.

This brings us to a third, theological, objection: the image of God does not refer to a human reflection of God's threeness-and-oneness. Thomas cites the objection as follows: "The name 'Image' does not fit any of the divine persons indifferently, but only the Son. . . . If then God's image in man had reference to the idea of person, there would be in man an image only of the Son, not of the whole Trinity."[50] Thomas again turns to Augustine for help, and responds to this objection by providing two reasons for thinking it is better to interpret

---

[46] Thomas Aquinas, *Summa Theologiae*, 1a.93.6, obj.1.

[47] Ibid., 1a.93.6, ad.1.

[48] Ibid., 1a.93.2, *sed contra*. Thomas quotes Augustine's *Gen. ad Litt.* VI, 12.

[49] Ibid., 1a.93.5, reply.

[50] Ibid., 1a.93.5, obj.4.

the image of God as the image of the Trinity: first, since the Son shares the essence of the Father, any image of the Son would be an image of the Father; second, Gen 1:26 indicates God's intention, in the plural, "Let *us* make human-kind in *our* image,"[51] which suggests that the image is an image of the plurality of divine persons. Unfortunately, neither of these reasons serves the purpose Thomas hopes it will. The first claim supports the idea that any likeness to the Son is also a likeness to the Father. Therefore, the image of God need not be a dual image, including likenesses to the Father and the Son in different ways. This supports the objection rather than Thomas's own conclusion. An image of the Son is an image of the Father and *vice versa.*

Furthermore, it appears that Thomas's argument rests on a confusion of God's essence and God's relations with reference to the image. God is "one na-ture in three persons (*tribus personis una existit natura*)."[52] The divine persons "are distinguished from one another in a way that suits the divine nature. So being in the image in the sense of imitating the divine nature does not exclude being in God's image in the sense of representing the three persons; indeed one follows from the other."[53] But in what way does one follow from the other? If the claim is simply that a human represents the three persons of the Trinity by representing the divine essence such that when they love they represent the God who is love, then this must be accepted. If, however, the claim is that there must be an analogical threeness-and-oneness in human nature in order for humans to represent the unity of the divine essence and the differentiation of the three divine relations, then this is misguided.[54] In this case, human psy-chology would have to be patterned after God's intra-Trinitarian life.[55] Howev-er, while human psychology may adequately demonstrate how we can think of one thing as a unity with internal relations, it does not provide a faithful por-trayal of the intra-Trinitarian relations since it refers generically to one thing with three aspects.[56] God, as Thomas knows well, is not a thing; nor does God have parts.[57]

---

[51] Ibid., 1a.93.5, ad.4 (emphasis added).

[52] Ibid., 1a.93.5, reply.

[53] Ibid., 1a.93.5, reply.

[54] A qualifying phrase in 1a.93.7, reply, lets on that Thomas is aware of the theological difficulty. "If then we are to observe an image of the divine Trinity in the soul, it must be looked for principally at the point where the soul approaches most closely, *in so far as this is possible at all*, to a portrayal of the divine persons in kind" (emphasis added).

[55] Matthew Levering points out that Thomas in no way intended human psychology to prove the Trinity (*Scripture and Metaphysics: Aquinas and the Renewal of Trinitarian Theolo-gy* [CCT; Malden, Mass.: Blackwell, 2004], 155).

[56] For example, Augustine's various models seek to demonstrate how one thing, the soul, can have three distinct aspects to it. However, these distinct aspects are not dis-tinguished by their relations but by the fact that they are different operations of the one soul. So, the manner by which the different aspects are distinguished is not analo-gous to the intra-Trinitarian relations. Augustine is well aware that his models are im-perfect (see *De Trinitate*, IX–XIV). The pertinent question for this study is whether this

This aspect of the theological objection is not intended to debunk the intellectual exercises Thomas has appropriated for the sake of developing wisdom.[58] Rather, it is intended to point out that Thomas's specific articulation of the *imago Dei* as Trinitarian is insufficient for the purposes of this study. Thomas is right that a human made in God's image is made in the image of the triune God. However, there is no reason to think that God's intention is for an individual human to be an image of the Trinity according to the intra-Trinitarian relations. It is just as likely that humans will image the triune God according to God's character or activity or function in the world or some combination of these.

## 2.3. Conclusions

For substantialistic interpretations more broadly conceived, it is easy to avoid the theological objection by arguing that the image of God is a spiritual image of the divine essence rather than an image of the divine relations. The exegetical, methodological, and metaphysical objections pertain, however, and they provide enough reason to pursue another approach.

In order to maintain the proper distinction between the divine essence and human substance it is necessary not only to preserve the ontological distinction between God and creation as Thomas does, but also to distinguish between the human manner of being and God's own manner of being. The effort to seek a likeness of kind is implicated here, if one intends this likeness of kind as a likeness to God's manner of being defined rationally or spiritually. By naming a part of human existence as made in the image of God, the substantialistic interpretation is required to analyze the human person in terms of disparate parts, some of which are elevated over the others. I suggest that such efforts are misguided. The image of God refers to humankind as a whole, as Gen 1:26–30 demonstrates. To maintain the proper distinction between the divine essence and human substance, one's definition of the image must not be derived by comparing humans to the immanent Trinity directly. Doing so would bypass the epistemological basis for the knowledge of God given to us in the divine economy. God can only be known through his covenantal revelation. Nor can a definition of the image of God be derived by comparison to other creatures. Rather, God's intention for humanity must be revealed in coordination with divine self-revelation and God's intention for creation as a whole.

---

kind of Trinitarian imaging is what is intended by the phrase "image of God" in Scripture. It is unlikely that this is what Scripture intends at all. It is worth noting that Augustine was engaged in an extended spiritual exercise of contemplation of the triune God. He did not intend to provide a doctrine of humanity *per se*. See chapter 6 for a discussion of Augustine's *De Trinitate*.

[57] Levering, *Scripture and Metaphysics*, 159; Gilles Emery, *The Trinitarian Theology of Saint Thomas Aquinas* (trans. Francesca Aran Murphy; Oxford University Press, 2007), 89–96.

[58] See Levering, *Scripture and Metaphysics*, 28–39.

# 3. Creation and Function: *Imago Dei* as Human Action?

If the substantialistic interpretation *simpliciter* is unsuitable, then two other possibilities must be evaluated: the functional/royal interpretation and the relational interpretation. First, I will discuss the functional/royal interpretation. J. Richard Middleton's presentation will be the focus of analysis, but, as with Thomas's substantialistic interpretation, it will also serve as a point of engagement with the functional interpretation more broadly conceived. The particular strength of Middleton's exegetical and intertextual study is his attention to the divine subject in Gen 1:1–2:3, and the biblical portrayal of God as King and Artisan who creates and orders a cosmic sanctuary by his word. His understanding of the relation of this portrayal to the *imago Dei* will be useful in the exegetical section in chapter 3. For my purposes in this chapter, I will focus narrowly on Middleton's exegesis of Gen 1:26 since it motivates his functional interpretation of the *imago Dei*.

The crux of Middleton's understanding of the meaning of the image is found in the following comment:

> . . . the royal function or purpose of humanity in [Gen] 1:26 is not a mere add-on to their creation in God's image, separable in some way from their essence or nature. On the contrary, rule defines image as its 'permanent implication.' I am thus inclined to agree with D. J. A. Clines that while rule may well be grammatically only the purpose and not the definition of the image in 1:26, an initial look at the overall rhetorical world of the text suggests that it is a necessary and inseparable purpose and hence virtually constitutive of the image.[59]

Middleton explains his rationale more fully in a footnote: "If rule is indeed a 'permanent implication' of the image, such that one cannot be the image of God without exercising rule, then from the point of view of sentential logic, image and rule are equivalent."[60] It is important to note the ways that Middleton situates this claim. First, he argues that ruling is not merely "a subsidiary component of the image."[61] In other words, human rule is not a mere consequence or result of the image. For support, Middleton appeals to the Hebrew syntax of the statement "Let us make . . .; and let them rule . . . ." Whenever a Hebrew jussive with unconverted *wāw* follows a cohortative, the jussive expresses the intention of the first-person perspective represented by the cohortative. Thus, Middleton concludes that God's purpose for humanity is to rule. Middleton acknowledges that the syntax alone does not permit one to interpret image and rule as equivalents, however. He offers a second argument: since, in Genesis 1, the natures of certain other creatures are defined explicitly

---

[59] Middleton, *The Liberating Image*, 54.
[60] Ibid., 54 n. 27.
[61] Ibid., 53.

by the functions of those creatures, the expectation of the text is that human function will reveal human nature, or at least something inseparable from human nature.[62] Rule is the necessary and inseparable purpose of humanity, so rule is "virtually constitutive of the image."[63] For Middleton, then, careful attention to the syntax of Gen 1:26 and the pattern of creation throughout Genesis 1 demonstrates that human dominion is the explicit definition of human existence.

### 3.1. Logical and Exegetical Objections to Middleton's Interpretation

I will raise two objections to Middleton's conclusions, one logical and one exegetical. The first objection regards Middleton's claim that sentential logic can be used to show that image and rule are equivalent if rule is a permanent implication of the image. This is of critical importance, for if sentential logic proves that the image is equivalent to rule, then no further search for the meaning of the *imago Dei* is necessary. In that case, Middleton has discovered the full meaning of the image through a strong logical and permanent implication.

To be as precise as possible, it is helpful to attend to Middleton's own words once again: "If rule is indeed a 'permanent implication' of the image, such that one cannot be the image of God without exercising rule, then from the point of view of sentential logic, image and rule are equivalent."[64] Sentential logic is intended to show the logical relationships between propositions. In this case, unfortunately, Middleton overstates the connection by misconstruing the logical relationship between the propositions he is working with. Middleton's antecedent claim does not guarantee the equivalence of image and rule; nor does it make equivalence likely. Let me show why this is the case by drawing some formal (not material) parallels. Consider the following statement using the same form:

(1) If breathing is indeed a permanent implication of earthly human existence, such that one cannot exist on earth as a human without breathing, then existing on earth as a human and breathing are equivalent.

While breathing is an implication of earthly human existence such that breathing is necessary for humans to live on earth, breathing itself is not a sufficient condition for human existence. Other conditions are necessary.

---

[62] Middleton refers to the firmament and the sun and moon as examples of this pattern. The existence of the *rāqîaʿ* that separates the waters is defined by its function of "opening up a habitable space for earthly life to flourish." "The greater light" and "the lesser light" have their existences defined by functioning in such a way as to separate day from night, light from darkness, by serving as signs to mark seasons, days, and years, by being lights in the sky, giving light on earth, and governing the day and night (*The Liberating Image*, 54).

[63] Ibid., 55.

[64] Ibid., 54 n. 27.

Moreover, breathing is not unique; some non-human creatures also breathe. Therefore, (1) does not express equivalence. Consider another statement:

(2)   If being male is indeed a permanent implication of being a human father, such that one cannot be a human father without being male, then father and male are equivalent.

While it is true that human fathers must be males, not all males are fathers. So, (2) does not express equivalence either. Therefore, (1) and (2) are false. In both cases, the antecedent claims are true, but the antecedents do not establish the truth of the consequent claims. The form of Middleton's claim is the same as the examples above, implying that the consequent is unproven even if the antecedent is true. Therefore, from a logical perspective it is unnecessary to affirm Middleton's claim that image and rule are equivalent.

In order for Middleton to demonstrate material equivalence between image and rule, he would need to show not only that the image necessarily indicates rule, but that rule necessarily indicates image, such that a being that rules is the image of God on that basis alone. This would establish the co-extension of the terms.[65] But there is no exegetical basis for this thoroughgoing material equivalence.

Despite the logical imprecision in Middleton's claim that image is equivalent to rule, Middleton's interpretation is especially useful because he attempts to trace carefully the implications of his exegesis for the relationships between the image and other human tasks and roles mentioned in Gen 1:1–2:3. At the end of his exegetical section, Middleton concludes,

> Said one way, humans are *like God* in exercising royal power on earth. Said in another way, the divine ruler *delegated* to humans a share in his rule of the earth. Both are important ways of expressing the meaning of the *imago Dei*. The first expression—the notion of likeness to the divine ruler—suggests the image as 'representational,' indicating a *similarity or analogy* between God and humans. The second expression—the delegation of, or sharing in, God's rule—suggests the image as 'representative,' designating the responsible *office and task* entrusted to humanity in administering the earthly realm on God's behalf. . . . It is precisely *because* the representational aspect of the image consists in a functional similarity or analogy between God and humanity, specifically concerning the exercise of (royal) power, that the image can be articulated also as representative, referring to the human office of representing God's rule/power in the world.[66]

Middleton is disciplined in his method. He resists speculating about the meaning of the image in the NT except to mention that NT references to the image primarily occur in the context of salvation rather than original

---

[65] I owe thanks to Shawn Graves for providing helpful insight on this point.

[66] Middleton, *The Liberating Image*, 88 (emphasis original).

creation.[67] Because of this methodological limitation, he does not address the possible relationship between the NT texts and Genesis 1. Middleton includes wisdom, artful construction, procreation, and a priestly dimension in his definition of the image.[68] Middleton hopes to include these diverse dimensions under his definition of image as rule, but there is reason to question whether he has outlined the correct relationships between human rule and these various aspects of human existence. If his understanding of these relationships is mistaken, then the proper ordering of human qualities such as wisdom and procreation will need to be revisited.

For Middleton, the functional similarity between God's rule and human rule establishes humanity as the image of God. Humanity can then be called God's representative since God has designated humanity for this purpose and entrusted humanity with this task. In other words, the representational function of humanity *is the basis for* its status as a representative of God.

However, this is not the logic of Genesis 1; as Clines and many others have argued, ruling is an implication of humanity's existence as God's image.[69] God's decision to create a representative logically precedes humanity's representational task of ruling. The implication of human dominion, therefore, follows from the fact that humanity is the image of God, and not *vice versa*.

The relationship between humanity's status as representative and its representational function as ruler is better understood as follows: since God determined to create a representative of God on the earth, it is fitting for this representative to share in God's rule representationally.[70] In this case, image and rule are not equivalent. Understanding the relationship between representative status and representational function in this way is fruitful. The advantages will be developed in chapter 3.

---

[67] Ibid., 17 and n. 6.

[68] Ibid., 89–90.

[69] Clines, "The Image of God in Man," 97.

[70] Conceptual clarification regarding the meaning of "representation" is required. G. C. Berkouwer's analysis is worth quoting at length: "If we examine what is meant by this concept, we must indeed admit that it has the essence of the image of God in view. This does not, of course, mean that the use of precisely this word will give us the key to an understanding of the image of God, but the content with which this concept is concerned is without a doubt central to Scripture. The idea of representation refers to man in the concreteness and visibility of his earthly life; to man, who was created in God's image and likeness and who is called to represent and portray this image here on earth, and after the Fall is again called away from the deformation of his entire life, and elected to become similar to the image of Christ. Being in the image of God refers to *this* representation, and therein to the reality of the creature's analogy—a word which, despite all the historical difficulties surrounding the 'analogia entis,' we can here hardly do without. Analogy (as the analogy of the creature) is implied in representation" (*Man: The Image of God* [Studies in Dogmatics; trans. Dirk Jellema; Grand Rapids: Eerdmans, 1962], 114). Therefore, humanity is not merely God's designated representative; the life of the representative is also intended to be representational.

It appears that Middleton confuses an epistemological clue to the meaning of the image with an ontological one. In Gen 1:26, it is apparent that being the image of God is intimately connected with ruling the earth in some way. Middleton correctly sees there the theological identification of God as Ruler of creation. The coordination of this revelation of God's rule with the implication that God's image should have a creaturely rule sheds light on the meaning of the image of God. Humanity is created in the image of God and represents God analogously in the world. Human rule is meant to be a picture of divine rule that follows from humanity's identity as God's image.

However, the image should not be defined by rule to any greater degree than God should be defined by his being the Ruler of creation. God is, in fact, rightly described as the Ruler of creation, but this is not an exhaustive description. It is vital and must be affirmed from the outset. But it is incomplete.[71] Likewise, the image of God is not exhaustively described by referring to humanity's rule. Rather, the image is given meaning by humanity's existence as a representative of God. In Gen 1:1–2:3, this is manifested as follows: since God is Ruler, humanity rules. But this is merely an introductory description. The *pattern* of relationship between God and humanity is expressed in Gen 1:26— humanity is the *imago Dei*, God's creaturely representative. The manner in which humanity represents God on earth is *partly* expressed in Gen 1:26— humanity rules over the earth. The image is human identity; rule is partial realization of human identity.

### 3.2. Conclusions

Middleton argues that the basis for human rule is God's rule. Moreover, God's rule provides the appropriate paradigm for human rule, and human rule is intended as a created analogy to God's rule. This is all very convincing. Indeed, I have suggested that Middleton's argument traces the first implication of the *imago Dei*, which remains a permanent implication.

However, Middleton's analysis is also subject to a number of confusions. First, Middleton's effort to establish the material equivalence of image and rule is unsuccessful. A creature's identity and function are not necessarily identical even if they are mutually dependent. Nor has Middleton successfully argued for the co-extension of image and rule. Rule may be one consequence of the image among many. Second, Middleton's exegesis does not establish his claim that humanity is God's representative because humanity functions in a

---

[71] Moreover, describing God as Ruler of creation is to provide a contingent description since creation must exist for God to be the Ruler of it! Understanding that God is sovereign is much like understanding that God is transcendent. Many things go wrong if this truth is forgotten. But much more intimate divine revelation is needed for humanity to know the triune God of the gospel. God's sovereignty and transcendence are permanent but introductory doctrines that provide boundaries within which theology functions as true theology. In like manner, the *imago Dei* is a crucial but introductory description of humanity.

manner that is like God. In order to defend his claim successfully, he would need to provide an ontological argument concerning the relationship between image and rule rather than the epistemological argument he does in fact provide. To the extent that other functional interpretations strictly define the image by humanity's rule over the earth, they are subject to the same objections put against Middleton's interpretation.

The limits of Middleton's interpretive method are a source of these confusions. By focusing only on Genesis 1 and its ancient Near Eastern backgrounds, Middleton has cut himself off from the other implications of humanity's existence as the *imago Dei* that may be provided in other canonical contexts. Since Middleton limits himself to the rhetorical world of Genesis 1, and Genesis 1 explicitly mentions that the image of God implies human rule over the earth, then Middleton concludes that representative human rule over the earth is virtually constitutive of the image.[72] As will be shown in chapters 3 and 5, other canonical texts suggest that human existence in/as the *imago Dei* has other implications as well.

## 4. *Analogia Relationis*: Intra-Trinitarian Relations and Human Relationships

There is another strong option for interpreting the image of God, one that has received the majority of attention from systematic theologians since Barth: the relational interpretation. Because Barth's theology has been a major impetus for reflection on the *imago Dei* along relational lines, his interpretation of the *imago Dei* will be considered here with an eye to the relevance that these considerations will have for the variety of relational interpretations that have been offered. The *Church Dogmatics* (hereafter *CD*) represents Barth's most complete and mature dogmatic work. And because it is in conversation with *CD* that most subsequent theologians have developed their relational interpretations, I will focus my attention on Barth's interpretation there. Barth's interpretation of the *imago Dei* is situated within his broader doctrine of creation in §40–42 (III/1) which is followed by Barth's theological anthropology in §43–47 (III/2). Specifically, his closest treatment is located in §41.2, "Creation as the External Basis for the Covenant." These broad and narrow contexts are important for understanding the method and content of Barth's interpretation.[73]

---

[72] Middleton, *The Liberating Image*, 55.
[73] See MacDonald, "The *Imago Dei* and Election," 309–10.

*4.1. Christ as the* Imago Dei *for Barth*

Ultimately, Barth locates his interpretation of the *imago Dei* in a Christological context, and therefore in a Trinitarian context.[74] Barth summarizes the logic of his interpretation as follows:

> In God's own being and sphere there is a counterpart: a genuine but harmonious self-encounter and self-discovery; a free co-existence and co-operation; an open confrontation and reciprocity. Man is the repetition of this divine form of life; its copy and reflection. He is this first in the fact that he is a counterpart of God, the encounter and discovery in God Himself being copied and imitated in God's relation to man. But he is it also in the fact that he is himself the counterpart of his fellows and has in them a counterpart, the co-existence and co-operation in God Himself being repeated in the relation of man to man. Thus the *tertium comparationis,* the analogy between God and man, is simply the existence of the I and the Thou in confrontation.[75]

In God himself is a real counterpart. This is the theological and ontological basis for the existence of humanity. Because God's existence includes a "history," "a divine movement to and from a divine Other," God "can become the Creator and therefore have a counterpart outside Himself without any contradiction with His own inner essence, but in confirmation and glorification of His inner essence."[76] The intra-Trinitarian encounter is the basis for humanity's creation and also the prototype and original of which humanity is a copy and imitation.

Barth's method, often referred to as Christocentrism, requires that the *imago Dei* testifies first and last to Jesus Christ.[77] "The whole Bible speaks figuratively and prophetically of Him, of Jesus Christ, when it speaks of creation, the Creator and the creature."[78] In Jesus Christ, the Creator is reconciled to the creature. And because the man Jesus is one in nature with humanity, "we are

---

[74] Several critics of Barth's interpretation fail to take the Christological context into consideration. See, for one example among many, Nicholas Wolterstorff, *Justice: Right and Wrongs* (Princeton University Press, 2008), 344–45. These rather thin critiques fail to attend to Henri Blocher's warning that "one should beware . . . of an oversimplified understanding" of Barth's interpretation ("Karl Barth's Anthropology," 116).

[75] Barth, *CD,* III/1, 185.

[76] Ibid., 183.

[77] For an apt analysis of the terms used for describing Barth's method, see Henri Blocher, "Karl Barth's Christocentric Method" in *Engaging with Barth: Contemporary Evangelical Critiques* (ed. David Gibson and Daniel Strange; Nottingham: Apollos, 2008), 26–27. For an excellent description of Barth's Christocentrism, see Marc Cortez, *Embodied Souls, Ensouled Bodies: An Exercise in Christological Anthropology and Its Significance for the Mind/Body Debate* (SST 1; London: T&T Clark, 2008), 16–39.

[78] Barth, *CD,* III/1, 23.

invited to infer from His human nature our own."[79] Barth even suggests that it may be due to

> a remaining trace of Docetism . . . that our appreciation of the bearing of the divine election effected in Jesus Christ, the institution of the covenant fulfilled in Him, and the reconciliation accomplished in Him, has been so small that it still strikes us as strange that in Jesus Christ we should have to do not only with the order and the revelation of the redeeming grace of God the Creator, but also with the order and revelation of the creature, and therefore of the truth of man.[80]

Both ontologically and noetically, humanity is Christologically determined.[81]

For Barth, therefore, Jesus Christ is the real image of God.[82] The "humanity of Jesus is . . . the repetition and reflection of God Himself, no more and no less. It is the image of God, the *imago Dei*."[83] But Jesus is the image with his community, and the community is "present in all that Jesus Christ is, and therefore in the fact that He is the image of God."[84]

### 4.2. The Community as Pointer to Jesus Christ

The community who finds its basis in Jesus Christ is created in and after the image of God.[85] Humanity exists as God's covenantal counterpart by being elected in Jesus Christ. Wolf Krötke explains, "The eternal election of all human beings in the man Jesus gives their human existence an indelible determination which through God always precedes the enactment of their own lives."[86] Therefore, the *imago Dei* is not a human attribute, quality, attitude, or function.[87] It is never a possession of humanity, and therefore humanity has no independent purchase on the image. Humanity is the image of God simply be-

---

[79] Barth, *CD*, III/2, 54 (English translation amended according to Blocher's observation that "the character of" is an addition ["Karl Barth's Anthropology," 101]).

[80] Ibid.

[81] Barth, *CD*, III/1, 28. See John Webster, *Barth's Ethics of Reconciliation* (Cambridge University Press, 1995), 65; Blocher, "Karl Barth's Christocentric Method," 30–31.

[82] Barth, *CD*, III/1, 203.

[83] Barth, *CD*, III/2, 219. Cited by Wolf Krötke, "The humanity of the human person in Karl Barth's anthropology" in *The Cambridge Companion to Karl Barth* (ed. John Webster; CCR; Cambridge University Press, 2000), 167.

[84] Barth, *CD*, III/1, 205. Somewhat valiantly, Barth seeks to interpret a number of Pauline texts in coordination with his interpretation of Gen 1:26. The result, however, is a set of tenuous readings and a strained argument. So John Webster, *Barth* (London: Continuum, 2000), 99. Nathan MacDonald confirmed through personal communication that Webster had Barth's interpretation of the *imago Dei* in mind (MacDonald, "The *Imago Dei* and Election," 321).

[85] Ibid., 199.

[86] Krötke, "The humanity of the human person in Karl Barth's anthropology," 167.

[87] Barth, *CD*, III/1, 184.

cause God wills it to be so.[88] The nature of God's will in this matter is perspicuous, and Barth can even explain God's purpose:

> [The creature] is the image of God in the fact that he is man. For the meaning and purpose of God at his creation were as follows. He willed the existence of a being which in all its non-deity and therefore its differentiation can be a real partner; which is capable of action and responsibility in relation to Him; to which His own divine form of life is not alien; which in a creaturely repetition, as a copy and imitation, can be a bearer of this form of life.[89]

The *analogia relationis* is found in humanity's "free differentiation and relation," first expressed in God's relation to the human and second in the human-to-human relationship.[90] Within humanity, free differentiation and relation is most fundamentally manifested in the inter-relatedness of male and female. The danger for Barth at this point is that it appears that this inter-relatedness "belongs" to humanity—that humanity possesses it. So, Barth coins the term *analogia relationis* in an effort to distinguish his interpretation from a relational *analogia entis*.[91] He argues that the distinction between an *analogia relationis* and an *analogia entis* must be maintained because the human relationship is pure gift. "As God is free for man, so man is free for man; but only in as much as God is for him."[92] This gift is not merely the bare fact of an *analogia relationis*; God enables the divine image to be actualized.[93] Humanity hears the friendly Word of God and so receives God's blessing. The propagation of humanity shows that God's will is confirmed since it requires both God's blessing and promise and the partnership of male and female.[94] So humanity relies on God in hope and faith rather than on any appeal to a quality of its own. Human existence in the image of God is a blessing from God, and as such it will "essentially and properly be salvation history. . . . Because it rests on a divine blessing, at bottom it must always be a history of peace and covenant."[95] All that humanity is is meant to serve the purpose of God's will that humanity exist as a covenantal counterpart to God.

In Barth's interpretation of 1 Cor 11:7, for example, he makes an effort to coordinate "the man" who in 1 Cor 7:11 *is* the image and glory of God with the "last Adam" and "the second man from heaven" in 1 Cor 15:45–49. Barth returns to his assertion that Jesus only is the image of God, but Jesus's exclusive status is actually inclusive. Because there is a man who is the image of God,

---

[88] Barth, *CD*, III/1, 197.
[89] Ibid., 184–85.
[90] Ibid., 185.
[91] Ibid., 195.
[92] Ibid., 195.
[93] Ibid., 195.
[94] Ibid., 189–90.
[95] Ibid., 189–90.

then "the same can be said of all men."[96] Moreover, Jesus is the image and glory of God with his wife. "This man together with this woman is the man who is the image of God." Therefore, "from the standpoint of this woman, or rather of her Husband, the same can be said of every woman."[97]

From another angle, one can see that humanity, created after the image, indicates or points to Jesus Christ. The creation of humanity establishes the physical and earthly possibility of the real image—the hope that is fulfilled in Jesus. Since God created humanity in the image, it is "the promise and guarantee and even presupposition of the 'man from heaven' who was to come according to the divine disposing and promise."[98] More specifically, "the fact that he was created and exists as male and female will also prove to be not only a copy and imitation of his Creator as such, but at the same time a type of the history of the covenant and salvation which will take place between him and his Creator."[99] The wife of the man is a pointer to her husband.

It is clear, at this point, that there are two interrelated aspects of Barth's interpretation. First, Barth is concerned with the dogmatic basis for humanity's being made in the image of God which is located in Jesus Christ, who is the *imago Dei* with his community. Second, Barth identifies an *analogia relationis* that constitutes humanity's existence in the image. Logical, and ontological, priority belongs to the first of these aspects, and the first includes the second. Krötke explains the relationship between the two aspects:

> [T]he triune God himself exists as Father, Son, and Spirit in relations, namely in the relation of love. In the man Jesus, God turns this love of his *ad extra* in such a way that, in the first instance, the relation of God and Jesus corresponds to God's own inner self-relation. As God is for him, so Jesus is the man for God. But he is the man for God in a definite form of humanity, namely in his being for other human beings.[100]

Ultimately, God's election is the theological basis for the creation of humanity in the *imago Dei*. God elects Jesus Christ, and Jesus Christ implies humanity.

## 4.3. Evaluation

Barth's interpretation requires careful evaluation. A number of strengths can be noted, four of which I will mention here. First, Barth distances the *imago Dei* from any particular human power, possession, or activity. Rather, the image consists always and only in the intention and action of God, in God's will

---

[96] Ibid., 203.
[97] Ibid., 203.
[98] Ibid., 203.
[99] Ibid., 186–87.
[100] Krötke, "The humanity of the human person in Karl Barth's anthropology," 168.

that humanity exist in his image.[101] More can and must be said of the image—indeed, Barth says more than this—but Barth's distinction between the image and any particular innate human property must be a presupposition of whatever else is said. Second, in line with Gen 1:26–28 Barth refers to the whole of humanity as made in God's image. Barth distinguishes between soul and body, but his interpretation of the image does not unduly separate the two "parts."[102] Third, Barth discerns that all Scripture is important for understanding the image, even though the image is explicitly mentioned in but a few passages. Barth even traces the *imago Dei* through God's covenantal relationship with Israel: "[T]he image of God, and therefore the divine likeness of man, is revealed in God's dealings with Israel and therefore in the history of Israel."[103] Barth also emphasizes the fulfillment of the *imago Dei* in Jesus Christ according to the relevant NT texts.[104] Fourth, Barth rightly describes the textual relationship between rule and image; rule is a consequence of image.[105] Despite these strengths, objections must be raised regarding Barth's exegesis, his explication of the creation-fall-redemption sequence, and his manner of analogy.

### 4.4. Two Exegetical Objections

Interpretation of Gen 1:26–28 is notoriously difficult. Nevertheless, Barth's reading of 1:27 is confident and determinative, especially since Gen 5:1 repeats the relevant material.

> And God created man in his image,
> in the image of God created he him;
> male and female created he them. (Gen 1:27)

> In the day that God created man, in the likeness of God made he him.
> Male and female created he them. (Gen 5:1–2)[106]

Barth credits Bonhoeffer in this context, and expresses his surprise that the connection between the *imago Dei* and human existence in differentiation and relationship had not been more often noticed: "Is it not astonishing that again and again expositors have ignored *the definitive explanation given by the text itself* . . .? Could anything be more obvious than to conclude from this clear indication that the image and likeness of the being created by God signifies existence in confrontation . . .?"[107] Despite Barth's confidence, alternative explanations of the parallelism in Gen 1:27 and the relationship between humanity's being

---

[101] Barth, *CD*, III/1, 197.

[102] For an analysis of Barth's understanding of human ontology, see Cortez, *Embodied Souls, Ensouled Bodies*, 75–92.

[103] Barth, *CD*, III/1, 200.

[104] Ibid., 201–3.

[105] Ibid., 187.

[106] Translations taken from Barth, *CD*, III/I, 195.

[107] Ibid., 195 (emphasis added). On the same page, Barth qualifies the strength of his claim, commenting that the meaning of the image in Gen 1:27 and 5:1 is in "almost definitive form."

male and female and God's blessing to "be fruitful and multiply" have led many scholars to eschew Barth's exegesis here. There is a legitimate exegetical challenge to Barth's claim that the phrase "male and female he created them" provides "the definitive explanation given by the text itself."[108] Rather than seeing the differentiation between male and female as the material content of the text's claim that humans are made in the image of God, it is possible that this differentiation makes it clear that all humans, male and female, are made in God's image. In other words, it may be that "male and female he created them" is a democratizing clarification rather than an indication of the meaning of the image.

This challenge has implications for a second exegetical objection regarding Barth's interpretation of Gen 5:3. With Bonhoeffer, Barth suggests that in 1:27 the threefold use of *bara'* connects the meaning of the three lines of poetry together. The meaning of the first and second lines should be interpreted by the further information provided in the third. Contrarily, Claus Westermann has convincingly argued that the third line of 1:27 is a precursor to the blessing in 1:28, which is then worked out in Genesis 5.[109] This reading is confirmed by Paul-E. Dion, who also argues that Gen 5:1–3 should be read as the transmission of humanity's divine likeness.[110] Read in this way, Gen 5:3 counters Barth's interpretation. Barth was aware of the possibility of interpreting Gen 5:1–3 in this manner, but rejects it decisively: "It is not at all the case that God's activity now finds as it were renewal and continuation in Adam's procreation."[111] He suggests that the reversal of the nouns and the interchange of prepositions from the pattern in Gen 1:26 may be a sign that "the text does not see this process in the same light as that of Gen 1:26."[112] *Contra* Barth, however, it is much more likely that the occurrence of בִּדְמוּת in 5:1 carries the same meaning as the occurrence in 5:3 so that the texts are mutually informing. MacDonald's observation is telling: "Indeed, [Barth's] interpretation of Genesis 5:3 appears very strained, an impression that Barth's two pages of detailed discussion serve only to reinforce."[113] These exegetical considerations indicate that Barth's reading of Gen 1:27 and 5:1–3 is not as definitive as he thought.[114] Nevertheless, one could accept the general shape of Barth's Christological analysis

---

[108] Once again, it is important to note that the male-female relationship does not *constitute* the meaning of the image of God for Barth. Rather, the male-female relationship *indicates* the meaning of the image.

[109] Westermann, *Genesis 1-11*, 160–61.

[110] Dion, "Ressemblance et image de Dieu," cols. 391–92.

[111] Barth, CD, III/1, 198.

[112] Ibid.

[113] MacDonald, "The *Imago Dei* and Election," 321.

[114] Moreover, the exegetical gymnastics Barth attempts in his interpretation of 1 Cor 11:7 are even more incredible. Blocher has even referred to Barth's effort as an "impossible exegesis" (Blocher, *In the Beginning*, 92).

of the image of God without endorsing his particular exegesis of Gen 1:27 or
5:1–3. Further analysis of Barth's interpretation is therefore necessary.

### 4.5. A Biblical-Theological Objection

Barth does not accept the traditional creation-fall-redemption sequence.
For Barth, theology begins with Jesus Christ, and therefore, with reconciliation.[115] Yet, Jesus Christ grounds every "stage" of the biblical narrative. What is
true of humanity is "true first of all in Jesus Christ."[116] Underlying Barth's interpretation of each of the "stages" in the biblical narrative is Barth's proposal
for understanding God's election and time. Jesus Christ is the result of God's
determination in eternity to be God for humanity. Therefore, Jesus Christ exists in God's "time." Because Jesus is the "real man," and his existence is eternal, the diversity of human times is relativized. Blocher summarizes the significance of this understanding for Barth's theology: In light of Barth's theology
of time

> the affirmation of Jesus' pre-existence is easily understood. The
> tendency to interpret creation, reconciliation and redemption as
> one, with a symmetrical arrangement (very much Barth's taste) of
> the first and the third terms, naturally flows from the same. It illu-
> minates the Barthian coalescence of history and ontology. On the
> one hand, history is considered in a predominantly ontological per-
> spective (a sign of which is the fusion of Christ's Person—or union
> in him of deity and humanity—and of his work for reconciliation):
> the all-inclusive Event is the key and ground of all reality, all be-
> ing—hence the complaint that history, so ontologized, is lost as his-
> tory. On the other hand, ontology is 'historicized,' an 'actualistic'
> ontology of becoming, 'if the eternal being of God is constituted by
> His eternal act of turning towards the human race.'[117]

As for the creation of humanity in God's image, Barth's theology of time implies that the existence of Jesus Christ, in his human nature, is prior to the
creation of other human beings. From another perspective, Jesus Christ, as
man, is the image after which the rest of humanity is created. Barth's Christological re-ordering of the biblical narrative on the basis of his understanding
of election and time is worked out in his treatments of creation, sin, evil,
death, reconciliation, and atonement.

Despite the inner consistency and powerful scope of Barth's logic, Barth's
relativization of the creation-fall-redemption sequence is problematic. In particular, problems arise in Barth's understanding of sin and evil.[118] In the biblical portrayal, God's good creation is compromised by sin and, therefore, death.
Redemption and reconciliation are required because of sin and its

---

[115] Barth, *CD*, IV/1, 22.
[116] See Barth, *CD*, II/2, 739–40.
[117] Blocher, "Karl Barth's Anthropology," 127.
[118] Ibid., 52.

consequences. For Barth, however, the logic is reversed. He recognizes, rightly, that redemption and reconciliation presuppose sin and alienation. But because reconciliation is theologically primary and is located in God's "time," God's judgment and wrath against sin must also exist in God's eternal relation with Jesus Christ. For Barth, even describing the human condition in terms of a "fall" is mistaken, since, as Blocher notes, "there never was a superior state from which to fall."[119] God's grace implies the existence of evil alongside God's good creation.

It is important to note that Barth in no way affirms that evil is a direct creation of God. Rather, evil, Barth's "Nothingness," "is that which God does not will. It lives only by the fact that it is that which God does not will. But it does live by that fact. For not only what God wills, but what God does not will, is potent, and must have a real correspondence."[120] Yet, Blocher suggests that Barth's effort to comprehend evil, to "rationally master its presence within God's creation," begins to "neutralize the evilness of evil." *Contra* Barth, Blocher argues that "theology is unable to go beyond the sequence of Creation-Sin-Redemption, and must therefore renounce symmetry," this being "a sign of the scandal of evil."[121] If Blocher is correct that the biblical portrayal of sin is that it is *atopos*, and I believe he is, then Barth's incorporation of sin and alienation into the eternal relation of God with Jesus Christ is mistaken. But if Barth's reversal of the creation-fall-redemption sequence fails at this point, then the reversal simply fails. One may easily agree with Barth that redemption is the theological ground of God's grace in the OT, and even that God's creation of humanity and God's covenant with humanity are mutually dependent, without reversing the revealed order of creation and redemption and thus relativizing the significance of this order.[122]

### 4.6. An Analogical Objection?

Several scholars have drawn upon Barth's interpretation of the image of God without subscribing to his exegetical conclusions or his reversal of the creation-fall-redemption sequence. Barth's *analogia relationis* in particular has caught the attention of scholars who have developed a variety of relational models of the image. Therefore, the character of Barth's analogy of relation deserves attention. In this context, there are three relations that Barth discusses: (1) the intra-Trinitarian relations; (2) the relation between God and humanity; (3) and the relation between human persons, male and female.[123] As noted above, the *tertium comparationis* is the encounter of an I and a Thou. The very being of humanity is found in the "confrontation and conjunction of man

---

[119] Ibid., 131.

[120] Barth, *CD*, III/3, 352.

[121] Blocher, "Karl Barth's Christocentric Method," 53.

[122] Ibid., 52.

[123] Barth, *CD*, III/1, 196.

and woman," and therefore it is also the divine image and likeness.[124] The fact that the relation takes the form it does in humanity, the form of male and female, is due to humanity's existence as a creature. Sexuality cannot be projected back onto God, of course; humanity is only an analogy, and the analogy "does not entail likeness but the correspondence of the unlike."[125]

Barth coins the term *analogia relationis* to refer to the analogy he has described, but what is the nature of the analogy? Blocher has surmised that "the correspondence between I-Thou in the Godhead and I-Thou in humankind, rather resembles the *analogia proportionalitatis!*"[126] Is Barth not saying that God and humanity share a similar manner of existence? This is how some have interpreted him, declaring that the key feature of human existence is that humans exist as persons-in-relation. In this case, we would have a form of the *analogia entis*, since Barth describes the relation as the being of humanity. Would this not lead us to a very anthropological understanding of God's triune existence? Characteristically, Barth appeals to God's freedom in order to keep his interpretation from lapsing into an *analogia entis*.[127] But surely Thomas Aquinas, who is criticized by Barth at this point, would affirm God's freedom as well!

Perhaps there is another explanation of the *analogia relationis'* uniqueness. Blocher suggests that Barth's originality is found in his conception that the analogy of relation is an event—human existence is interpreted as history rather than as a state of being.[128] This is indicated by Barth's inclusion of the relation between God and humanity in his interpretation. The analogy is not merely drawn between the I-Thou relation in God and the I-Thou relation in humanity. There is also a God-humanity relation. In this case, the analogy is, indeed, a correspondence of the ontologically unlike. The bare fact in view is that humans stand in a relation to God and one another. The manner of these relations is not described further except to note that they are personal relations: "This God can and will say to man 'Thou,' and the man who corresponds to Him can also be responsible before Him as an 'I.'"[129] Since the intra-Trinitarian relation, the God-humanity relation, and the male-female relation are all very different in form and content, it is unclear what the *analogia relationis* would imply for any further correspondence of these relations. And this would ultimately frustrate the efforts of one who would like to pattern human relationships upon intra-Trinitarian relations. In the end, then, the analogical

---

[124] Ibid. Those who argue for a relational ontology may believe they are able to find an ally in Barth here. However, Barth does not emphasize the relation over against the *relata*. Relation, of course, logically presupposes the *relata*, even if the *relata* never exist without the relation, as Barth argues (see Blocher, "Karl Barth's Anthropology," 118).

[125] Barth, *CD*, III/1, 196.

[126] Blocher, "Karl Barth's Anthropology," 118.

[127] Barth, *CD*, III/1, 195.

[128] Blocher, "Karl Barth's Anthropology," 118.

[129] Barth, *CD*, III/1, 196.

objection does not pertain to Barth specifically. Rather, it is directed at those who would use his *analogia relationis* to construct an ontological or ethical system by gazing upon the immanent Trinity to discern directly the contours of human existence.

*4.7. Conclusions*

The problems involved with Barth's exegesis of Gen 1:27 and Gen 5:1–3 lead to the conclusion that it is improbable that his precise explication of the image of God is correct. Moreover, his reversal of the creation-fall-redemption sequence runs against the grain of Scripture by making the existence of evil inevitable. Barth's articulation of the *analogia relationis*, however, is not objectionable *per se*. And when the broader context of Barth's interpretation is taken into consideration, there is promise for a re-reading of the relevant biblical texts with Barth. Accordingly, MacDonald has suggested that Barth's hermeneutic should have led him to understand the *imago Dei* as analogous to God's election of humanity.[130] This suggestion deserves further attention.

# 5. Looking Ahead

In this chapter, I have evaluated the substantialistic, functional, and relational interpretations of the image of God through an analysis of the particular interpretations offered by Thomas Aquinas, J. Richard Middleton, and Karl Barth. There are significant strengths in each of these readings, and these strengths will help to shape the interpretation I will offer in the next chapter of this study. However, I have also shown that significant methodological, exegetical, and material weaknesses exist in these readings of the *imago Dei*. None of the particular interpretations analyzed can be accepted wholesale; moreover, there is reason to believe that other versions of the substantialistic, functional, and relational interpretations will suffer similar or related weaknesses. Therefore, in chapter 3 I will argue for an alternative interpretation of the *imago Dei*—image as human identity. To support my interpretation, I will provide a close reading of Gen 1:26–30. On the basis of this "identity interpretation," I will then describe the manner in which humanity's substance, function, and relations are logically related to the *imago Dei*.

---

[130] MacDonald, "The *Imago Dei* and Election," 326.

# Chapter 3

# Image as Identity

In the first two chapters, I demonstrated the need for a canonical re-reading of the *imago Dei*. In this chapter I will begin to take up the challenge of offering this re-reading, in three parts. First, I will clarify the term "identity" and describe just how this term applies to the *imago Dei*. Second, I will argue for an interpretation of the *imago Dei* as human identity through a close reading of Gen 1:26–30 in its theological and cultural context. Third, I will describe the relationship between the *imago Dei* and various aspects of humanity, including personhood, substance, function, and relations.

## 1. Scripture, Divine Identity, and Human Identity

Since the word "identity" is used multifariously, it is first necessary to offer a description of the specific use made of the term here. Otherwise, its diverse uses may cloud the theological waters. Because of this initial ambiguity, one might wonder if there is no better term than "identity" for elucidating the meaning of the *imago Dei*. I have found no better term, and will therefore demonstrate the suitability of the term in three ways. First, I will refer to the *Oxford English Dictionary* (*OED*) definitions of "identity" to articulate its common uses and their relation to my use here. Second, I will draw upon a helpful conceptual analysis of "identity" provided within the social sciences by Rogers Brubaker and Frederick Cooper. "Identity" as a concept is used pervasively in the social sciences and its use in the social sciences shapes its meaning in other academic literature. Third, I will relate my use of the term to the way others have used it in recent theological literature. As mentioned in the first chapter, there are helpful parallels between the discussion of identity required here and Richard Bauckham's discussion of Jesus Christ's divine identity as described in the NT. Bauckham's use of "identity" is informed by a number of others that will also receive attention here, including studies by Paul Ricoeur, Hans Frei, Robert Jenson, and Kevin Vanhoozer. In *nuce*, my claim is that in Scripture the portrayal of the divine identity has formal similarity to the biblical claim that humanity is made in the image of God.[1] The implications of this claim will be explored in the third part of this chapter and in chapter 4.

The following points characterize my use of the term "identity": (1) a strong, corporate, conception of identity, which implies that the *imago Dei* is a common identity shared by all individual human beings. "Human identity" refers to that which uniquely identifies humanity as the particular creature that it is, defined by its relation to God. This identity is real whether or not an individual human being knows her identity since human identity is determined by the transcendent God who makes each creature, and all of creation, what it ultimately is. (2) Knowledge of the meaning of the *imago Dei* is acquired on the basis of the narrative identity of humanity developed within the OT and NT biblical literature. (3) Human identity is discerned in a manner parallel to the way one can discern Jesus's divine identity—through careful attention to the specific portrayal of that identity in the relevant biblical texts.

### 1.1. Common Uses of "Identity"

The *OED* includes no fewer than ten definitions of the word identity. However, the first two definitions are most important here: "1.a. The quality or condition of being the same in substance, composition, nature, properties, or in particular qualities under consideration; absolute or essential sameness; oneness"; "2.a. The sameness of a person or thing at all times or in all circumstances; the condition or fact that a person or thing is itself and not something else; individuality, personality." Of these two definitions, 2.a. is the closest to my use in this study. By the word "identity," I do not intend sameness of substance or properties. Rather, I pick up the middle clause of definition 2.a.: "the condition or fact that a person or thing is itself and not something else." I do not intend this to indicate the ways that individual humans are distinguished from each other. Instead, I am using "human identity" to refer to that which distinguishes humans from all other creatures. In the creation narrative, God determines the particular existence of humanity—the thing that makes humanity what it is and not something else. As will be shown by the exegesis of Gen 1:26–30 below, this particular existence is determined by the position of humanity in God's plan for creation.

Turning back to the *OED*, there is further help in the second definition of "identification": "2. The determination of identity; the action or process of determining what a thing is; the recognition of a thing as being what it is." In Genesis 1, God makes clear what humanity is—what its identity is—so that humans, and the people of Israel specifically, may recognize themselves (and everything else!) for what they truly are. In Gen 1:26, God determines humanity's particular existence, and in Gen 1:27 this particular existence is created.

---

[1] However, because the similarity is between divine identity and human identity, the comparison is fundamentally a comparison of the unlike. God is in no way confused with the human creature, but the human creature finds its identity through reference to God.

The fact that humanity is the image of God motivates God's persistent interest in this creature. If one is to understand properly God's creation, and particularly God's intention for humanity, then one must recognize humanity's designated position as image of God.

## 1.2. *"Identity" in the Social Sciences*

The *OED* definitions of "identity" and "identification" offer a helpful place to start with the concept of identity, but further attention to the term is necessary for understanding the full meaning. In the social sciences, identity has taken on diverse meanings, many of which have found their way into theological literature. Rogers Brubaker and Frederick Cooper analyze the uses of "identity" in the social sciences and help to make clear the conceptual context for my claim that the image of God is human identity.[2] Brubaker and Cooper provide five common uses of the term identity in their academic field:

> 1. Understood as a ground or basis of social or political action, "identity" is often opposed to "interest" in an effort to highlight and conceptualize *non-instrumental* modes of social and political action. With a slightly different analytical emphasis, it is used to underscore the manner in which action—individual or collective—may be governed by *particularistic self-understandings* rather than by *putatively universal self-interest*. This is probably the most general use of the term; it is frequently found in combination with other uses. It involves three related but distinct contrasts in ways of conceptualizing and explaining action. The first is between understanding and (narrowly understood) self-interest. The second is between particularity and (putative) universality. The third is between two ways of construing social location. Many (though not all) strands of identitarian theorizing see social and political action as powerfully shaped by position in social space. For identitarian theorizing, it means position in a multidimensional space defined by *particularistic categorical attributes* (race, ethnicity, gender, sexual orientation). For instrumentalist theorizing, it means position in a *universalistically conceived social structure* (for example, position in the market, the occupational structure, or the mode of production).
>
> 2. Understood as a specifically *collective* phenomenon, "identity" denotes a fundamental and consequential *sameness* among members of a group or category. This may be understood objectively (as a sameness "in itself") or subjectively (as an experienced, felt, or perceived sameness). This sameness is expected to manifest itself in solidarity, in shared dispositions or consciousness, or in collective action. This usage is found especially in the literature on social movements; on gender; and on race, ethnicity, and nationalism. In this usage, the line between "identity" as a category of analysis and as a category of practice is often blurred.

---

[2] Rogers Brubaker and Frederick Cooper, "Beyond 'identity'," *TheorSoc* 29 (2000): 1–47.

3. Understood as a core aspect of (individual and collective) "self-hood" or as a fundamental condition of social being, "identity" is invoked to point to something allegedly *deep, basic, abiding, or foundational*. This is distinguished from more superficial, accidental, fleeting, or contingent aspects or attributes of the self, and is understood as something to be valued, cultivated, supported, recognized, and preserved. This usage is characteristic of certain strands of psychological (or psychologizing) literature, especially as influenced by Erikson, though it also appears in the literature on race, ethnicity, and nationalism. Here too the practical and analytical uses of "identity" are frequently conflated.

4. Understood as a product of social or political action, "identity" is invoked to highlight the *processual, interactive* development of the kind of collective self-understanding, solidarity, or "groupness" that can make collective action possible. In this usage, found in certain strands of the "new social movement" literature, "identity" is understood both as a *contingent product* of social or political action and as a ground or basis of further action.

5. Understood as the evanescent product of multiple and competing discourses, "identity" is invoked to highlight the *unstable, multiple, fluctuating, and fragmented* nature of the contemporary "self." This usage is found especially in the literature influenced by Foucault, post-structuralism, and post-modernism. In somewhat different form, without post-structuralist trappings, it is also found in certain strands of the literature on ethnicity—notably in "situationalist" or "contextualist" accounts of ethnicity.[3]

Of the five usages surveyed by Brubaker and Cooper, the first four have something to contribute to my study. The fifth may be ruled out since I am not interested here in the human experience of an unstable and fluctuating "self." In order to discern how the other four usages contribute, it is helpful to draw upon a distinction made by Brubaker and Cooper between strong and weak conceptions of identity. Strong conceptions, they state, "preserve the common-sense meaning of the term—the emphasis on sameness over time and across persons."[4] Underlying this strong conception of identity are four assumptions, which Brubaker and Cooper take to be problematic.

1. Identity is something all people have, or ought to have, or are searching for.

2. Identity is something all groups (at least groups of a certain kind—e.g., ethnic, racial, or national) have, or ought to have.

3. Identity is something people (and groups) can have without being aware of it. In this perspective, identity is something to be *discov-*

---

[3] Ibid., 6–8 (emphasis original).
[4] Ibid., 10.

*ered,* and something about which one can be *mistaken.* The strong conception of identity thus replicates the Marxian epistemology of class.[5]

4. Strong notions of collective identity imply strong notions of group boundedness and homogeneity. They imply high degrees of groupness, an "identity" or sameness among group members, a sharp distinctiveness from nonmembers, a clear boundary between inside and outside.[6]

The reason these assumptions are problematic for political and social analysis of gender, race, ethnicity, and nationalism is clear. "'Identity' bears a multivalent, even contradictory theoretical burden" in the social sciences since it is used to "highlight *fundamental* sameness" and to "*reject* notions of fundamental or abiding sameness."[7] In these contexts a strong notion of identity is too prescriptive.

But it is precisely this strong sense of the term identity that I wish to use here. If the image of God is human identity and this identity is given by God to all humanity, then, indeed, all individual humans and all groups of humans have this identity. If Gen 1:26–30 makes God's people aware of their identity within creation, then this identity may be discovered. If some people substitute an alternative identity for their God-given identity, then they are either unaware of their identity or mistaken or both.[8] And if the image of God is *human* identity, then there is a clear boundary between those inside and outside—humans are inside and other creatures are outside. Brubaker and Cooper's analysis indicates that identity is an appropriate descriptor for my thesis. In fact, much of the rest of their article is devoted to showing why other uses of the word are problematic. Since the assumptions underlying the term are unacceptable for the purposes of the social sciences, and since other uses of the term leave "us without a rationale for talking about 'identities' at all," Brubaker and Cooper suggest that their academic discipline should use other terms that are "less ambiguous, and unencumbered by the reifying connotations of 'identity.'"[9] My use of the term "identity," however, intentionally absorbs those implications of the term deemed unfit for the social sciences. By using the term in the strong sense, its meaning is disambiguated. The theological content of the term will be clarified in the following paragraphs.

---

[5] It is important to note that this Marxist epistemology of class assumes that human beings have differing and competing identities. My claim is that the *imago Dei* is the identity of all humanity; because this identity comes from a transcendent source, God, to all humans, there are no class distinctions in the *imago Dei.*

[6] Brubaker and Cooper, "Beyond 'identity'," 10.

[7] Ibid., 8 (emphasis original).

[8] Psychologically, in other words, it is possible for someone to be unaware of their God-given identity or mistaken about it. After the fall, the effects of sin make this lack of awareness or misunderstanding likely.

[9] Brubaker and Cooper, "Beyond 'identity'," 10.

## 1.3. Narrative Identity

Before transitioning to theological uses of the term "identity," it is important to consider Paul Ricoeur's distinction, in *Oneself as Another*, between *idem*-identity and *ipse*-identity, which highlights the differences between the identity of substance and personal identity.[10] In the *OED*, definitions 1.a. and 2.a. use the word "same" or "sameness" to describe quite different phenomena—the former refers to the identity of substance and the latter to the identity of persons. In personal and impersonal cases, the *OED* uses the word "same" to define identity. Unlike the *OED* definitions, Ricoeur is interested in the difference between sameness (*idem*) and selfhood (*ipse*). Ricoeur argues that *ipse*-identity is more helpful than *idem*-identity for understanding human persons. *Ipse* suggests rich personal self-constancy rather than flattening out human existence into permanence of the same. Self-constancy, or faithfulness to one's word, requires a narrative through which one persists.[11] So, Ricoeur develops his understanding of *ipse*-identity in tandem with narrative identity.

> When we speak of ourselves, we in fact have available to us two models of permanence in time which can be summed up in two expressions that are at once descriptive and emblematic: *character* and *keeping one's word*. In both of these, we easily recognize a permanence which we say belongs to us. My hypothesis is that the polarity of these two models of permanence with respect to persons results from the fact that the permanence of character expresses the almost complete mutual overlapping of the problematic of *idem* and *ipse*, while faithfulness to one's word marks the extreme gap between the permanence of the self and that of the same and so attests fully to the irreducibility of the two problematics one to the other. I hasten to complete my hypothesis: the polarity I am going to examine suggests an intervention of narrative identity in the conceptual constitution of personal identity in the manner of a specific mediator between the pole of character, where *idem* and *ipse* tend to coincide, and the pole of self-maintenance, where selfhood frees itself from sameness.[12]

Conceptually, narrative identity stands between character and self-constancy in that it introduces movement into established dispositions while at the same time asserting one's self-constancy through the narrative. There is movement, but this movement is developed from something already established rather than being untethered or wildly "free."

Two uses of the word "character" show how narrative functions to mediate these two poles. Character, understood as one's settled dispositions and

---

[10] Paul Ricoeur, *Oneself as Another* (trans. Kathleen Blamey; University of Chicago Press, 1992).
[11] Ibid., 165.
[12] Ibid., 118–19 (emphasis original).

habits, "is truly the 'what' of the 'who.'"[13] This "what" is not external but internal to the person, and it is a persistence of the same. But character has a history. And in this history we can speak of a person as *a* character, understood as a protagonist in a story. Dispositional character belongs, therefore, to a storied character, one who persists through time. On the other hand, the fact that a person can make and keep promises requires persistence through time. As Ricoeur notes, this persistence is a commitment to hold fast into the future: "Even if my desire were to change, even if I were to change my opinion or my inclination, 'I will hold firm.'"[14] Such faithfulness belongs "solely within the dimension of 'who?' . . . The continuity of character is one thing, the constancy of friendship is quite another."[15] "Identity" applies to the persistence of character and of faithfulness, despite the fact that having settled dispositions and keeping one's word are distinct ways of referring to one's persistence through time.

Narrative identity mediates between these two poles through its attention to the "who" of the narrative. The character of the narrative is tied to her actions such that she is identified by the interweaving of her motives and her role in the plot of the story. Ricoeur explains the implications of this confluence as follows:

> From this correlation between action and character in a narrative there results a dialectic internal to the character which is the exact corollary of the dialectic of concordance and discordance developed by the emplotment of action. The dialectic consists in the fact that, following the line of concordance, the character draws his or her singularity from the unity of life considered a temporal totality which is itself singular and distinguished from all others. Following the line of discordance, this temporal totality is threatened by the disruptive effect of the unforeseeable events that punctuate it (encounters, accidents, etc.). Because of the concordant-discordant synthesis, the contingency of the event contributes to the necessity, retroactive so to speak, of the history of a life, to which is equated the identity of the character.[16]

A character's identity is discovered in her history, recognized through the continuities and discontinuities of her experiences. Ricoeur's subsequent comments also prove helpful:

> The person, understood as a character in a story, is not an entity distinct from his or her "experiences." Quite the opposite: the person shares the condition of dynamic identity peculiar to the story recounted. The narrative constructs the identity of the character,

---

[13] Ibid., 122.
[14] Ibid., 124.
[15] Ibid., 123.
[16] Ibid., 149.

what can be called his or her narrative identity, in constructing that
of the story told.[17]

A reflexive relationship exists, therefore, between the story and the character.
Despite such strong words, Ricoeur does not collapse the character into the
story.[18] Rather, the story must be attributed to someone—a "who."

Insightfully, Ricoeur notes that the farther one moves from notions of
identity, the farther one moves from narrative. So, in the case of several modern novels and autobiographies, the narrative form is eschewed. In these cases, the self remains, but there is no longer any clear continuity of experiences
that establish the protagonist's identity.[19] Ricoeur's point is that narrative is
necessary for bringing about the continuity required for one to have an identity. These novels and autobiographies expose the self which, without the support of sameness, is in flux. The continuing problem for personal identity is
that one's whole personal story is never available. The early years of one's life
are cloudy in one's memory and the future is unavailable. There is no beginning or ending to the story, so one's personal identity is never fully known. I
will return to this point after situating narrative identity in the theological
context necessary for this study.

Ricoeur argues, "Telling a story, we observed, is deploying an imaginary
space for thought experiments in which moral judgment operates in a hypo-
thetical mode."[20] But while Ricoeur rightly situates narration between description and prescription, it is unclear whether and how one's *personal* identity is
integrated with *human* identity more broadly conceived. Since my claim is that
humanity is identified in the biblical narrative as God's image in creation, I am
interested in a corporate identity prior to personal identity. Brubaker and
Cooper's articulation of "strong" identity is helpful here. Since, like Brubaker
and Cooper, Ricoeur is suspicious of strong notions of personal identity, my
claim may appear counterintuitive. It is important to note, however, that Ricoeur and Brubaker and Cooper are interested in an immanent description of
personal identities. If God, our transcendent Creator, has determined that humans will share a corporate identity upon which personal "identities" are developed, then the claim that humanity is made in God's image requires a
strong notion of identity. Moreover, if God has communicated the nature of
this transcendent creational act through God's covenantal relationship with
humanity, and if an authoritative account of that relationship is provided in
the OT and NT Scriptures, then the biblical narratives provide the appropriate
context for us to come to know God's identity and human identity. In order for

---

17 Ibid., 149–50.
18 Whether or not Ricoeur is consistent on this point is open for debate. To avoid col-
lapsing the character into the story, an underlying *who* must be posited so that the
selection of narrative events are bound together as *someone's* story.
19 Ricoeur, *Oneself as Another*, 149.
20 Ibid., 170.

this claim to become clearer, it is important now to turn to the theological literature focused on the identity of God.

### 1.4. Theological Uses of "Identity"

Kevin Vanhoozer has juxtaposed Ricoeur's analysis with Robert Jenson's.[21] Jenson's argument is theological; his interest is in identifying the God of the Gospel. God has, in fact, taught us his name: Father, Son, and Holy Spirit. "The doctrine of the Trinity comprises both a proper name, 'Father, Son, and Holy Spirit,' in several grammatical variants, and an elaborate development and analysis of corresponding identifying descriptions."[22] These identifying descriptions make clear who, exactly, one is speaking about when one refers to God. In the OT, God is known as "whoever got [Israel] out of Egypt." In the NT, God is known as "whoever raised Jesus from the dead."[23] Jenson is concerned to show that God is distinguished from other supposed gods by his name and the narrative associated with that name.

Jenson positions this triune name in relation to two ways of thinking about eternity: 1) Persistence of the Beginning; 2) Anticipation of the End. In the former, eternity relativizes time, cancelling its significance. In the latter, time is affirmed as essential for the development and realization of the world. "Therefore religion is either a refuge from time or confidence in it. God may be God because in him all that will be is already realized . . . Or, God may be God because in him all that has been is opened to transformation, so that the guilts of the past and immobilities of the present are rightly to be interpreted as opportunities of creation."[24] Jenson's claim is that the God of the Gospel must be understood in the latter sense, understood as eternal because he is faithful through time.[25]

Vanhoozer draws the connections, now apparent, between Ricoeur and Jenson. *Idem*-identity corresponds to Jenson's Persistence of the Beginning due to its emphasis on sameness. *Ipse*-identity corresponds to Jenson's Anticipation of the End due to its emphasis on faithfulness (self-constancy).[26] But there remains the crucial question of permanence through time. On this matter, Vanhoozer finds that Ricoeur supplements Jenson's analysis through his focus on the question "who?" rather than "what?" Instead of asking "what?" has persisted through time, the proper question is "who?" has persisted through

---

[21] See Kevin Vanhoozer, "Does the Trinity Belong in a Theology of Religions?" in *The Trinity in a Pluralistic Age: Theological Essays on Culture and Religion* (ed. Kevin Vanhoozer; Grand Rapids: Eerdmans, 1997), 41–71.

[22] Robert Jenson, *The Triune Identity: God According to the Gospel* (Minneapolis: Fortress, 1982), 4.

[23] Jenson, *The Triune Identity*, 7–8.

[24] Ibid., 4.

[25] While Jenson's distinction between being and becoming presents a helpful polarity, in the end a *tertium datur* is required in order to rightly conceive of God's transcendence and immanence.

[26] Vanhoozer, "Does the Trinity Belong in a Theology of Religions?" 48–49.

time. But at just this point Vanhoozer provides an important theological qualification to Ricoeur's narrative analysis of identity. "It is important to note that
the stories of God's acts do not make him what he is, but reveal him for what
he has been from all eternity and always will be."[27] For Ricoeur and Jenson,
identity and character is not something that exists prior to one's acting it out.
Ricoeur is interested in human identity rather than divine identity. Jenson
goes so far as to argue that this union of identity and character requires a revi-
sionary metaphysic for understanding God's eternal being. For Vanhoozer, on
the other hand, the biblical narratives "are a necessary mediation: ontological
reflection alone does not allow us to identify the Christian God over against
the others."[28] Jenson had already noted as much: "Indeed, Christianity's entire
soteriological message can be put so: God's self-identification with the Crucified One frees us from having to find God by projection of our own perfections."[29] But Vanhoozer's interest is to protect God from being constituted by
the narrative: "The narrative does not constitute God's being, but reveals it."[30]
With this qualification in mind, it is possible for Vanhoozer to conceive of
identity as being constituted within narratives in a particular sense. The constitution of identity, in this sense, is not one of being but of "self"; it refers to a
personal character or a group of personal characters. Since personal narratives overlap, one's "life history is 'entangled' in the histories of others."[31] The
narrative identity of God—Father, Son, and Holy Spirit—is made complex by
the fact that it is known only by the interrelation of three life histories. "Who
God is, and what God is like, is a function of the entangled life histories of Father, Son, and Spirit related in the Gospels."[32] So, God is identified through the
divine economy as testified in Scripture.[33]

Vanhoozer further develops the implications of this conclusion: "God's
unity can be determined only by a configuration of the works of Father, Son,
and Spirit in salvation history."[34] This configuration must be Christocentric;

---

[27] Ibid., 49 n. 26.

[28] Ibid.

[29] Jenson, *The Triune Identity*, 16.

[30] Vanhoozer, "Does the Trinity Belong in a Theology of Religions?" 49 n. 26. This point
is repeated on p. 65 n. 74 in the context of God's dynamic self-identity in the biblical
narratives: "God does not 'acquire' an identity as the plot of universal history develops.
Rather, the story of God's relations shows who God always was, is, and will be."

[31] Ibid., 64. The conception of "self" as constituted by narrative is contrary to the con-
ception found in Brubaker and Cooper's fifth definition of identity. Brubaker and
Cooper have in mind the human experience of an unreliable and fragmented self.
Vanhoozer is emphasizing the unity of the narrative self.

[32] Ibid., 65. Note that "what God is like" refers here to God's character as portrayed in
the biblical narratives. Thus, it is not equivalent to speaking of "what God is" essentially. Another theological argument is required if one wishes to speak of God's eternal
essence.

[33] It is important to note that Scripture includes both human and divine testimony
about God's identity.

[34] Vanhoozer, "Does the Trinity Belong in a Theology of Religions?" 66.

since Jesus Christ is the Word of the Father and the Holy Spirit is the Spirit of Christ, Jesus's life, death, and resurrection give shape to the entire narrative history of the world. "If Jesus is indeed the decisive revelation of God, then God can be true to his Word only if the whole of history manifests the same cross-and-resurrection shape."[35] Vanhoozer and Jenson, in coordination with Ricoeur's narrative theory, have demonstrated that God's identity is known in Scripture through narrative, which provides insight into who God is and what he is like.

Other theologians have focused on the portrayal of Jesus's identity in the Gospels. In two essays, Hans Frei develops a conception of Jesus's identity in relationship to his presence.[36] According to the Gospels, Jesus Christ is portrayed as the one and only savior of the world. This portrayal amounts to a description of Jesus's identity, an identity which is ultimately determined by the cross-resurrection sequence.[37] Here it is Jesus as a "who," as a character, who holds together the variety of his acts. In other words, the "who" is the basis for the action rather than *vice versa*. Yet, in narrative form, Jesus's identity is proclaimed and established by his acts. Frei defines identity as the "specific uniqueness of a person."[38] This is uninformative at first glance. But Frei points out its significance: "A person's identity is the total of his physical and personality characteristics referred neither to other persons for comparison or contrast nor to a common ideal type called human, but to himself."[39] One significant point of overlap can be mentioned regarding Frei's use of "identity" and the use of the term in this study. The overlap may be highlighted by amending his definition of the term as follows: human identity is not referred to other creatures for comparison or contrast, but to God. Frei's observation that identity is not established by comparison or contrast to other members of a group is significant. But, unlike Frei's, my use of the term denotes the uniqueness of humanity as a particular group of creatures who share an identity as God's image, not the uniqueness of a particular individual human creature in distinction from all others. Frei intends to indicate the particular identity of Jesus Christ; I intend to indicate the particular identity of humanity.

Therefore, while Frei's is a helpful means of discerning the way that one particular human has a personal identity, use of "identity" in this study will take a different shape. Richard Bauckham provides additional methodological

---

[35] Ibid., 66.
[36] Hans Frei, "Theological Reflections on the Accounts of Jesus' Death and Resurrection," *Christian Scholar* 49 (1966); idem, *The Identity of Jesus Christ: The Hermeneutical Bases of Dogmatic Theology* (Philadelphia: Fortress, 1975). Citations refer to the reprint of these essays in *The Identity of Jesus Christ* (Eugene, OR.: Wipf and Stock, 1997).
[37] Hans Frei, "Theological Reflections on the Accounts of Jesus' Death and Resurrection," in *The Identity of Jesus Christ*, 14.
[38] Frei, *The Identity of Jesus Christ*, 95.
[39] Ibid., 95.

development of the manner in which identities are recognized in Scripture.[40] Bauckham attends carefully to the unique characterization of God in Jewish literature, especially during the Second Temple period. He demonstrates that the primary means of signifying God's identity is to refer to God as the sole Creator and sovereign Ruler of all things. He then shows that in the NT Jesus Christ is included in the divine identity. The pre-incarnate Christ participates in creation and the exalted Jesus exercises sovereignty over all things.[41] One of Bauckham's primary interests is to show that Jesus is identified in the NT fully with God; Jesus is not portrayed as merely a created intermediary figure somehow standing between God and humanity. The strong emphasis upon the ontological distinction between God and creation in Second Temple Jewish monotheism would never have allowed such a created intermediary. Bauckham argues:

> What Jewish monotheism could not accommodate were precisely semi-divine figures, subordinate deities, divinity by delegation or participation. The key to the way in which Jewish monotheism and high Christology were compatible in the early Christian movement is not the claim that Jewish monotheism left room for ambiguous semi-divinities, but the recognition that its understanding of the unique identity of the one God left room for the inclusion of Jesus in that identity.[42]

In Jewish monotheism, only God is referred to as Creator and sovereign Ruler. Thus, if Jesus is included in the divine identity in the NT through these significations, then he is portrayed as fully divine.

Because of dominant but misleading presuppositions and categories, the significance of Jesus's inclusion in the divine identity is often missed in NT studies. It is useful to consider Bauckham's argument further:

> The dominance of the distinction between 'functional' and 'ontic' Christology has made it seem unproblematic to say that for early Christology Jesus exercises the 'functions' of divine lordship without being regarded as 'ontically' divine. In fact, such a distinction is highly problematic from the point of view of early Jewish monotheism, for in this understanding of the unique divine identity, the unique sovereignty of God was not a mere 'function' which God could delegate to someone else. It was one of the key identifying characteristics of the unique divine identity, which distinguished the one God from all other reality. The unique divine sovereignty is a matter of *who God is*. Jesus' participation in the unique divine sov-

---

[40] Richard Bauckham, *God Crucified: Monotheism and Christology in the New Testament* (Grand Rapids: Eerdmans, 1998).
[41] See ibid., 28–32.
[42] See ibid., 27–28.

ereignty is therefore also not just a matter of what Jesus does, but of *who Jesus is* in relation to God.[43]

This identification of Jesus as God is extended by his being included in God's creative activity, and thus in divine transcendence. This rich description of Jesus's identity, which cannot be reduced to function or ontology, parallels the understanding of human identity as the *imago Dei* in a number of ways. First, the NT texts with which Bauckham is concerned aim to proclaim Jesus's identity, holistically understood, rather than making a merely functional or ontological claim about Jesus. The point of interest is "who Jesus is in relation to God." In the same way, the interest of Gen 1:26–30 is to make clear human identity rather than making a merely functional or ontological claim about humanity. The point of interest is who humanity is in relation to God. Second, Jesus's identity has functional and ontological implications. In the same way, human identity carries certain functional and ontological implications. Third, the identifying characteristics of God's identity distinguish God from all other reality. In the same way, humanity's identifying characteristics distinguish it as the particular creature that it is. God's identity is unique, and human identity as God's earthly image is unique amongst creatures.

Another of Bauckham's claims is important to my thesis: "worship in the Jewish tradition is recognition of the unique divine identity."[44] In other words, it is only when God has been recognized as absolutely distinct from creation that God can be worshipped exclusively.[45] Building on this observation, it can also be true that it is important to identify, and name, creation itself correctly in order to recognize God's unique identity. Further, it is important to be able to identify correctly the various created realities in order to know how they relate to God and each other. Genesis 1 is concerned to express the divine and created identities necessary for Jewish and Christian monotheism.

As Bauckham points out regarding Jesus Christ, identity is logically prior to function even if function is often epistemologically prior to identity. Identity has functional and ontological implications, but it cannot be collapsed into those implications. The distinctions between identity, function, and ontology will be important throughout the rest of this study.

## 1.5 Conclusions

I can now summarize the use of the term "identity" here. First, according to the strong conception of identity summarized by Brubaker and Cooper, the *imago Dei* is the common identity shared by all particular human beings. This is true whether or not a particular human being knows their identity, since human identity is determined by the transcendent God who makes creation what it is. Second, knowledge of the meaning of the *imago Dei* as human identity is

---

[43] Ibid., 41.
[44] Ibid., 34.
[45] Ibid., 14.

acquired on the basis of the narrative identity of humanity as developed within the OT and NT literature. Ricoeur's narrative notion of ipse-identity is in view, with his focus upon the "who" rather than the "what" of the subject. Third, in coordination with the studies by Jenson, Vanhoozer, Frei, and Bauckham, I refer "human identity" to that which uniquely identifies humanity as the particular creature that it is, defined by its relation to God. However, since humanity is a creature, and these previous uses of "identity" refer to God's unique identity, there are important differences between my use and these other uses which will be explored below. Fourth, human identity is discerned in a manner parallel to the way one can discern Jesus's divine identity—through careful attention to the specific portrayal of that identity in the relevant biblical texts. Fifth, as with NT Christology, one must continuously distinguish between (though not separate) identity, function, and ontology if the proper order of theological language about the *imago Dei* is to be achieved. The theological and anthropological implications of "identity" for the meaning of the *imago Dei* will become clear through careful engagement with the relevant biblical texts, specifically Genesis 1 and those texts taken up in chapter 5. With the foregoing conception of "identity" in place, I will offer in the next section of this chapter an interpretation of Gen 1:26–30 in its literary and theological contexts.

## 2. Genesis 1:26–30 in Its Literary and Theological Contexts

There are a number of interpretive issues encountered in Gen 1:26–30, and they have received an abundance of attention. Gordon Wenham highlights three issues in particular, all pertaining initially to 1:26: 1) the use of the plural; 2) the meaning of the prepositions ב and כ; 3) the meaning of צלם and דמות.[46] These traditional points of departure have generally led into the morass of ambiguities associated with investigations into the meaning of the *imago Dei*. I will comment on these aspects of the text when necessary, but only in relation to a broader theological interpretation of Genesis 1. There are two reasons for this decision. First, the debates surrounding these issues tend to eclipse the larger theological statement that is made in Genesis 1 concerning creation and humanity's place within it. Second, in the end it is not altogether clear what exactly should be concluded about any of these three issues merely on the basis of critical exegesis of Gen 1:26–30. The meaning of the text is in some measure ambiguous even upon close inspection. James Barr goes so far as to say, "There is no reason to believe that this writer had in his mind any definite idea about the content or the location of the image of God."[47] If this is even partly true, then the immediate context of Gen 1:26 cannot be expected

---

[46] Gordon Wenham, *Genesis 1–15* (WBC 1; Nashville: Thomas Nelson, 1987), 27–29.
[47] James Barr, "The Image of God in the Book of Genesis: A Study of Terminology," *BJRL* 51 (1968): 13.

to provide the needed information for understanding the meaning of the image of God. In fact, I will argue that the meaning of the *imago Dei* is not ultimately determined by the three issues mentioned above. As will be shown, a range of interpretive decisions are consistent with understanding the image of God as human identity.

Barr's conclusions, one of which is noted in the preceding paragraph, present a significant challenge to those who wish to describe the meaning of the image of God. His studies represent the skeptical pole of interpretation, a pole rarely visited. The excesses have generally been in the other direction, excesses of anthropological speculation. Yet, Barr's conclusions represent a different kind of excess, and it is important to address his skepticism at this point. Barr's method is to examine the lexical stock of Hebrew words that could have been chosen by the author or editor of Gen 1:26 to say that humanity is made in God's image. Barr is hopeful that comparing צלם to other possible word choices will shed light on the choice made by the author. "[I]t is the choice, rather than the word itself, which signifies."[48] Barr argues that צלם is an opaque word, ambivalent in meaning. It is this ambivalence which makes the word suitable. The term indicates the relation between God and humanity but, since the term is ambiguous, it does not come with the conceptual "baggage" that would have been carried by other terms, especially terms used regularly of idols.[49] Barr concludes, "What I suggest is that . . . the choice of *selem* as a major word for the relation between God and man becomes intelligible, even at a stage at which we have still not determined what entity constituted the image of God in man, and even granting the possibility that the P writer himself did not know."[50] Barr argues that דמות limits the meaning of צלם since it indicates "that the sense intended for *selem* must lie within the part of its range which overlaps with the range of *demut*."[51] When reflecting on the image of God in his Gifford lectures some years later, Barr summarizes his interpretation: "The image of God in humanity is not something that can be *defined*, as if we could point out this or that characteristic which clearly exists and to which the phrase expressly refers."[52] But Barr adds that the image of God might refer the reader to God: "It may thus be possible to say that, though the image of God is attached to the story of the creation of humanity, its primary function and purpose is to say something about God. Its dynamics develop from the need to clarify speech about *him*. Precisely for that reason one cannot necessarily locate the elements in human existence to which it applies."[53] In this later

---

[48] Barr, "The Image of God in the Book of Genesis," 15.
[49] See ibid., 21–22.
[50] Ibid., 22.
[51] Ibid., 24.
[52] James Barr, *Biblical Faith and Natural Theology* (Oxford: Clarendon, 1993), 169 (emphasis original).
[53] Ibid., 170 (emphasis original).

analysis, Barr's conclusions point tentatively toward a theological reading of the image of God. Yet the theological suggestion goes undeveloped.

Barr's technical study in *BJRL* is focused on the prepositions and terms used by the author of Genesis. His chosen method is to focus exclusively on these terms, and he concludes that the meanings of the terms are ambiguous. In his Gifford lectures, Barr suggested that the text may be theologically rather than anthropologically motivated. Both studies act as a corrective to various misreadings based upon poor interpretive strategies. However, Barr does not attempt to discern the meaning of the image of God by attending to the theology of Genesis 1–11 or a broader OT theology. In some ways, Barr succeeds in demonstrating what the author of Genesis 1 was not saying, but he does not offer an explanation of what the author may have meant by the image. Barr's method leads to excessive attention to discrete terms rather than to the theological use to which these terms were put. Claus Westermann's study, cited in Barr's Gifford lectures, offers an alternative.

Westermann notes the remarkable lack of attention to the whole creation narrative when interpreting Gen 1:26–30: "As far as I know there has been no attempt to derive the principles for the understanding of Gen 1:26f. from the passage as a whole. It is usually said: the immediate context says nothing about the meaning of the image and likeness; the text presumes it and the hearers knew what was meant."[54] The question he puts to the text is helpful: "What can a narrative mean that wants to tell about the creation of humanity and which has as its kernel the creation of a human being in the image of God? What is the purpose of the creator God when he decides to create a person in his image?" Westermann contrasts this question with the possibility of asking a question disconnected from the creation narrative, the narrative context in which the claim about humanity being made in the image of God is embedded. The mere question of how humanity is described in Gen 1:26 does not take the creation narrative seriously enough since "When it is said in the context of primeval event that 'God created man. . . .', then something is being said about the beginning of humanity that is not accessible to our understanding."[55] We have no experience of the beginning that would yield the divine perspective pronounced by Gen 1:26.

Juxtaposing Westermann's concern with Barr's conclusions yields a helpful insight. While, as Barr concludes, the terms צלם and דמות are somewhat ambiguous, this does not necessarily imply that the narrative is ambiguous regarding what one ought to think of humanity in light of the fact that God has decided to make an image of himself and that God then created humankind to be that image. To begin with, the image of God provides a context for understanding the relationship between God and humanity. This is the case because God's decision to make an earthly image of himself is intimately related to God's decision to create humanity. The logic flows from God's will that an im-

---

[54] Westermann, *Genesis 1–11*, 156.
[55] Ibid.

age of himself should exist to God's act of creation in bringing humanity into existence. God was not faced with a pre-existent humanity that was then determined to be God's image. Nor did God make humankind and subsequently add his image to it. Rather, God decided to put an image of himself into the cosmic sanctuary to serve as God's representative. It is fitting, even "very good," that a creature exist in this position. Therefore, God creates humanity as this image.[56]

Of significance here is the logical order; God's decision to create an image of God is logically prior to the decision to create humanity.[57] This particular creature is what it is because it is identified by God as God's image. The various powers and attributes belonging to humanity follow from God's determination that humanity will be God's image. This identity explains in large part the form that humanity takes, why the relationship between God and humanity takes the particular shape that it does, and how human life is intended to be lived on the earth. Indeed, the identity is teleological, and the teleological dimension of being made in God's image is the identifying characteristic of this particular creature that sets the context for all other aspects of theological anthropology.[58]

This way of putting the matter is reminiscent of Bauckham's analysis of the identity of Jesus Christ as portrayed in the NT. Gen 1:26–30 reveals the character of the human creature and situates it appropriately in relation to God and creation. As for humanity's place within creation, the text describes the appropriate order for human relationships, both with one another and with the creatures over which they rule. In all of these relationships humanity is God's image.[59]

It will now be helpful to describe the theological narrative of Gen 1:1–2:4 and the place that Gen 1:26–30 has within this narrative. This will be

---

[56] The fittingness of this existence of an earthly image of God is only known to us after God makes this decision. Nevertheless, the fact that God did make this decision is a sign of its fittingness. Even more important to note is the shape of God's determination that humanity be the image. No particular human attribute has *a priori* likeness to divinity. Humanity is known to be God's image only insofar as humanity is understood in relation to the divine creator.

[57] Logical priority does not imply temporal priority, of course.

[58] Most interpretations of the *imago Dei* start with humanity as the given and inquire about the content of the image. The procedure here will be to start with the image as the given and wonder about the being of the human creature identified as God's image. This will be shown to be a faithful reading of Gen 1:26–28 as the case is made that creation is portrayed in Genesis 1 as a cosmic temple in which the existence of an image of God is appropriate.

[59] One major reason the functional interpretation is overly reductionistic is that Gen 1:26–30 is interested in ordering the full range of human relationships; the text is not merely interested in humanity's rule over the earth, or even God's rule over the earth through humanity. Of course, human rule over the earth is one of the things mentioned in the text. But, as Barth rightly emphasized, the text is also important for understanding a human's relationship to God and other humans.

accomplished in two ways. First, I will briefly outline contributions from comparative studies of Genesis 1 and other ancient Near Eastern texts, while commenting in the process on the limits of such endeavors. Second, I will outline the theological and literary context in which Gen 1:26–30 is embedded. An interpretation of Gen 1:26–30 will then be offered.

### 2.1. Genesis 1 and the Ancient Near Eastern Cognitive Environment

Ancient Near Eastern parallel texts provide an intellectual context for interpreting Genesis 1. In his monograph on Genesis 1 and its ancient Near Eastern conceptual context, John Walton argues that Israel shared important aspects of its view of the world with other ancient Near Eastern cultures, and that this common cognitive environment is more important for understanding the parallels between Genesis 1 and ancient Egyptian and Mesopotamian literature than textual dependence.[60] Likewise, drawing upon Richard Hays's notion of intertexual echo, Middleton argues that the textual meaning of Genesis 1 is constrained by common cultural codes, patterns of meaning, and ideologies found elsewhere in the biblical canon and in other ancient Near Eastern documents.[61]

---

[60] John Walton, *Genesis 1 as Ancient Cosmology* (Winona Lake, Ind.: Eisenbrauns, 2011).

[61] See Middleton, *The Liberating Image*, 43–231. Middleton's *The Liberating Image* is the most thorough recent attempt to read the *imago Dei* in light of the ancient Near Eastern material, and as such his conclusions must be engaged here. *Contra* Edward Curtis, Middleton convincingly argues that the differences between Egyptian and Mesopotamian royal ideologies, while real, were smaller than they might first appear. In his PhD dissertation ("Man as the Image of God in Genesis in the Light of Ancient Near Eastern Parallels," University of Pennsylvania, 1984), Curtis had argued that the difference between Egyptian and Mesopotamian royal ideologies was fundamental: Egyptian kings were thought to be an image of a deity by nature while Mesopotamian kings were merely chosen by the deity, endowed with kingship and its requisite functions. Middleton's response is well stated: "Whether grounded in nature or grace (if we may so put it), it is the intermediary or representative function of Egyptian and Mesopotamian kings that provides the basis for referring to such kings as the image of God" (*The Liberating Image*, 127). Still, the distinction noted by Curtis may bear some conceptual weight. It is true, as Middleton states, that the representative *function* of Egyptian and Mesopotamian kings is similar. However, Curtis's distinction shows that there is a difference for the standing of the king *in relation to deity*. Egyptian kings were thought to be "divine"; Mesopotamian kings were not. This is significant, even if the functions exercised by the kings were similar.

However, for this study the particular significance of each ancient text is not the manner in which it affirms shared assumptions, but the manner in which it incorporates these shared assumptions into a distinct interpretation of the relationship between deity and creation. The distinctive features of ancient Israel's understanding of God's relation to creation are recognized as Genesis 1 is interpreted in the context of Genesis 1–11 and as creation is referred to canonically. For as Walton concludes, Israel's conception of God and God's relation to the world is unique. "In Genesis, God is outside the cosmos, not inside or a part of it, and he has no origin" (*Genesis 1 as Ancient Cosmology*, 177). Walton summarizes the relation between Genesis and other ancient Near Eastern

One area where the common patterns of ancient Near Eastern cultural practices is helpful for informing the distinctive theological teaching of Genesis 1 is in the records of temple construction and dedication. Studies of these records suggest that God's creative action in Genesis 1 is portrayed as the construction of a cosmic temple. The seven-day structure has parallels in ancient Near Eastern temple building and temple dedication accounts. Moreover, 1 Kgs 8:65 and 2 Chron 7:8–9 record the seven-day dedication of Solomon's temple after the seven-year period of its construction. The dedication was followed by an additional banquet celebration lasting seven days. Jon Levenson has suggested that the seven-year construction of Solomon's temple and the seven-day dedication and banquet periods were modeled on the seven days of creation.[62] *Contra* Levenson, Walton argues that "the association is the reverse— namely, that the Genesis 1 account is modeled after a temple-inauguration account."[63] For my purposes, there is no need to decide between Levenson and Walton on this point. The relevant point here is that there is an important conceptual connection between temple and creation in Genesis 1, in which God rests after establishing the functions and functionaries belonging to a place of worship in which he is present. Walton also supports this conclusion by showing the significance of the Garden of Eden as the place of God's presence, out of which flows the life-giving power of God. Walton concludes that the seventh day of rest is the culmination of the creation week, when God assumes rule over the functional cosmos that he has ordered on the previous days.[64]

Middleton is like-minded, and he develops the connection between creation and temple alongside other OT texts, specifically those that describe

---

texts thusly: "Though the shape of the cosmos is seen in terms quite similar to the literature of the ancient Near East, the elements of the cosmos have no corresponding deities, and the structure of the cosmos is radically different. By the way in which Genesis 1 uses the shared ancient Near Eastern cognitive environment, it asks the same questions that lie behind all of the other ancient cosmologies and operates from the same metaphysical platform but gives quite different answers that reflect the uniqueness of the Israelite world view and theology" (*Genesis 1 as Ancient Cosmology*, 178). Since it is the unique theology and worldview of Israel that is of interest in this study, I will primarily restrict my exegetical comments to the biblical text. But the questions and metaphysical assumptions of the ancient Near East will help to shape interpretation insofar as they inform our understanding of the conceptual interests of Genesis 1.

[62] Jon Levenson, "The Temple and the World," *JR* 64 (1984): 275–98. Cited by Walton, *Genesis 1 as Ancient Cosmology*, 182.

[63] Walton, *Genesis 1 as Ancient Cosmology*, 182. See also Middleton, *The Liberating Image*, 83–85, where Middleton draws a number of additional connections between the heptadic structure of Genesis 1 and other OT texts, such as the seven speeches that include the instructions from God to Moses regarding the tabernacle in Exodus 25–31. Important here is that "the seventh speech is devoted to the theme of Sabbath observance, which is there rooted in God's rest on the seventh day" (85).

[64] Walton, *Genesis 1 as Ancient Cosmology*, 190.

creation as a building.[65] He presses the point by linking creation and tabernacle construction. The key biblical text is Isa 66:1–2:

> Thus says the LORD:
> Heaven is my throne
> and the earth is my footstool;
> what is the house that you would build for me,
> and what is my resting-place?
> All these things my hand has made,
> and so all these things are mine,
> says the Lord.

God is portrayed as enthroned in heaven with the whole earth under his feet; an earthly temple cannot contain God's presence. Yet, argues Middleton, the whole earth is a place of God's presence, a divine sanctuary. Middleton takes the reference to God's Spirit (רוּחַ אֱלֹהִים) in Gen 1:2 to emphasize God's presence in creation, similar to Exod 40:34 when God's presence was signaled by the glory of the LORD filling the newly constructed tabernacle. It is worth quoting Middleton at length:

> If the cosmos can be understood as indwelt by the creator, then the language of Psalm 119:91 ("all things are your servants"; NRSV) might well refer not only to the obedience of creatures to their cosmic ruler, but also to the liturgical service in the cosmic sanctuary. This is consistent with Psalm 148, which exhorts all creatures—humans, angels, animals, even the sun, moon, mountains, and trees—to praise the creator, as if all creatures constituted a host of worshippers in the cosmic temple, over which God is exalted as king. This picture of creation as a cosmic temple also suggests the appropriateness of humanity as God's image in the symbolic world of Genesis 1. For just as no pagan temple in the ancient Near East could be complete without the installation of the cult image of the deity to whom the temple was dedicated, so creation in Genesis 1 is not complete (or "very good") until God creates humanity on the sixth day as imago Dei, in order to represent and mediate the divine presence on earth.[66]

The construction of the tabernacle parallels creation in several other ways also, including the qualities attributed to a chosen craftsman of the tabernacle, Bazalel (Exod 31:3). In Prov 3:19–20 God's wisdom, understanding, and knowledge are mentioned as the means by which God constructed the heavens and the earth, and these same attributes are given to Bazalel as he is filled with the Spirit of God.[67]

The theological connection between creation and tabernacle/temple functions on two levels. First, God's presence and activity are the same in creation

---

[65] Middleton, *The Liberating Image*, 77–81.
[66] Ibid., 87.
[67] Middleton, *The Liberating Image*, 87.

and tabernacle/temple construction. Second, the appropriate response to God's presence and activity in both cases is worship. The temple, therefore, can be conceived of as a microcosm of "the macrocosmic sanctuary of the entire created order."[68] As Walton concludes, with Moshe Weinfeld, "The *Sitz im Leben* of Gen. 1:1–2:3 is to be sought in Temple liturgy."[69] Again, it is unnecessary to ask whether the temple is patterned after creation or *vice versa* in this case. Of significance is the plain fact that there are clear literary and conceptual connections between creation and temple.

Much of Walton's comparative study focuses on the ontological presuppositions Israel shared with its neighbors; in other words, Walton aims to expound the ancient Israelite cognitive environment that would have informed both the author and original readers of Genesis 1. Ancient Near Eastern ontology has received very little attention, so Walton's thorough and measured study is extraordinarily useful. Walton argues that the ancient Near Eastern cultures had a "functional ontology" in which "everything exists by virtue of its having been assigned a function and given a role in the ordered cosmos."[70] Thus, for God to "create" in Genesis 1 is to order and assign functions to the objects of creation; this is how they come into existence. According to Walton, whether or not God created *ex nihilo* is of little or no importance to Genesis 1. Rather, the author of the text is interested in communicating the origins of the cosmos in light of the functional ontology of the ancient Israelite cognitive environment.

Walton's study raises a different set of questions than those often asked of the Genesis 1 text. Modern readers may wonder, "Why is there something rather than nothing?" By posing that question one would normally intend to inquire into why things exist materially. Walton argues that in the ancient Near Eastern cognitive environment, however, the "precosmic world was understood not as a world absent of matter but as a world absent of function, order, diversity and identity."[71] The questions in this case would be: "Why are things ordered rather than chaotic? How did things become what they are, distinct from other things? Why do things have differentiated functions and how were these assigned?" In the relevant literature of the ancient Near East,

---

[68] Ibid.

[69] Walton, *Genesis 1 as Ancient Cosmology*, 191. Walton details here Moshe Weinfeld's seven points found in "Sabbath, Temple and the Enthronement of the Lord: The Problem of the Sitz im Leben of Genesis 1.1-2.3," in *Mélanges bibliques et orientaux en l'honneur de M. Henri Cazelles* (ed. A. Caquot and M. Delcor; AOAT 212; Kevelaer: Butzon & Bercker/Neukirchen-Vluyn: Neukirchener Verlag, 1981), 512. The sentence quoted is point seven.

[70] Walton, *Genesis 1 as Ancient Cosmology*, 24.

[71] Ibid., 42. This is not to say that the ancient Near Eastern cognitive environment requires that things exist materially in a pre-cosmic state. Rather, Walton's concern is to demonstrate the appropriate context for interpreting Genesis 1. From Walton's perspective, a faithful reading of Genesis 1 does not require belief either in pre-cosmic material existence or *creatio ex nihilo* materially understood.

these questions are always answered through reference to divine, personal, causation.[72] This is clearly the case in Genesis 1.

The ancient Near Eastern cosmological texts support an understanding of creation that is coordinated with the assignment of a creature's function and role. Function and role are connected teleologically. Summarizing the ancient Near Eastern understanding of divine causation and teleology, Walton maintains, "The perspective of the ancients on the nature of the material world and causation firmly support what is patently obvious to anyone reading the texts—that they viewed cosmic origins and operations in teleological terms. Purpose and intentionality characterized the work of the gods."[73] This is also true of Genesis 1.

Construing creation in terms of functions and roles correlates well with Middleton's royal-functional interpretation of the *imago Dei* in which humanity is assigned the function of ruling and on that basis is given the role of representing God's rule in the world.[74] There is good reason to believe that function and role are conceptually intertwined. But one may question whether "function" and "role" are the most helpful terms, since they tend to be conceived of reductionistically. For example, in a given day I may function in the roles of husband, father, teacher, writer, cook, gardener, etc. Some of these roles are commonly perceived as being weightier than others, and rightly so. But none of these roles is necessarily conceived as fundamental to my very existence as a human creature in the way that the *imago Dei* is portrayed to be in Genesis 1. In Genesis 1 the *imago Dei* is the justification and explanation of the human creature. So Westermann argues: "This means that the creation of human beings in the image of God is not saying that something has been added to the created person, but is explaining what the person is."[75] Westermann refers to Barth's claim that the image of God "consists as man himself consists as the creature of God."[76] It seems to me, therefore, that "function" and "role" are insufficient terms since humans can function in a role without that function or role being fundamental to who and what they are.

The question at this point, then, is how the function and role assigned to humanity in Genesis 1 can be coordinated with God's purpose in making humans in God's image without relativizing the importance of other human functions, roles, and activities. Both Walton and Middleton conclude that humanity is in the image of God as it rules. Seeing the potential for a reductionistic interpretation, however, Middleton attempts to make the function of ruling nearly all-encompassing in order to avoid relativizing what appear on the surface to be other human activities. My contention is that we should understand God's action in Genesis 1 as establishing the *identity* of the creatures made and

---

[72] Ibid., 37–38.
[73] Ibid.
[74] Middleton, *The Liberating Image*, 88.
[75] Westermann, *Genesis 1–11*, 157.
[76] Barth, *CD* III/1, 184.

that this identity implies *various* functions and roles fundamental to the creature's existence. On this account, the emphasis upon divinely assigned teleological functions is maintained without reducing the human creature to being merely the functionary intended for that sole purpose. In other words, understanding the *imago Dei* as human identity allows ruling to have a significant place within biblical anthropology without reducing "humanity" to "ruler." The canonical witness describes the relationship between God and humanity in various ways, and understanding the *imago Dei* as human identity allows for each of these various aspects of the divine-human relationship to take shape on the basis of God's intention for the human creature rather than in addition to God's intention.

Put theologically, although there are ancient Near Eastern parallels to how and what God creates in Genesis 1, there is no extrabiblical parallel to the God of Israel who does the creating. The particularity of Israel's God requires that the meaning of the image of God in Genesis 1 be bound to the God of Israel and no other. It is this God in whose image humanity was made.

Walton's and Middleton's analyses of the ancient Near Eastern material point in a similar direction. Specifically, they emphasize the portrayal of God as Ruler of all created things which are so ordered to exist as a cosmic temple or sanctuary with humanity ruling as God's representative. With this in mind, I will now explore the immediate literary context in which Gen 1:26–30 is embedded.

## 2.2. Reading Gen 1:26–30 in Its Literary Context

According to Blocher, Genesis 1 is composed in two literary panels. The first panel contains days 1–3. On these days God makes the various spaces or regions of existence. This is accomplished by "divine acts of separation."[77] The second panel contains days 4–6. On these days God peoples or fills these regions with living or mobile beings.[78] The course of these panels is symmetrical: "Day 1 corresponds to Day 4, Day 2 to Day 5, Day 3 to Day 6."[79] Genesis 2:1 summarizes the divine accomplishment according to the acts recorded in the two panels: "Thus the heavens and the earth were finished," [Days 1–3] "and all their multitude" [Days 4–6].[80]

Within this multitude of living and mobile creatures, humanity is the particular creature made in God's image. The purpose of Genesis 1 is primarily theological—it provides an introductory account of what God is like and what God's intentions are for his creation. Genesis 1 also provides an account of the origin and identity of the various cosmic realities, situating them appropriately in relation to God. Therefore, Genesis 1 communicates the fundamental

---

[77] Blocher, *In the Beginning*, 51.
[78] Blocher, *In the Beginning*, 51; Middleton, *The Liberating Image*, 74.
[79] Blocher, *In the Beginning*, 51.
[80] See Blocher, *In the Beginning*, 51–52; Middleton, *The Liberating Image*, 75–76.

relation between God and all other realities. God is the creator of all things. In the following paragraphs, this claim will be explored in more detail.

As noted above, Israel's monotheism is an important distinctive feature of Genesis 1. Its nature is developed along a number of lines. First, there is only one God, the creator. There are no other gods mentioned in the creation narrative.[81] The רוּחַ אֱלֹהִים is mentioned in 1:2 due to the Spirit's being *of God*—this is God's Spirit, participating in God's work. And God creates through his Word. There are no other participants in the creative act; only אֱלֹהִים creates. Second, none of the created realities shares in God's divinity. There are no divine or semi-divine creatures. Creation is no emanation from God.[82] The creation is given its own being, distinct from God yet related to him. Objects in the cosmos that were worshipped as deities in the ancient Near East (i.e., the sun and moon) are called into existence by the fiat of Israel's God. God has no competitors; he did not need to conquer any other gods in order to stake his claim over the world. This radical monotheism establishes the uniqueness of God and his position over all other realities. As Bauckham's research demonstrates, God's being the creator of all things is an identifying characteristic uniquely

---

[81]Some have argued that the plural in Gen 1:26 ("Let us") should be read as God's address to a heavenly court. Despite the fact that several OT texts refer to a heavenly court of created angels, it is problematic to suppose that the plural is an address to the heavenly court in this case. As Clines noted, "If 'we' includes the heavenly court, man must be made in the image of the *elohim*." But in the very next verse the author of Genesis 1 writes in the singular, "So God created humankind in his image." The other problem with this explanation is that it introduces other beings into the creative act. Again Clines's comment is useful: "The Old Testament quite consistently represents creation as the act of Yahweh alone, and we cannot avoid the force of 'let us' by explaining it as a mere consultation before the work of creation begins" ("The Image of God in Man," 67). Others have understood the plural as an address from one god to another, drawn unassimilated from an ancient Near Eastern myth. Again, I agree with Clines: "[W]e think it extremely unlikely, in spite of the superficial similarity of these texts, that the use of the plural in Genesis 1.26 is in any way dependent on such mythological descriptions. If the author of Genesis 1 was in every other instance able to remove all trace of polytheism from the traditional material he was handling, as he is generally agreed to have done, why did he not manage to expunge the plural of 'let us'? Did he not realize the contradiction between 'let us' and 'God created'?" (64). It is generally agreed now that the author of Genesis 1 was too careful and deliberate in his work to have missed such an obvious contradiction.

Cf. Middleton, *The Liberating Image*, 56. He lists the following texts as those which refer to a heavenly court: Job 1:6; 2:1; 5:1; 15:8; 38:7; Ps 29:1; 82:1; 89:5–7 (MT 89:6–8); 95:3; 96:4 (= 1 Chron 16:25); Ps 97:7; Exod 15:11; 2 Sam 5:22–25; 1 Kgs 22:19; Isa 6:2, 8; Jer 23:18, 21–22; Ezek 1; 3:12–13; 10; Dan 4:17 (MT 4:14). None of these texts necessarily has a direct bearing on the meaning of Gen 1:26, however.

[82] In the *Memphite Theology*, Ptah is said to be the one god from whom the other gods emanated. Ptah also creates by his word. The crucial difference between Genesis 1 and the *Memphite Theology* on this point is that Israel's God creates all other realities, and they remain distinct from him. No other realities arise out of God's divinity or share in it.

ascribed to God in each layer of the biblical material, both OT and NT. It is a fundamental presupposition of all subsequent Jewish and Christian thought.

God's position over all other realities should be understood in coordination with God's relation to all other realities as their divine Ruler. There is no aspect of creation outside of God's purview. God's governance over creation is first indicated in Genesis 1 by his creative act. Since God has the authority to make the cosmos what it is, then it continues to exist under God's authority. Creation "obeys" God's Word as he pronounces and so determines creation's existence.[83] God's rule is also indicated by his prerogative to name the beings under his rule, and the whole cosmos (day, night, sky, sea, earth) is named by God.

Middleton elaborates on God's cosmic rule in terms of divine kingship. He opens the parameters of the royal metaphor beyond their usual boundaries. "While I do not believe there is any significant question of the presence of the royal metaphor in Genesis 1, this metaphor must not be understood simplistically, but rather as a complex metaphor, incorporating elements that we might not usually think of as relevant to kingship."[84] He mentions the portrayal of God as artisan specifically. This is telling—it illustrates Middleton's desire to organize what appear to be multiple, but complementary, portrayals of God under, or as aspects of, the portrayal of God as king. Middleton's interpretation of the image of God is organized similarly. For Middleton, humanity is the image of God in that humanity rules, but this rule includes aspects of human existence that we would not normally consider relevant to the function of ruling.

As previously noted, Middleton rightly draws attention to the relationship between God's rule and human rule. But for Middleton, this relationship between God's rule and human rule determines *in toto* the shape of the *imago Dei*. My suggestion is that the relationship between God's rule and human rule *illustrates* the *imago Dei* and establishes one of its aspects. For Gen 1:26 does not say, "let humanity image me *only* in this . . . let him rule." Rather, "Let us make humankind in our image, according to our likeness; *and* let them have dominion over the fish of the sea, and over the birds of the air, and over the cattle, and over all the wild animals of the earth, and over every creeping thing that creeps upon the earth" (italics mine).[85] The connection between image and ruling is not one of definition.[86] On the contrary, the connection is

---

[83] Middleton, *The Liberating Image*, 72.

[84] Ibid., 74.

[85] Even if one chooses to translate וירדו "so that they may rule," the text does not say that humanity is made in the image of God *only* for the purpose of ruling. God may have additional purposes in mind.

[86] Humanity is the object of creation in Gen 1:26–27, and we are told three things about it: (1) Humanity is made in the image of God; (2) Humanity is intended to rule; (3) Humanity is made male and female. These descriptive terms are not interchangeable in content. So, the text does not imply: the image of God is to rule; the image of God is male and female; the rulers are the image of God; the rulers are male and female; the male and female are the image of God (together); or the male and female are the rulers.

paradigmatic. The logic of the text seems to be thus: God is Creator and Ruler of all things; let God's image rule over the earth. Divine self-revelation suggests something about the shape of human existence because humanity is God's image. The text leaves room for fuller understanding of what it means to be God's image *as more about God is revealed*. In Gen 1:26–28 humanity is called to image God by having dominion over the earth precisely because it is God's dominion over the earth that has been revealed thus far.

God, in giving humanity the identity "image of God," leaves humanity without a self-directed definition or goal. Humanity is intended to move toward God. Humans can only know themselves truly in light of God as God is for the world. To use a different idiom, one could even say that God disciples humanity through God's Being-for-the-world to the end that humanity will image God in its being-in-the-world.

Therefore, the Genesis narrative establishes that God, as creator of all things, has determined that the human creature be "in his image." In Genesis 1, the implication drawn from this fact is that humanity, male and female, will rule over the non-human creatures on earth. But human identity is also underdetermined to the extent that God, the one imaged, is not yet fully revealed to humanity in his being creator. There is much more to know about God and the humans made to represent God. For example, while God is fully who God is in being creator, knowledge of God's character arises also from God's covenantal promises revealed by the particularities of God's relation to/with his creatures.

My interpretation suggests a more definitive covenantal basis for the *imago Dei* than the dominion view allows. Genesis 1 is interested in providing the necessary and fundamental identifying descriptions of God and all other realities, including humanity, in order to provide the proper context for understanding God's relationship with Israel and the church. These descriptions do not need to be organized under one theme (e.g., kingship). There is no *a priori* reason for thinking they would not be organized in this manner, but the complex portrayals of God and humanity in Genesis 1 and across the canon suggest that a more inclusive account is preferable. As the covenantal realities add to what we know of God, humanity's knowledge of its own identity is also enlarged.

---

To the question, "who is the image of God?" the only answer that can be given is: the human creature. But to the question, "what is humanity?" three answers must be given: humanity is the image of God, humanity is the creaturely ruler of the earth, and humanity exists as two sexes.

To what do these various descriptions refer? The *imago Dei* is human identity. Rule is an activity, a consequence of the image. Regarding humanity's sexual differentiation, Gen 1:27 states, "Male and female he created them." The pronoun אתם refers back to האדם, describing the distinct but complementary ways of existing as a human being. The comment relates specifically to the manner by which humans will be fruitful and multiply in accordance with God's command and blessing in 1:28.

Blocher has aptly noted the connection between "image" and "son" in Gen 5:1–3, and drawn the implication for Gen 1:26f.: "God created man as a sort of earthly son, who represents him and responds to him."[87] But this raises a question: why would the author not have said as much in Genesis 1? Blocher offers two reasons: (1) "'Son' rather than 'image' could have suggested that mankind possessed divinity"; (2) Scripture reserved the word 'son' "for the closer, indissoluble relationship of communion that God established with us in Jesus Christ, the Son who became the new man."[88] Yet there may be still another reason why "image" and "son" are distinguished. The image of God is the external basis of covenantal sonship; covenantal sonship is the internal basis of the image of God.[89]

## 3. *Imago Dei* and Personhood

By arguing that the *imago Dei* is human identity and not some human capacity, attribute, or activity, it may appear that I am siding with those who equate the image with "personhood." Gerald Bray, for example, argues that being God's image means being a person: "Relationships are only possible between persons, and it is this elusive concept, the thing which defines man as a 'who', and not a 'what', which gives the image its meaning."[90] In the first part of this chapter, I explored the way in which narrative identity is likewise shaped by reference to a "who." However, it is also necessary to demarcate my "identity interpretation" from those interpretations that understand image and the fact of personhood to be equivalent. In the following paragraphs, therefore, I will describe the manner in which human substance, function, and relationships are logically related to the *imago Dei* with the intention of dogmatically ordering the canonical language of the image of God and providing the appropriate conceptual context for clarifying exegesis of the relevant OT and NT texts that will be considered in chapter 5.

---

[87] Blocher, *In the Beginning*, 89–90.

[88] Ibid., 90.

[89] The shape of this language is borrowed from Barth (see *CD* III/1, 42–329). While I do not intend to affirm Barth's reversal of the creation-fall-redemption sequence, much of Barth's language insightfully expresses the connection between creation and covenant. For example, Barth argues, "The history of this covenant is the goal of creation as creation itself is the beginning of this history" (*CD* III/1, 42). However, for Barth this covenant is God's covenant with the Man, Jesus Christ—the beginning of the covenant of redemption between God and humanity. Covenantal sonship is indeed the *telos* of humanity and the internal basis of the *imago Dei*, but this is true first within the covenant of creation and second within the covenant of redemption. The advantage of this language is that it indicates the interconnection of creation, covenant, and eschatology (see Michael Horton, *Lord and Servant: A Covenant Christology* [Louisville: Westminster John Knox, 2005], 93–112).

[90] Bray, "The Significance of God's Image in Man," 222.

Human personhood should not be equated with the image of God. Rather, personhood is a condition of possibility for the realization of the image of God. In other words, humans could not live successfully as God's image without being persons. Though not mentioned specifically by Barth, personhood can be added to the "phenomena of the human" that he describes.[91] Other phenomena to include are rationality, creativity, freedom, physicality, and spirituality. These phenomena can be observed as properties of human existence, but merely describing them as such can yield no unified or compelling vision of human being-in-the-world. Barth argues that such phenomenological self-understanding is incomplete:

> while the conclusions of autonomous human self-understanding are not necessarily false, but in their limits may well be accurate and important, they are all bracketed, and no decisive enlightenment about man is to be expected from within these brackets, but only from a source outside. This source is God. He, the Creator of man, knows who and what man is. For man is His creature, and therefore in the last resort known to Him alone. He must tell man who and what he really is if this is to be known to him.[92]

Barth rightly insists that knowledge of real humanity comes from God. Self-understanding is limited to description of the phenomena of the human without any guidance for how to situate those phenomena in an integrated fashion.

> The point is that the man who can teach himself well or badly about the phenomena of the human finds that in respect of his reality he must receive and accept the instruction of God; that the autonomy of his self-understanding is limited, at the decisive point where phenomena and reality are to be distinguished, by the instruction which is to be received and accepted from God.[93]

Fundamentally, this instruction includes the divine perspective on human identity and the proper shape of human being-in-the-world. As suggested in the second section of this chapter, the manner in which divine revelation is necessary for understanding human identity is even more radical than Barth proposed. There is a positive sense of this: humanity is made for revelation.

Barth's effort to reorder theological language concerning human nature leads him so far as to call these human abilities "symptoms of the human."[94] In other words, they are symptoms of humanity's particular creaturely condition.

---

[91] Barth, *CD* III/2, 122. Because of Barth's emphasis on the relational nature of humanity, it may be that Barth himself would resist such inclusion of personhood as a phenomenon of the human. I include his insight here for two reasons: first, to situate personhood in a manner similar to the way Barth situates rationality; second, to draw upon his claim that humanity is finally known only by God; human personhood, as far as it can be clearly articulated, is still anthropology "from below."

[92] Ibid., 122.

[93] Ibid., 123.

[94] Ibid., 122.

Once these "phenomena of the human" are recognized as subordinate to divine revelation for understanding human identity, Barth reintroduces them into his theological anthropology. Ian McFarland explains:

> At this point, Barth is quite happy to reintroduce the "phenomena of the human" he had earlier dismissed as anthropologically inconclusive as containing value and important insights in the character of the human being. To be sure, they can be reintroduced *only* at this point, once the fundamental determination of human being for God has been secured in Jesus Christ, because it is only when human beings have received definite knowledge of their status before God that they are able to determine which of the many "phenomena of the human" are genuine *symptoms* of human being. Even though such symptoms neither establish that nor explain why human beings have been elected for covenant partnership with God, they do tell us how this covenant partnership is to be lived out. In other words . . . if none of these symptoms constitute the ground of our personhood, they do define its form. They establish that we are persons *as* human beings and not in spite of that fact.[95]

McFarland's claim that "the fundamental determination of human being for God has been secured in Jesus Christ" requires further attention. However, it is important, first, to note the way that the phenomena of the human relate to human identity. These phenomena do not define human identity, but they are the creaturely properties by which human identity is given shape in the world. For example, I have suggested that dominion over the earth is a partial realization of human identity as God's image.[96] God is Ruler of all things, and God's image rules over the earth. Dominion, as McFarland points out, presupposes "those cognitive capacities that have so often been seen as the distinguishing features of human being."[97] Exercising dominion requires the "ability to analyze our situation over against our environment, and to manipulate the latter on an other than purely instinctual basis."[98] Freedom and creativity are also required in this case. Moreover, freedom and creativity enable humans to improvise upon our knowledge of our identity in creation so that after considering examples of the fruitful outworking of that identity, humans can faithfully perform this divinely ordained identity in new ways and in new contexts.

Like the "symptoms" of rationality, creativity, and freedom, human personhood can be properly appreciated and situated only when human identity is understood in light of humanity's relation to God. The mere phenomena of human personhood provide no intrinsic knowledge of what personhood is *for*.

---

[95] Ian McFarland, *Difference and Identity: A Theological Anthropology* (Cleveland: Pilgrim, 2001), 147–48.

[96] *Contra* McFarland, who sees dominion as one of the symptoms of the human (*Difference and Identity*, 149–52).

[97] McFarland, *Difference and Identity*, 151.

[98] Ibid.

Understanding human personhood as a created reality entails that it serves God's purpose for humanity within creation. In other words, human personhood serves the ends of human existence, including the ability for humans to represent God on earth. Personhood is a condition of possibility for the realization of human identity in the world.

Following the pattern of this insight, I will now briefly explain how the physicality and spirituality of humanity enable the realization of human identity. The human creature is in continuity with the rest of creation ontologically. This continuity is necessary in order for humanity to have a concrete presence in the world. Since this is a physical creation, it is fitting that God's image in this world is also physical. This makes the human body a condition of the possibility of being God's *image*.[99] It is also fitting that an image of the living God be a living image. The particular kind of life unique to this physical human creature is personal, responsive, responsible, and self-transcendent. These are spiritual features, and, as the next chapter will demonstrate, the nature of human reception of and response to God's self-revelation is dependent upon the aspects of humanity attributed in Scripture to the human soul.[100] This implies that the human soul is a condition for the possibility of being *God's image*.

Michael Horton argues along similar lines, and he includes "intentional relationality" as a "prerequisite characteristic for human image-bearing."[101] This pits Horton's interpretation against Barth's relational model since for Horton relationality is a prerequisite to being the image and not the archetypical instance of the image:

---

[99] In Col 1:15, it is said that Jesus is the "εἰκὼν τοῦ θεοῦ τοῦ ἀοράτου." The incarnation makes this possible, since "ὁ λόγος σὰρξ ἐγένετο καὶ ἐσκήνωσεν ἐν ἡμῖν, καὶ ἐθεασάμεθα τὴν δόξαν αὐτοῦ, δόξαν ὡς μονογενοῦς παρὰ πατρός, πλήρης χάριτος καὶ ἀληθείας" and "Θεὸν οὐδεὶς ἑώρακεν πώποτε· μονογενὴς θεὸς ὁ ὢν εἰς τὸν κόλπον τοῦ πατρὸς ἐκεῖνος ἐξηγήσατο" (John 1:14; 18).

[100] I do not intend to engage the question of the structure of the human soul here. Irrespective of whether body-soul dualism, holism, emergentism, or some other interpretation of the relation between body and soul is found to be most convincing, Scripture frequently refers to a human soul. I am simply referring to the aspect of humanity picked out by the biblical use. See John Cooper, *Body, Soul and Life Everlasting: Biblical Anthropology and the Monism-Dualism Debate*, new ed. (Grand Rapids: Eerdmans, 2000) for a summary of the relevant arguments concerning the relationship of the soul to the body and a defense of holistic dualism. For a similar conclusion, see Robert Gundry, *Sōma in Biblical Theology: With Emphasis on Pauline Anthropology* (Cambridge University Press, 1976). Likewise Blocher concludes, "Duality stands out unambiguously in the New Testament, just as it does in the Judaism of that era. Furthermore, it is presupposed by the doctrine of the intermediate state. . . . But even in the Old Testament, despite the haziness of the concepts and the different meanings that words can have, it would be wrong to suppose that it was absent. The idea of an inner life is often expressed, with the help, among other things, of the concept of the heart" (*In the Beginning*, 88). The aspect of humanity described here is the one intended by using the term "soul."

[101] Horton, *Lord and Servant*, 104.

While my proposal rejects any identification of the image of God with any faculty or substance, mental or physical, can there be any doubt that human beings are uniquely suited among the creation to be covenant partners with God? And can we not point out fairly obvious prerequisites such as certain natural capacities for deliberative reason, intentional relationality, moral agency, and linguisticality? Yet, none of these capacities exists prior to the covenant of creation, but all are already presupposed by it.[102]

While Horton's "prerequisite characteristics" parallel Barth's "phenomena of the human," Horton's language situates these capacities more clearly in service of human identity. "Condition of possibility" is even more precise since functional capacities, ontological features, and phenomenological orientations can then be included as "conditions." Also, there is an ethical rationale for "conditions of possibility." I am concerned to show that one may have the identity "image of God" even when the conditions of possibility required for *realization* of that identity in the world are not present. Being a person with the identity "image of God" does not require this identity to be expressed clearly prior to the resurrection.[103] It may be the case that one cannot express her identity due to certain conditions of realization not being met. Yet, she still has the identity "image of God." "Prerequisite characteristics for Human Image-Bearing," the full title of Horton's section, can be read as saying that someone cannot be God's image unless they have all of these characteristics.

All of the aspects of human existence that enable it to be and become God's image can fruitfully be understood within the category of "conditions of possibility"—even human substance and relationality. Particular human relationships, with God, other humans, and the rest of creation, provide the context in which the *imago Dei* is realized. Human functions also enable the realization of the *imago Dei* in that they orient human being-in-the-world toward the fulfillment of human identity.

If the interpretation suggested in this chapter is a faithful reading of Genesis 1, then it is necessary to consider further the Christian doctrine of revelation and its implications for the realization of human identity. In chapter 4, I will investigate the relationship between divine revelation and human identity as God's image. The theological basis for this inquiry into divine revelation is God's decision to elect a people, reveal himself to them, and transform them through his presence.

---

[102] Ibid.

[103] After the resurrection, redeemed humans will fully express their identity as God's image. This will be possible because all the conditions for the possibility of expressing this identity fully will be met.

# Chapter 4

# Divine Revelation and Canonical Interpretation of the *Imago Dei*

In chapter 3 I argued that in Genesis 1 the *imago Dei* is best interpreted as human identity. In this chapter, I will describe two theological implications for canonical interpretation of the *imago Dei*. First, human identity is revealed by God. Second, human identity involves becoming like God. These two implications are related, since *imitatio Dei* is dependent upon divine revelation. In the first part of this chapter, therefore, I will provide an account of divine revelation and human reception that will situate dogmatically the remainder of my canonical re-reading of the *imago Dei*. In the second part, I will clarify the manner in which the image of God is related to the imitation of God, particularly in the OT. This will prepare the way for chapter 5, in which I will undertake theological exegesis of the relevant OT and NT texts that inform my interpretation of the *imago Dei*.

## 1. Revelation and the Image of God

Of particular importance in this part of the chapter is the manner by which human identity takes shape in response to divine revelation. In this context, John Calvin's judgment that "without knowledge of God there is no knowledge of self" is entirely correct.[1] Though I make use of Calvin's claim somewhat differently than he did early in the *Institutes*, I believe that my own use is more than accidentally related to Calvin's intent, for as he observed:

> [I]f all men are born and live to the end that they may know God, and yet if knowledge of God is unstable and fleeting unless it progresses to this degree, it is clear that all those who do not direct every thought and action in their lives to this goal degenerate from the law of their creation. This was not unknown to the philoso-

---

[1] John Calvin, *Institutes of the Christian Religion*, vol. 1 (ed. John McNeill; trans. Ford Lewis Battles; LCC; Louisville: Westminster John Knox, 1960), 37–38.

phers. Plato meant nothing but this when he often taught that the highest good of the soul is likeness to God, where, when the soul has grasped the knowledge of God, it is wholly transformed into his likeness.[2]

My proposal is similar to what Calvin affirms here.[3]

Another of Calvin's reflections is helpful in noting the shape of the human pursuit of the knowledge of God:

> [W]e know the most perfect way of seeking God, and the most suitable order, is not for us to attempt with bold curiosity to penetrate to the investigation of his essence, which we ought more to adore than meticulously search out, but for us to contemplate him in his works whereby he renders himself near and familiar to us, and in some manner communicates himself.[4]

While Calvin had God's revelation through creation in view specifically, his comments have a broader application. In every case, knowledge of God is communicated, and mediated, by God. Also, Christian theological reflection primarily attends to God's acts, and only through God's acts considers God's essence, since humans cannot comprehend God's essence directly. Knowledge of God is sought and received through directed contemplation of God's works.[5]

Three theological propositions are at work in Calvin's insights: first, there is a connection between the knowledge of God and human transformation into God-likeness; second, God communicates himself through his works; third, revelation is received by humans through contemplation of God's works. Holding these three propositions together, I will critically engage a number of contemporary proposals on the doctrine of revelation. I wish to focus attention appropriately upon a theology of the knowledge of God without distorting its systematic weight. To rightly situate my evaluation of these contemporary proposals, I will begin this chapter by considering the basis for human knowledge of God and its ends. Human knowledge of God is ectypal, patterned upon God's archetypal knowledge of himself. Therefore revelation must be understood first with reference to God's self-knowledge.

## 1.1. *God's Intra-Trinitarian Knowledge*

God is known because God knows himself. This is a necessary starting point. So, 1 Cor 2:10–11 explains: "For the Spirit searches everything, even the

---

[2] Ibid., 46–47 (Book 1, ch 2.3).

[3] Ford Battles connects Calvin's comments to Plato's *Theaetetus* (*Institutes*, 47 n. 12). "To escape evil and attain true wisdom, men must 'become like God . . . righteous, holy, and wise' (LCL Plato II. 128 f.)."

[4] Calvin, *Institutes*, 62 (Book 1, ch 5.9).

[5] Undirected contemplation of God's works is not sufficient (or even possible). The Scriptures include not only accounts of God's works but also interpretations of those works. Scripture mediates and directs one's understanding of God's economy. So, humans receive knowledge of God through directed contemplation.

depths of God. For who knows a person's thoughts except the spirit of that person, which is in him? So also no one comprehends the thoughts of God except the Spirit of God" (ESV). Any knowledge of God that is given to creatures is derivative of God's own self-knowledge and self-revelation. Lest one think that this knowledge is purely introspective and uncommunicated within God's life, Matt 11:27 states: "[N]o one knows the Son except the Father, and no one knows the Father except the Son." The Father is known by the Son and the Spirit. The Son is known by the Father and the Spirit. And the Spirit is known by the Father and the Son. This movement of God's self-knowing is the eternal act that provides the basis for temporal and creaturely knowledge of God.

### 1.2. The Fruit of God's Self-Knowledge in God's Life

To discern the ends of the knowledge of God for humanity, it is helpful to first consider the fruit of the knowledge of God in God's own triune life. Jesus's prayer in John 17 is instructive: "[Y]ou have given him [your Son] authority over all people, to give eternal life to all whom you have given him. And this is eternal life, that they know you, the only true God, and Jesus Christ whom you have sent. I glorified you on earth by finishing the work that you gave me to do" (John 17:2-4). Eternal life is knowing God. Jesus makes the Father known, thereby bringing eternal life to God's people. Because the Father is known, he is glorified. Jesus wishes to return to his eternal life with the Father: "So now, Father, glorify me in your own presence with the glory that I had in your presence before the world existed" (John 17:5). This glory comes from the Father and is related to the identity of the Son. Jesus explains: this is "my glory, which you have given me because you loved me before the foundation of the world" (John 17:24). It is the Son's knowledge of the Father, given because of the Father's love, that brings about the Son's glorification of the Father and the Father's glorification of the Son.

God's self-knowledge is also God's wisdom. In the divine economy, Christ is revealed as the wisdom of God. This is Paul's argument in 1 Corinthians 1, where Christ is identified as "the power of God and the wisdom of God" (1 Cor 1:24). "He [God] is the source of your life in Christ Jesus, who became for us wisdom from God, and righteousness and sanctification and redemption" (1 Cor 1:30). The important thing to note here is that Christ Jesus became "*for us*" wisdom from God. Yet, before Christ Jesus became wisdom for us, he was already the very wisdom and power of God through whom all things were made (John 1:3).[6] The divine economy reveals what was already the case—the eternal Son is the wisdom of God since he is the image of the Father who exists also as the Father's Word. The Spirit of God is the Spirit of wisdom (Eph 1:17) because he is the Spirit *of* the Father and the Son, who searches the depths of God and

---

[6] Athanasius, *On the Incarnation of the Word of God*, §48. See Daniel Treier's treatment of Prov 8 for a Christological and Pneumatological understanding of wisdom in conversation with patristic observations [Daniel J. Treier, "Proverb 8" in R. Michael Allen, ed., *Theological Commentary: Evangelical Perspectives* (New York: T&T Clark, 2011), 57–72].

knows God's thoughts (1 Cor 2:11). God's self-knowledge and its fruit—glory and wisdom—are the basis for the human knowledge of God and its proper ends.

### 1.3. Human Knowledge of God

Creatures are invited to know God. Creatures cannot demand knowledge of their Creator in any way that forces God to act. If God is known by human creatures, it is only because God wants to be known and therefore accommodates himself to human ways of knowing. A number of biblical passages emphasize the Son's communication of his knowledge of the Father. Matt 11:27: "All things have been handed over to me by my Father; and no one knows the Son except the Father, and no one knows the Father except the Son and anyone to whom the Son chooses to reveal him." This communication of knowledge is possible because of God's self-knowledge. So John 1:18: "No one has ever seen God; it is God the only Son, who is close to the Father's heart, who has made him known." Jesus's prayer in John 17:25-26 extends the insight: "Righteous Father, the world does not know you, but I know you; and these know that you have sent me. I made your name known to them, and I will make it known, so that the love with which you have loved me may be in them, and I in them." As John Webster notes, the revelation of God in Christ is the *verbum externum*—"the presence and action of the eternal Word."[7] The Word reveals the Father to the world.

Second, God sanctifies the human intellect so that it can receive the knowledge of God. In 1 Corinthians 2, Paul says: "as it is written:

> 'What no eye has seen, nor ear heard,
>   nor human heart conceived
> what God has prepared for those who love him'—

these things God has revealed to us through the Spirit" (1 Cor 2:9-10). Paul offers this further explanation: "Now we have received not the spirit of the world, but the Spirit that is from God, so that we may understand the gifts bestowed on us by God. And we speak of these things in words not taught by human wisdom but taught by the Spirit, interpreting spiritual things to those who are spiritual" (1 Cor 2: 12-13). This work of the Spirit corresponds to the presence of the Word; the Spirit's work is the *verbum internum*—"the presence and action of the Holy Spirit by whom cognitive fellowship between God and creatures is consummated."[8] Webster argues:

> In relation to the gospel, created intelligence is not directive but directed. Put more materially, understanding of the gospel arises as the Father of glory gives a spirit of understanding (Eph. 1.17), so enlightening the eyes of the heart (Eph. 1.18). What sets in motion

---

[7] John Webster, *The Domain of the Word: Scripture and Theological Reason* (New York: T&T Clark, 2012), 119.
[8] Ibid., 119.

> creaturely apprehension of the gospel is God himself: the inner glo-
> ry of God in its outward splendour, the inner wisdom of the Spirit
> who knows God's depths and is in himself infinitely wise, and who
> communicates this to creatures.[9]

The relationship between God's gift of knowledge and the powers of the human knower is asymmetrical. God's gift of knowledge is accommodated to human knowing, but human knowing is never able to accommodate itself to God. Webster comments insightfully: "There can be no relaxation from the creaturely side of the rule *finitum non capax infiniti*. . . . Yet, for all its interim importance, this emphasis on finite incapacity is no resting place. The missions of Son and Spirit overrule creaturely inadequacy and make it possible for knowledge of God to take creaturely form."[10] In fact,

> God loves creaturely nature and capacities and desires their full use,
> and so reveals himself in ways which are fitting to that nature and
> gives occasion for the exercise of those capacities. . . . Revelation is
> accommodation, its modes proportionate to its recipients; and ac-
> commodation is the exercise of charity (God working in and
> through and to the benefit of the created nature which he loves)
> and of power (God making creaturely words fitting and effective).[11]

God's self-knowledge is the basis for humanity's knowledge of God, and it is also the surety of that knowledge. Human knowledge of God relies upon God's eternal act of intra-Trinitarian knowing and God's determination to accommodate the knowledge of God to human intelligence. As human knowledge is dependent upon God's self-knowing, so the *teloi* of human knowledge of God are dependent upon the fruit of God's self-knowledge in the divine life. These *teloi* can now be considered.

### 1.4. The Ends of the Human Knowledge of God: Worship

I have argued that divine self-knowledge is the ontological fount of revelation. It is precisely because the Son knows the Father from before the creation of the world that the Son can reveal the Father in the world. So Jesus says: "I have made your name known to those whom you gave me from the world." (John 17:6). When this revelation is received, it leads to the glorification of God by those to whom the revelation is given. "[F]or the words that you gave me I have given to them, and they have received them and know in truth that I came from you; and they have believed that you sent me. . . . All mine are yours, and yours are mine; and I have been glorified in them" (John 17:8, 10). The people of God glorify Jesus because they know the Father through the Son and believe that the Son is from the Father. It is this knowledge of God, through the gospel, that glorifies God in the world. When God's Name is

---

[9] Ibid., 61.
[10] Ibid., 138.
[11] Ibid., 59.

known, when the Name shared by the Father and Son is known, God is glorified. The recognition of God's Name by human creatures leads to worship; it is the communication of God's own self-knowledge within creation that leads creation to worship. Human worship—embracing God's Name and so giving God glory—is a creaturely act patterned upon the eternal, mutual glorification of the Father, Son, and Spirit which is rooted in God's self-knowledge. God's revelation conforms human intelligence to his own Word such that humans can offer fitting worship.

## 1.5. The Ends of the Knowledge of God: Wisdom

The Spirit of wisdom turns divine wisdom toward the creature. Christ Jesus has become the wisdom of God for us but it is through the Spirit that this wisdom is revealed (1 Cor 2:10). And the Spirit gives God's people "the mind of Christ" (1 Cor 2:16). What is the mind of Christ? It is the mind that knows God through Christ by the power of the Spirit.

Wisdom, in Proverbs 3:18, is pictured as the tree of life, and "those who hold her fast are called happy." Note the contrast with Genesis 3, where the effort to establish a creaturely wisdom apart from God led to humanity's being cursed. As Daniel Treier argues, "Rather than being told by God what was good and evil, [Eve] would decide as much herself (or so the serpent falsely advertised)."[12] The creational context of wisdom in Proverbs 3 and 8 reveals the way that divine wisdom sets the pattern for human wisdom. Human wisdom exists within divine wisdom; it takes the same shape as divine wisdom and submits to the boundaries set for it by divine wisdom. "The LORD by wisdom founded the earth; by understanding he established the heavens; by his knowledge the deeps broke open, and the clouds drop down the dew" (Prov 3:19–20). "The LORD possessed me at the beginning of his work, the first of his acts of old. Ages ago I was set up, at the first, before the beginning of the earth" (Prov 8:22–23, ESV). Because creational wisdom is derived from divine wisdom, wisdom demands faith in God: "Trust in the Lord with all your heart, and do not lean on your own understanding" (Prov 3:5). For "[t]he fear of the Lord is the principle of wisdom, and the knowledge of the Holy One is insight" (Prov 9:10).[13] Knowledge of the Holy One *is* insight, and it must be pursued in the fear of the Lord rather than in a way that sees wisdom as merely immanent in creation.

Creaturely worship and wisdom find their ontological justification within God's own life. God's self-knowledge brings the divine Persons glory and constitutes God's wisdom. Creaturely knowledge of God produces worship and

---

[12] Daniel J. Treier, *Virtue and the Voice of God: Toward Theology as Wisdom* (Grand Rapids: Eerdmans, 2006), 47.

[13] Translation amended to cohere with Henri Blocher's argument that the fear of the Lord is the "principle" of wisdom from beginning to end [Henri Blocher, "The Fear of the Lord as the 'Principle' of Wisdom" *TynBul* 28:1 (1977)].

wisdom since these ends are, eternally, the fruit of the knowledge of God. Yet, further reflection on human reception of divine revelation is required.

*1.6. How the Knowledge of God and Its Ends are Given and Received*

The epistemological basis for human knowledge of God is divine revelation. God knows himself, and therefore God can make himself known. Divine revelation is the accommodating instruction given by God so that creatures come to the knowledge of God and are moved by that knowledge toward its proper ends. Theology, understood as contemplation of God and God's relation to creation, is crucial for successful realization of the *imago Dei* in the world because appropriate creaturely representations of God's character in human action rely upon sound judgments about who God is and what God's character is like. Theology is the vigorous and joyful task of attending to God's self-revelation, intellectually tracing its contours, so that human worship, wisdom, and action take on a fitting shape.

Karl Barth's *Anselm: Fides Quaerens Intellectum* is particularly enlightening with respect to the nature of the theological task.[14] Theological understanding, he argues, can only proceed upon the basis of faith. God is known by faith, and that knowledge can be made a matter of intelligence. For Anselm, "*intelligere* is itself and remains *credere* while the *credere* in and by itself . . . is also an embryonic *intelligere*. But *intelligere* is more than that: to read and ponder what has already been said—that is to say, in the appropriation of truth, actually to traverse that intervening distance (between recognition and assent) and so therefore to understand the truth as truth."[15] The question is how this distance is traversed. What human activity is required for faith to become understanding? Barth observes:

> Anselm is distinguished from the 'liberal' theologians of his time in that his *intelligere* is really intended to be no more than a deepened form of *legere*. But—and this distinguished him just as definitely from the 'positivists', the traditionalists of his day—it does involve a deepened *legere*, an *intus legere*, a reflecting upon. So as sons and heirs of Adam we are not confronted by the truth of Scripture in such a way that, when the hearing or reading of the outward text is crowned by faith (certain as it is that this text is the full revealed truth), we are then absolved from the task of understanding it as truth, which, though divinely given, has still to be sought by human means.[16]

The problem, then, is how one should describe the human means of receiving divine revelation. This is where Barth recognizes in Anselm the convergence of the human knowledge of God and divine knowledge of God. Anselm uses the

---

[14] Karl Barth, *Anselm: Fides Quaerens Intellectum: Anselm's Proof of the Existence of God in the Context of His Theological Scheme* (Eugene, OR: Pickwick, 2009).

[15] Ibid., 40.

[16] Ibid., 41.

word *ratio* to denote both the means and the end of his search for understanding.[17] The means of arriving at understanding is humanity's knowing *ratio*. The goal of his search for understanding is "the *ratio* that is to be known, the *ratio* that belongs to the object of faith itself."[18] Human *ratio* is aimed at understanding our faith.

The problem, now, is that the human *ratio* is so frail on its own, as Anselm himself recognizes: "I acknowledge, Lord, and I give thanks that you have created Your image in me, so that I may remember You, think of You, love You. But this image in me is so effaced and worn away by vice, so darkened by the smoke of sin, that it cannot do what it was made to do unless You renew it and reform it."[19] It is this prayer that concludes with Anselm's conviction that belief and love may be led, little by little, to understanding.

Barth argues that Anselm recognizes a "third and ultimate *ratio*, a *ratio veritatis*."[20] It is at this point that Anselm takes the path of our investigation above, rooting *ratio* in the life of God himself. Barth explains: "Strictly understood the *ratio veritatis* is identical . . . with the divine Word consubstantial with the Father. It is the *ratio* of God. It is not because it is *ratio* that it has truth but because God, Truth, has it."[21] This claim has two implications. First, human *ratio* stands under the truth and is guided by it. "The way in which the right use of the human *ratio* is determined primarily by its object is therefore, as it were, only the operation by means of which Truth, that is God himself, makes this decision. What is meant by the human *ratio* with regard to truth can therefore in no circumstances be one that is creative and normative." Second, God's own Truth, his Word, is the basis for God's Word to humanity, and it is also the basis for humanity's understanding of that Word, an understanding which can only be seen through the eyes of faith. "[B]ecause it is truth that disposes of all *rationes* and not *vice versa*, the revelation must ensue first and foremost in the form of authority, in the form of the outward text: above all the *ratio veritatis* can be nothing more than something dictated."[22] In a characteristic sentence, Barth states: "It is in the Truth and by the Truth, in God and by God that the basis is a basis and that rationality possesses rationality."[23] When rightly ordered, human reasoning is a creaturely reflection of God's own *ratio*, which is the product of the reality that God is truth. Human understanding, which is the product of well-ordered human *ratio*, is aimed at God himself and finds its fulfillment in the knowledge of God.

---

[17] Ibid., 44.
[18] Ibid.
[19] Anselm of Canterbury, *Major Works: Proslogion* (Oxford: Oxford University Press, 2008), 87 (§1).
[20] Barth, *Anslem*, 45.
[21] Ibid.
[22] Ibid., 48.
[23] Ibid., 51.

Both the ontological and epistemological bases for the knowledge of God, then, are located in God himself. Ontologically, God's self-knowledge and its fruit within the triune life of God is the basis for human knowledge of God and its fruit within human life. God's self-glorification is the basis for and justification of human worship, and divine wisdom is the basis for and justification of human wisdom.

Epistemologically, God's self-knowledge is the basis for divine revelation. The economic Trinity is the expression and disclosure of the immanent Trinity. God's self-knowledge is also the Truth, the Word that produces divine *ratio*. Human *ratio* seeks to trace the logic of divine *ratio*, holding to its determined contours as it contemplates God in response to divine revelation.[24] Theology is, therefore, not merely the reproduction of divine revelation in human form but human contemplation of and reasoning through divine revelation. This is important to the theological implications of the *imago Dei*. The task of patterning our thoughts after God's thoughts and patterning our acts after God's character revealed through God's acts follows upon God's invitation to know and glorify God analogically in wisdom and worship. Given that the realization of the *imago Dei* relies upon divine revelation, it is important to examine the human reception of divine revelation in more detail. Therefore, with the foregoing account in view, I will now assess a number of recent proposals on the doctrine of revelation.

### 1.7. Contemporary Proposals on the Doctrine of Revelation

Barth's account of divine revelation in the *Church Dogmatics* looms large in the background of any serious contemporary discussion of the doctrine of revelation. While it is unnecessary here to offer a detailed study of Barth's doctrine of revelation, it is useful to summarize his contribution since Ronald Thiemann's and Gunton's proposals come in response to Barth's influence. Gabriel Fackre summarizes the discussion of revelation in *CD* IV/3/1 in the following way: "Here is the heart of Barth's theology of revelation, Jesus Christ, the 'one and only Word of God', spoken as preceding 'all reception on our part', reconciliation *as* revelation."[25] Fackre explains the broad scope of this point for Barth:

> Barth's christological concentration cannot be separated from the entire sweep of the drama of God's deeds. He tracks the revelatory reconciliation in the historical event of Jesus Christ back to its origins in the inner-trinitarian Life, and then follows the course of the electing Love there present forwards into the covenant with creation, the call and expectation of Israel, to the Word enfleshed—and

---

[24] This process finds its fulfillment eschatologically when we see God face to face (1 Cor 13:12), when we are like him because we see him as he is (1 Jn 3:2).

[25] Gabriel Fackre, *The Doctrine of Revelation: A Narrative Interpretation* (ECTS; Edinburgh University Press, 1997), 125 (emphasis original). It might be argued that a reversal of terms would be more accurate: revelation *as* reconciliation.

from there again to the witness of Scripture, the recollective life and tradition of the church and finally to the full light of eschatological radiance. The echoes of narrative interpretation of Christian doctrine can be heard in this encompassing epistemology.[26]

Barth's emphasis on the self-revealing triune God has received much attention. God is Revealer, Revelation and Revealedness.[27] "*God* reveals Himself. He reveals Himself *through Himself.* He reveals *Himself.* . . . God . . . is identical with His act in revelation and also identical with its effect."[28] God reconciles humanity to himself through his self-revelation in Jesus Christ; for Barth, this is the first principle of theology.

The manner by which humanity receives and appropriates revelation receives less attention from Barth, as Ben Quash criticizes: "[Barth] stops short of showing how revelation can be something with which human beings are in a collectively creative relationship through time, inasmuch as he isolates the revelatory event from any historical conditioning (it occurs in, but not as part of history)."[29] Drawing upon Rowan Williams's description of the tradition of Christian thought as "learning about learning," Quash asks, "Might it not be possible to see 'learning about learning' . . . as being God's work?"[30] God reveals himself, and God unfolds "the truth of revelation over time and in the life of the community of the redeemed."[31] Further consideration of how the church receives God's self-revelation is useful.

Ronald Thiemann and Colin Gunton have recently offered significant constructive proposals on the doctrine of revelation, and both are interested in identifying the ways in which God's revelation is received and appropriated by the church.[32] Thiemann develops his doctrine of revelation in concert with narrative identity understood similarly to the portrayal in the third chapter. "[T]he category of narrative is useful for theology because it integrates a central literary genre in scripture with an organizing theological image. But narrative has the further significance of providing the language by which we specify personal identity."[33] Thiemann analyzes the personal identity of Jesus Christ as it is portrayed in the Gospel of Matthew in order to demonstrate the

---

[26] Ibid., 125.

[27] Barth, *CD* I/1, 295.

[28] Ibid., 296.

[29] Ben Quash, "Revelation," in *The Oxford Handbook of Systematic Theology* (ed. John Webster, Kathryn Tanner, and Iain Torrance; OHRT; Oxford University Press, 2007), 336. Barth does direct the reader to his book on Anselm, discussed above. I believe that Barth's argument in *Anselm* goes some way toward answering Quash's criticism.

[30] Ibid., 336. The phrase "learning about learning" comes from Rowan Williams's *On Christian Theology* (CCT; Oxford: Blackwell, 2000).

[31] Quash, "Revelation," 336.

[32] Ronald Thiemann, *Revelation and Theology: The Gospel as Narrated Promise* (University of Notre Dame Press, 1985); Colin Gunton, *A Brief Theology of Revelation* (New York: T&T Clark, 1995).

[33] Thiemann, *Revelation and Theology*, 112.

manner by which identity description has theological implications. Thiemann summarizes the fruits of his approach: "At the Gospel's ending the careful reader will have discovered the identity not only of the Son of God but also of the one he calls 'Abba, Father.'"[34] The revelation of God the Father occurs as Jesus fulfills his formal identity as the Son of God. Jesus's individual personal identity is established by the narrative identifications provided in the Gospel.[35] To develop Thiemann's insight, one could say that Jesus's performance of his identity reveals both who is the Son of God and who is God the Father. Jesus is shown forth as the one who truthfully performs his identity as Son of God. His performance of this identity is the proof that Son of God is indeed Jesus's identity. Yet, it is not as though Jesus's individual personal identity is entirely free from ambiguity throughout the narrative. Rather, in 4:18–20:34, "Matthew stresses the ambiguity which characterizes Jesus' personal identity."[36] Confirmation of Jesus's identity as the Son of God awaits the end of the narrative. "In an artful literary and theological conclusion Matthew shows the unity between the intentions of God and Jesus as manifested in the events of crucifixion and resurrection. In obediently submitting to his crucifixion Jesus of Nazareth shows himself most clearly to be God's Son, an identification which is confirmed and completed in the resurrection."[37] So, Jesus's identity as Son of God is made known through the performance of that identity and then through the narrative directions communicated in Scripture.

Thiemann argues that the God identified by the narratives of the Gospel of Matthew is ultimately concerned to include the reader in his promise; God invites the reader to recognize God's promise of salvation described in the Gospel. The reader comes to know the identity of the God of promise through Jesus Christ and is then invited by Jesus to participate in God's promise. In Matt 28:16–20, as Jesus sends his followers to make disciples of all nations and promises to be with his disciples to the end of the age, he proclaims the promise to the reader. "Thus the reader is invited to respond to this narrated promise by entering the world of the narrative and joining with those on the mountain who worship him."[38] Thiemann comments on the significant implications that follow from this narrative reading of the doctrine of revelation:

> That extension of the narrative's textuality in the world of common human reality provides the crucial context for the final formulation of a revised doctrine of revelation. . . . In that transition from narrative identification to narrative address the Gospel story announces that it seeks to embrace the whole of human reality within its purview. The God identified within this narrative now addresses his promise of salvation through this narrative to those who read the

---

[34] Ibid., 115.
[35] Ibid., 114.
[36] Ibid., 114.
[37] Ibid., 115.
[38] Ibid., 143.

text and hear his promise. The promises of God depicted within the text now become his promises to those who stand outside the text.[39]

Because knowledge of God's identity comes through "narrated promise," Thiemann argues for an alternative way of formulating the doctrine of revelation. The traditional conversation has inquired primarily into whether God can be known. Thiemann suggests that the following replace the traditional inquiry: "*A doctrine of revelation is an account of God's identifiability.*"[40] Instead of taking up the doctrine of revelation in theological prolegomena or methodology, Thiemann suggests that the doctrine must be addressed within the doctrine of God. He hopes that this dogmatic reorganization will accomplish two things. First, this move will save Christian theology from being enslaved to foreign epistemologies that require epistemic justification prior to engagement with the narrative content of Scripture. Second, Thiemann hopes that this will provide a more holistic understanding of the ways that the locution and illocution of the biblical text are related to the "interlocutionary act" that marks successful communication.[41]

Thiemann is right to be wary of the demands put to Christian theology from foreign epistemologies, but there is reason to question whether he has rightly understood the "threat" of "foundationalism," which Thiemann says is the cause of the misguided efforts to speak of revelation faithfully. I will address this point in more detail below. A strength of Thiemann's approach is his insistence that God's identity is known on the basis of the narrative content of Scripture. Moreover, the vast scope of Thiemann's doctrine of revelation is remarkable. In the end, however, the component aspects of a doctrine of revelation must be more carefully situated in relation to knowledge and reception. For example, Thiemann claims that "[a] doctrine of revelation, understood as an account of God's identifiability and recast under the category of narrated promise, provides an appropriate rationale for the Christian belief that the universe is God's, created, redeemed and reconciled by his grace, i.e., for belief in God's provenience."[42] But one is left to wonder how the "appropriate rationale" for God's identifiability is, in fact, established and for whom it is established. Thiemann hopes to offer a solid alternative to modern construals which are too dependent upon modern epistemology, and he has made several helpful suggestions in this direction. But it is not clear that he has supported his analysis with a theological rationale that fully accounts for the knowledge of God in Christian theology. Gunton presses Thiemann's proposal in the following way: "To base theology on narrative, that is to say, to turn the narrative into the revelation, appears to preclude any discussion of the grounds for preferring one narrative to another, whether in question are rival versions of the

---

[39] Ibid., 143–44.
[40] Ibid., 153 (emphasis original).
[41] Ibid. "By 'interlocutionary act' I mean the successful act of communication which elicits an appropriate response from the addressee" (144).
[42] Ibid., 156.

Christian narrative, and they will, of course, be various, especially under modern conditions, or the narratives told by different religions."[43] Gunton argues that Thiemann's account is missing a robust doctrine of creation, noting especially the lack of a theology of nature and its attendant epistemological implications.

Gunton seeks to establish a theological rationale for thinking that divine revelation fits in the broader context of human knowing. To do this, he suggests that all human knowing is dependent upon some form of revelation; humans have no immediate knowledge of other human persons, the world, or God.[44]

> My theological concern here, therefore, is that there can be no recovery of a doctrine of theological revelation—revelation of God—in the absence of what I would call a general theology of revelation. By that is meant a recovery of the Coleridgean doctrine that 'all Truth is a species of Revelation', and that means not only divine revelation but that revelation without which we should know nothing at all.[45]

Revelation is needed since knowledge must be mediated to humanity. On the other hand, on the basis of the doctrine of creation Gunton asserts that the structures for revelation are present in creation so that the world may be known. "[T]here can be revelation because the world is so made that it may be known."[46] The convergence of these two points requires anthropological and pneumatological development since the mediation of revelation "requires not only a doctrine of creation, but involves us in a particular teaching about ourselves, the kind of beings we are, and about the way God the Spirit works toward and in the world."[47] The argument is dependent upon the theological claim that God has made humanity to be a knowing creature. Humans are meant to know God, other humans, and the world—not comprehensively but adequately. This raises the question of what human knowledge is adequate for, and it may now be suggested that human knowledge must be adequate for the outworking of human identity as God's image in the world. Knowledge is intrinsically and not only instrumentally good. The pursuit of knowledge is good because humans are oriented toward knowing by God. Ultimately, as argued in the final section of the previous chapter, the various structures and orientations belonging to human existence are what they are because they facilitate humanity's existence as the creature designed by God for the specific purpose of being his image. That humanity is a knowing creature is a condition of possibility for its existence as God's image. I have now added my own claim concerning the *imago Dei* to Gunton's insight that God intends the world to be

---

[43] Gunton, *A Brief Theology of Revelation*, 49.
[44] Ibid., 22–39.
[45] Ibid., 32.
[46] Ibid., 33 (emphasis original).
[47] Ibid., 34.

known. This complements the anthropological clarification that is necessary for the development of a theology of revelation.

Throughout his study, Gunton distinguishes between what is revealed and the reception of that revelation. When this is applied to the context of bibliology, Gunton resists the conflation of the God who is known through Scripture and the medium of Scripture itself. This distinction appears obvious when stated in these terms, but Gunton sees this conflation as the danger inherent in narrative theology. Moreover, Gunton is suspicious that narrative theology is guilty of seeking an unmediated knowledge of a God constituted by the biblical text.[48] Gunton is also wary of accounts that diminish the significance of the mode of mediation necessary for human knowledge, such as Barth's. Gunton argues that Barth's theology portrays revelation as epistemically unmediated since Barth underplays the significance of the humanity of Christ and the place and function of the Spirit.[49] Gunton counters all such claims to epistemic immediacy; rather than seeking to bypass the mediation of divine revelation, Gunton attempts a proper dogmatic description of the mediation of revelation.

Gunton concludes with four points in this regard. First, one must differentiate between a Christian theological epistemology and the philosophical assumption that "like is only known by like," and "we can only know God by means of something Godlike."[50] Second, the work of the Spirit mediates knowledge of God through Christ's humanity, so one could say that knowledge of God is mediated through that which is not God. Third, the Spirit mediates knowledge of God through more general means than the humanity of Christ, namely through "the humanity of scripture."[51] Fourth, in that Christ is the mediator of creation, he also mediates human rationality and human knowledge which is taken up by the perfecting work of the Spirit so that humans can and do know. Ultimately, therefore, Gunton concludes that revelation is mediated by Jesus Christ and the Holy Spirit.

Gunton, like Thiemann, is dubious of foundationalism, and seeks a non-foundationalist theology of revelation. It is important to note that a great deal of conceptual baggage is often illegitimately piled upon foundationalism, which is ultimately a theory of epistemic justification. Non-foundationalist epistemologies can also be falsely maligned. The doctrine of creation provides the requisite context for navigating through the relevant questions; attacking foundationalism or non-foundationalism on their own terms often leads to a misunderstanding of the theological context for human knowing.[52] In order to

---

[48] Ibid., 5–7.

[49] Ibid., 119. Gunton notes that Barth speaks frequently of the humanity of God but rarely of the humanity of the incarnate Son (123 n. 17).

[50] Ibid., 124 n. 20; 123.

[51] Ibid., 124.

[52] Kevin Vanhoozer points in the right direction when he observes of modernism and postmodernism, "precisely because it is a reaction against modernity, postmodernism inadvertently risks letting *modernity* set the agenda. . . ." ("Pilgrim's Digress: Christian Thinking on and about the Post/Modern Way", in *Christianity and the Postmodern Turn*

avoid misunderstanding, it is helpful to address briefly the appropriate dogmatic context for theological epistemology. First, the Christian doctrine of creation implies that humanity is designed to live in the world in successful ways measured according to God's purpose for the human creature. Humanity is always-already in the created world, and it is an appropriate environment for human functioning.[53] On this basis it is fair to conclude that humans are designed to know God and the world adequately enough to enable the fulfillment of humanity's particular vocation.[54] Second, the doctrine of creation implies that each human being inhabits a particular location in creation. It is from this historical, situated, created location that one learns, knows, and lives. A number of implications can be drawn at this point: (1) humanity is designed to function in the world successfully toward the end for which God designed us; (2) knowledge of God and the world is necessary for proper functioning such that proper functioning entails adequate knowledge of God and the world; (3) humans are situated in the world such that human knowledge is partial and is gained from a particular perspective.

If God has designed humanity and the human environment, then there will be beliefs and actions that are appropriate universally—not because they are the result of human transcendence but because creation in each of its parts and contexts is an appropriate historical and situational context for these beliefs and actions. There are also beliefs and actions that are only appropriate in a particular historical and situational context and not another. Attending well to humanity's creational location proscribes epistemologies that overlook either the wider or narrower epistemic contexts.

By suggesting that the doctrine of creation provides a rationale for the claims made above, I hope to avoid the quagmire into which debates about foundationalism and non-foundationalism often lead. Unfortunately, most theologians who comment on the matter are untrained in modern analytic and/or continental epistemology so the evaluations are often thin and one-sided. There are legitimate criticisms that can be leveled against particular

---

[ed. Myron Penner; Grand Rapids: Brazos, 2005], 81). The same can be said in this case; non-foundationalism risks letting foundationalism set the agenda precisely because it is a reaction against foundationalism, "even if only in a negative fashion." This critique can also be extended to modest or moderate forms of foundationalism. While they may represent nuanced responses to the differences between classic foundationalism and non-foundationalism, they fail to change the terms of the debate; classic foundationalism continues to set the agenda.

[53] See Alvin Plantinga, *Warranted Christian Belief* (New York: Oxford University Press, 2000).

[54] At this point, I am not addressing the corruption that has entered into human knowing because of sin. Of course this would need to be addressed if a thorough theological epistemology were developed, but here I am only interested in showing how the doctrine of creation sets the epistemological questions within a distinct conceptual context. A complete theological epistemology would need to take a Christological turn since Jesus, in his human nature, fulfilled humanity's identity and vocation as *imago Dei*.

foundationalist or non-foundationalist accounts, but it is unhelpful to engage in holistic criticisms of all foundationalist or all non-foundationalist episte-mologies. Although my thesis is not wed to a particular theory of epistemic justification, it is theologically instructive to note that the doctrine of creation provides the needed epistemological context for a broad theology of revela-tion. While Thiemann's and Gunton's criticisms of foundationalism are not careful enough to be decisive in the matter, Gunton's recognition of the im-portance of the doctrine of creation for analysis of the doctrine of revelation is correct.

In the end, Gunton appreciates Thiemann's emphasis on the knowledge of the God of promise gained through divine prevenience, but believes that this claim needs to be based on a broader theology of revelation. Gunton's empha-sis on the mediation of all knowledge is helpful for accounting for the various forms of mediation present in the church's reception of divine revelation.

Placher's description of the way divine revelation is shaped historically is similarly informative, and it is useful to add his insights to Gunton's. Placher's interests have to do with knowing the transcendent God in history. After pointing out the differences between the narratives of the Exodus, King Da-vid's reign, the stories about Elijah, and those of Acts, Placher observes,

> The texts as we have them assume that God is at work in *all* of this history and do not reflect on the different modes of divine action they report in different periods. If one were to try to extract a "bib-lical point of view" from these texts, therefore, it would have to be something like, "God works in history—sometimes more dramati-cally and sometimes through the more ordinary behavior of natural forces and human actors—and the differences do not much matter.[55]

This focus on history is important for clarifying the significance of those his-torical events that reveal God in a particularly acute way, most importantly the life, crucifixion, resurrection, and ascension of Jesus Christ. The narratives about Jesus take place within a canonical context that emphasizes the ubiquity of divine action in history. Placher summarizes his proposal concerning reve-lation in three propositions:

> (1) Some historical events can provide a luminous key to under-standing all things. (2) [T]hey do not just happen to do so for some people, but there is something about the events themselves such that in them was the special disclosure of the transcendent begin-ning and end of all things we call God. (3) When we ask how God was acting differently in such events, however, we quickly realize that we lack the categories to describe such differences.[56]

---

[55] Placher, *The Domestication of Transcendence,* 192.
[56] Ibid., 193.

The possibility of knowing God is based upon God's revelatory action in history.[57] Placher's insight corresponds to the significance of Barth's description of the God of the Gospel as Revealer, Revelation, and Revealedness.

To this point, I have taken note of Thiemann's emphasis upon the relationship between revelation and biblical narrative, Gunton's insistence that all knowledge is dependent upon revelation mediated in various ways, and the importance of history for understanding God's revelation as noted by Placher. These aspects of the doctrine of revelation provide the appropriate context for noting how God uses Scripture both to reveal himself and to shape human imitation of God's character.

### 1.8. *Divine Revelation and Holy Scripture*

Given the broader canonical re-reading of the *imago Dei* coming in chapter 5, it is important to clarify the relation of Scripture to divine revelation. As Webster argues, Holy Scripture is a creaturely reality elected and sanctified by God to serve a particular purpose in God's communicative divine economy—to bear testimony.[58] "Through Holy Scripture God addresses the church with the gospel of salvation."[59] Since it is God who addresses the church through Scripture, the authority of the biblical testimony is God's, but Scripture itself remains a creaturely reality. "It is *as*—not *despite*—the creaturely realities that they are that they serve God."[60]

Elsewhere, Webster argues that "[s]cripture is the availability of prophetic and apostolic ministry beyond its originating occasion"—availability of God's Word in the present.[61] The *telos* of reading and hearing God's Word is that creatures come to know and love God. "Scripture engenders such acts [of knowing and loving]; it is their occasion and regent. God's Word does not stun creatures into immobility; it moves them, it is a *path* (Ps. 119.35), a divine movement summoning and ruling a corresponding creaturely movement."[62] And this divine movement leads humans to rightly worship God and live wisely in creaturely reflection of his character.

The task of human reasoning through Scripture for moral decision-making is illuminated by Oliver O'Donovan:

> Ethics reflects on the conditions of obedience *to the realities which the Scriptures attest*—to those realities as a whole, that is, and not to selected parts of them which might seem specially apt for moral reflection. Obedience to Scripture can only be an exercise of faith—

---

[57] It should be noted that in this context I intend God's action to include speech-acts.

[58] John Webster, *Holy Scripture: A Dogmatic Sketch* (CIT; Cambridge University Press, 2003), esp. 11–29.

[59] Ibid., 32.

[60] Ibid., 28.

[61] Webster, *Domain of the Word*, 121.

[62] Ibid., 121–122.

not, that is, faith *in Scripture*, but faith in the creating and redeeming work of God, to which Scripture bears authoritative witness.[63]

The insights offered by Webster and O'Donovan are helpful for framing Scripture's role in divine revelation and human formation. By combining these insights with the arguments made earlier in the chapter, I want to emphasize (1)
the instrumental role that Scripture plays as it moves one made in God's image
toward worship and wisdom in response to divine revelation and (2) the corresponding human reasoning that, by the illumination of the Holy Spirit, traces
the logic of divine revelation and envisions human life in ways that are faithful
to God's own character.

## 1.9. Revelation and Identity

Vanhoozer's important observations about narrative, drama, revelation,
and identity are helpful for drawing together the various threads of the foregoing discussion.[64] Vanhoozer argues, "The vocation of being human follows
from God's prior evocation. We are called into existence through the triune
God's self-communicative activity. Being human thus involves both indicative
and imperative dimensions: what we should do follows from the kind of creatures we are."[65] Human action in the world is intended to take the particular
shape that it does because humans are the creatures made in God's image. The
divine determination to make humanity what it is is also the determination of
appropriate human activity. Note the union of ontology and ethics. In
Vanhoozer's elaboration on this claim, he touches on the relevant point for
this chapter: "The human creature is called above all to be a witness. It is the
vocation of human being to be echoes of God's evocative creative, reconciling
and redeeming action."[66] As God's image, humanity is a witness concerning the
divine Creator, Reconciler, and Redeemer.[67] In order to echo God's action, God

---

[63] Oliver O'Donovan, *Ethics as Theology, vol. 1: Self, World, and Time* (Grand Rapids: Eerdmans, 2013), 80.

[64] Kevin Vanhoozer, "Human Being, Individual and Social," in *The Cambridge Companion
to Christian Doctrine* (ed. Colin Gunton; Cambridge University Press, 1997), 158–88. After
surveying a number of important streams of thought on the nature of human being,
Vanhoozer posits his own interpretation of the *imago Dei*: "Humans are like God in their
ability to go out of themselves and enter into personal relations through communicative activity. . . . What it means to be in the image of God is best grasped by an auditory
rather than a visual analogy. The human creature is not so much ikon as an *echo* of the
divine being and of the trinitarian communicative relations."[64] This intriguing conception of the image holds together well the traditional emphases on rationality and relationality. According to the pattern suggested in this chapter, it seems that communicative agency is necessary but not sufficient for the realization of human identity as the
*imago Dei*, and, this being the case, communicative agency appears to be a condition of
possibility for this human identity.

[65] Ibid., 183.

[66] Ibid.

[67] While Vanhoozer's statement appears to allow for the failure of humans to be witnesses, I will suggest below that humans are always witnesses of that which they

must first act and reveal himself to the human creature. Humanity has been created as the kind of creature that can receive and respond to God's revelation. Vanhoozer describes the conceptual context for understanding divine revelation: "The human creature comes second to God, both in the order of being (namely, creation) and in the order of knowledge (namely, revelation)."[68]

Furthermore, in *The Drama of Doctrine*, Vanhoozer explains the relationship between vocation and identity.[69] Identity, for Vanhoozer, is something to be enacted and lived out. "[T]heology exhorts the faithful *to become something they already are*—to participate in the eschatological reality of the coming kingdom of God."[70] Vanhoozer focuses upon the Christian's identity in Christ, but the principles of identity and human vocation undergirding his discussion apply to the *imago Dei* also, especially in light of the fact that the Holy Spirit's work of conforming Christians to the image of Christ is in continuity with humanity's creation in the image of God, as will be shown in chapter 5. It is worth quoting Vanhoozer at length:

> One's identity 'in Christ' is both gift and task. While the divine call is decisive because it determines our identity, our response to the call also matters. The way we respond determines whether we will embrace our God-given identities or seek (foolishly) to forge our own, whether we accept our acceptance by God or, in attempting to become wise in our own eyes, become hypocrites. To realize one's identity 'in Christ' is therefore a task of the disciple, a task that requires practical wisdom and hence the diet of doctrine.[71]

Note that one's identity "in Christ" is not subject to change even if one seeks to forge their own identity; rather, such a person becomes a hypocrite. One's identity is determined by God and is performed either well or poorly, either truthfully or falsely. This shows that identity is both gift and task, determination and vocation. Vanhoozer draws the implications for realizing this identity as follows: "We are imitators of Christ not because we need to complete his mission but in order to witness to its *finality*. The purpose of doctrine is to conform us to the truth, and we conform to the truth by bearing true witness to what God has done and is doing in Christ through the Spirit." Just as one who is reconciled and redeemed to God the Father through Christ in the Holy Spirit is a witness to this action of God as they live out their identity "in Christ," human beings are witnesses to God's creative action by faithfully living out their

---

worship. It is not a question of whether humans are or are not witnesses but whether or not humans are witnessing faithfully or unfaithfully, whether in fact humans are true or false witnesses.

[68] Vanhoozer, "Human Being," 159.

[69] Kevin Vanhoozer, *The Drama of Doctrine: A Canonical-Linguistic Approach to Christian Theology* (Louisville: Westminster John Knox, 2005), 394–97.

[70] Ibid., 394.

[71] Ibid., 394–95 (emphasis original).

identity as God's image. While we can distinguish between human identity at creation and human identity in Christ, these are not ultimately different identities.[72] God has fulfilled and realized human identity as the *imago Dei* in Christ, and as the church is included in Christ the personal identities of its members are likewise realized.

Vanhoozer emphasizes the role of the biblical canon in shaping human identity. It is instructive to consider his reflection on Barth's theology of revelation:

> Why can't Jesus Christ be theology's first principle? I am sympathetic to Barth's insistence that our starting point must be God in self-revelation, namely, Jesus Christ. Though I would not for a moment dispute Jesus' status as God's Word, I do see a problem concerning access; we have no authorized version of Jesus Christ save that recorded in Scripture. Barth's point stands—the first principle of Christian theology must be God's self-revelation—yet . . . Scripture, too, is ultimately the work of the triune God in communicative action, a canonical showcase for Christ.[73]

This critique is in no way a reversal of Barth's conception of revelation, but instead it represents the kind of careful attention Quash recommends to the manner by which the church receives and appropriates divine revelation. The church knows and worships the God revealed in Scripture. As suggested near the beginning of this section, God's self-revelation in history, to which Scripture is a truthful witness, is therefore the basis for human self-understanding.

For the purposes of this study, the doctrine of revelation informs the relationship between God's self-revelation and human identity by affirming the following: first, God is known through God's triune action in the world, including divine speech-acts; second, divine revelation is mediated through Scripture, which is the authentic testimony to God's triune action in the world; third, human reception of divine revelation is dependent upon God's action, both in making himself known and in mediating this knowledge to created beings; fourth, human reception of divine revelation is also dependent upon God's creational intention for humanity, since humans are knowing creatures who arrive at knowledge on the basis of various forms of mediation. Chapter 5 attends to the particular ways human identity takes shape in relationship to God's self-revelation in Scripture.

Before attending to the relevant biblical texts in detail, however, a set of objections must be addressed. Divine revelation is necessary for the *imago Dei* to be realized, and the realization of the *imago Dei* entails the *imitatio Dei*, the imitation of God. There has been disagreement, however, about the viability of the *imitatio Dei* as a proper interpretive category in OT theological ethics. Since

---

[72] The word "ultimately" is important here; since the world is not identical to the church, these identities are now descriptively distinct. However, as far as Christ is the paradigmatic human person, prescriptively the identities are unified.
[73] Vanhoozer, *The Drama of Doctrine*, 63 n. 19.

I will argue that imitation of God is invited at various points in the OT, I must address the criticisms that have been raised against this interpretive strategy.

## 2. *Imago Dei* and *Imitatio Dei*

Based on exegesis of Genesis 1, I have argued that the invitation for humanity to share in God's dominion over the earth in a creaturely way is paradigmatic for understanding the further ways in which humanity is meant to pattern its being-in-the-world after God's economic action. In other words, human identity as the image of God is the theological basis for imitating God. Yet Cyril Rodd has argued that the imitation of God is almost completely absent from OT ethical thought.[74] John Barton has recently responded to Rodd's critique with an acknowledgement that imitation of God is certainly not a sufficient motivation for all OT ethics.[75] Likewise, Walter Houston argues that "*imitatio dei* is not a key to unlock all doors in the ethics of the Old Testament."[76] While Barton and Houston find more OT instances of ethical reasoning on the basis of the imitation of God than Rodd does, they both work under the assumption that Rodd's objections need to be addressed directly if a convincing case is to be made for understanding these instances of ethical reasoning as *imitatio Dei*.[77] The following paragraphs address Rodd's objections on a methodological level so as to open the way for a theological reading of OT texts in light of the developmental nature of humanity as God's image.

Rodd's criticisms are aimed most directly at Eryl Davies's "Walking in God's Ways: The Concept of *Imitatio Dei* in the Old Testament."[78] Davies finds imitation of God to be foundational to biblical ethics in general, and he finds references to it littered throughout the OT, especially noting imitation language in the Pentateuch, Psalms, and the prophets.

---

[74] Cyril Rodd, *Glimpses of a Strange Land: Studies in Old Testament Ethics* (OTS; Edinburgh: T&T Clark, 2001), esp. 65–76. Rodd qualifies his view by acknowledging that a certain similarity of human action to divine action may at times be promoted (68). Rodd himself does not rule out imitation of God completely; he discovers one true assertion that humans ought to imitate God in the OT (Deut 10:17–19). Primarily, however, Rodd argues that the motivation to imitate God, if it exists at all, is hidden behind other more pronounced ethical motivations.

[75] John Barton, "Imitation of God in the Old Testament," in *The God of Israel* (ed. Robert Gordon; UCOP 64; Cambridge University Press, 2007), 35–46.

[76] Walter Houston, "The Character of YHWH and the Ethics of the Old Testament: Is *Imitatio Dei* Appropriate?" *JTS* 58 (2007): 1–25.

[77] Barton states that "Rodd has constructed a hard-hitting case against *imitatio dei* in the Old Testament, which will have to be taken into account in any future discussion of the subject" ("Imitation of God," 42).

[78] Eryl Davies, "Walking in God's Ways: The Concept of *Imitatio Dei* in the Old Testament" in *In Search of True Wisdom: Essays in Old Testament Interpretation in Honour of Ronald E. Clements* (ed. Edward Ball; JSOTSup; Sheffield: Sheffield Academic, 1999), 99–115.

Similarly, Eckart Otto sees imitation of God as central to OT ethics. Otto argues, "Wie Gott mit dem Menschen umgeht, so soll sich der Mensch zum Menschen verhalten."[79] More specifically, Otto refers imitation to the whole pattern of God's saving action toward humanity: "Das heilsgeschichtliche Handeln Gottes dient als Vorbild für das ethische Handeln des Menschen."[80] For Otto, then, the specific instances of imitation language are reflective of an entire pattern established by God's relationship to his people and its implications for the people's relationship with one another. Rodd does not directly address Otto's arguments.

In his critique of Davies and Barton, Rodd takes pains to show that the biblical texts normally used to support the imitation of God are, in fact, misinterpreted when taken to support direct, or univocal, imitation of God. Among others, he picks out Lev 19:2 as a text particularly prone to being misinterpreted in this regard: "קְדֹשִׁים תִּהְיוּ כִּי קָדוֹשׁ אֲנִי יְהוָה אֱלֹהֵיכֶם." Rodd only raises one in principle objection to using imitation language for interpreting this text:

> [I]t is doubtful whether what is envisioned in Leviticus 19 is actually *imitating* God. Imitating involves copying an action, repeating it, reproducing it. This is not what is found in the chapter. Rather what is required of Israel is to be holy (in its own way) because God is holy (in his), and although human holiness and divine holiness as purity may be thought to coincide, the moral actions which are called out by it need not be.[81]

The objection, then, is two-pronged. First, Rodd makes a terminological distinction: imitation is not mere similarity but repetition or reproduction. As Rodd notes, in Lev 19:2 "The phrase is 'because (*kî*) I am holy', not 'according to my holiness'."[82] Second, the particular actions taken up by Israel in response to God's holy actions do not necessarily follow directly from God's holiness. "None of the social obligations which Davies lists has an original in the divine activity."[83] Rodd raises a couple of additional hermeneutical problems with interpreting Lev 19:2 in the context of imitation, but the objections outlined here are the ones by which he comes close to dismissing imitation language from OT ethics. It is important, therefore, to address these directly.

Barton has responded directly to Rodd's critique. In response to the first prong of Rodd's critique he says, simply, "that it is very much a matter of definition whether one calls this kind of 'similarity' with God 'imitation' or not. . . . I would not go to the stake for the term *imitatio dei*, but I still think it pointed

---

[79] "Human beings should behave towards each other as God behaves to them." Eckart Otto, *Theologische Ethik des Alten Testaments* (TW; Stuttgart: Verlag W. Kohlhammer, 1994), 185. Translated by Barton, "Imitation of God," 37.

[80] "God's action in salvation history serves as a model for the ethical action of human beings." Otto, *Theologische Ethik des Alten Testaments*, 185.

[81] Rodd, *Glimpses of a Strange Land*, 69 (emphasis original).

[82] Ibid., 69 n. 16.

[83] Ibid., 69.

to something worth saying."[84] Thus the terminological distinction is hardly a devastating criticism for the claim which Davies and Barton seek to develop by insisting that there is an important relationship between divine action and human ethics. Barton is happy to use a different term to describe this relationship if *imitatio Dei* is found objectionable. In order to answer the second prong, Barton appeals to the "scholastic doctrine of analogy." Barton explains that according to the doctrine of analogy,

> [H]umankind retains traces of its divine origin and therefore can offer some clues, however inadequate, to what God is like. This is true because God did indeed make us in his own image, and we are therefore not deluded when we suppose that he is in some very remote sense like ourselves. But, of course, from a God's-eye view this really means that we are like him: in the order of *knowing*, we reason from humans to God, but this is only legitimate because, in the order of *being* we derive all our good qualities from him in the first place.[85]

While Barton's explanation of the doctrine of analogy is not as careful as we might like, his appeal to this doctrine is appropriate.[86] When Rodd asserts that Israel should be holy (in its way) because God is holy (in his), the distinction he makes between the Creator and the creature is the same distinction made in the doctrine of analogy. God's manner of being is different from humanity's manner of being. Since this is the case, humanity can only imitate God analogously—there is no univocal *imitatio Dei* if the imitation is performed by a creature. That said, since humanity is intended to be a creaturely representative of God on the earth it is appropriate that humans imitate God in their own way. There is no hubris in human imitation of God, biblically conceived, since God has ordered humanity toward this end.

This claim runs up against another of Rodd's objections, one disconnected from Lev 19:2. Regarding the teleological aspect of OT ethics, Rodd asserts, "[I]n one sense, to be given teaching which leads to the goal God has in mind is to become conformed to the character of God and to live according to his ethical practice. But this is not the same as being invited (or even commanded) to *imitate* him, and in any case the goal which God has in mind for human beings is not necessarily the same as the goal for himself."[87] It is instructive that in his reply, Barton inserts his agreement with Rodd's first sentence, saying, "This is

---

[84] Barton, "Imitation of God," 39.
[85] Ibid., 40 (emphasis original).
[86] On analogical language see David Burrell, *Analogy and Philosophical Language* (New Haven: Yale University Press, 1973; *idem, Exercises in Religious Understanding*; see also the "Symposium on Freedom and Creation" in *FaithPhil* 25.2 (2008), esp. David Burrell, "Creator/Creatures Relation: 'The Distinction' vs. 'Onto-Theology'" and *idem*, "Response to Hasker and Cross"; see also Michael Horton, *Covenant and Eschatology: The Divine Drama* (Louisville: Westminster John Knox, 2002), esp. 7–9.
[87] Rodd, *Glimpses of a Strange Land*, 68 (emphasis original).

indeed more or less what I mean by *imitatio dei*."[88] Apparently Rodd is willing to grant that there is good precedent in the OT for the idea that human action should be conformed to the character of God, even if he is unwilling to use the term *imitatio Dei* to describe this. Barton's agreement shows that there is really no difference in principle between their views at this point since Rodd's objections are based upon a misunderstanding of the way others are using the term "imitation." A canonical perspective, one from which Rodd is not working, highlights this misunderstanding. Take Eph 5:1–2 for example: "Therefore be imitators (μιμηταὶ) of God, as beloved children, and live in love, as Christ loved us and gave himself up for us, a fragrant offering and sacrifice to God." Paul here affirms that God's people are meant to mirror intentionally God's love in relationship with one another. However, Paul does not have in view some kind of univocal imitation in which Christians give their sons over to be sacrificed for the salvation of humanity. Imitation language in Scripture takes on the analogical form given by Paul rather than the univocal meaning insisted upon by Rodd.[89]

However, the final sentence of Rodd's quotation raises an additional objection. Teleologically, God and humanity may have very different ends. Thus, the means to those ends may also be vastly different, and imitating God may not lead to the proper end of humanity. The *imago Dei* speaks directly to this concern since it is humanity's identity to be God's image on the earth. As shown in my exegesis of Genesis 1, human dominion over the earth is an analogical participation in God's own dominion. From the outset, then, the teleological trajectory for human existence is tied intimately to God's own relation with the world. Barton touches on this in his claim that according to the order of being all good things are derived from God.

But the relationship between *imago Dei* and *imitatio Dei* may also help address Rodd's final objection. Rodd's strongest argument against finding the ethical motive of the imitation of God in the OT is that there are a number of God's actions which, if copied by humans, would be humanly unethical.[90] Any defensible notion of the imitation of God needs to give an account of how Israel is intended to act in response to divine actions that seem to violate biblical ethics as applied to humanity. Barton concurs; as an example, he picks out the apparent injustice of God's actions in corporate judgment. God judges nations for the sins of their leaders without discerning between the innocent and the

---

[88] Barton, "Imitation of God," 40.
[89] Moreover, in the theological tradition the imitation of God has rarely been understood as univocal imitation. On the contrary, such an anthropomorphic interpretation has been considered naïve. One is not meant to reproduce literally divine actions. Rather, one is meant to display a character that has been analogously formed and patterned after the character of God, revealed in God's word and works. This way of understanding imitation has been maintained throughout the Christian tradition. Rodd appears to be unaware that Davies and Barton may be using the term "imitation" in this theological sense and so makes a straw man out of their claims.
[90] Rodd, *Glimpses of a Strange Land*, 75.

guilty. This goes contrary to the Deuteronomistic command to human leaders: "Parents shall not be put to death for their children, nor shall children be put to death for their parents; only for their own crimes may a person be put to death" (Deut 24:16). Barton takes these cases as convincing evidences that "God acts in ways human beings are forbidden to act," and concludes that in such cases it would be "entirely inappropriate for us to try to imitate him."[91] Therefore, while Barton remains convinced that imitation of God is a useful concept for understanding some aspects of OT ethics, he concludes that divine imitation is not always invited. The implication for OT ethics in general is that there are a variety of ethical motives represented in the OT, and the ethical motivation for each particular text should be interpreted on its own terms.[92] I am in agreement with Barton here. The image of God is one thread of the fabric that makes up the narrative of God's covenantal relationship with humanity. There is no need to insist that it is the only thread or even the central thread.

Because one does not need to force every text into the mold of *imitatio Dei*, one is free to ask what criteria there are for determining which texts should be read in light of the *imitatio Dei* and which should not. The texts addressed in chapter 5 are primarily shaped by an invitation, command, or expectation of analogical imitation as evidenced by the literary context in which the invitation, command, or expectation is situated. For example, Davies makes an impressive case for interpreting Psalms 111 and 112 in the light of *imitatio Dei*.

> The attributes of God set forth in Psalm 111 are regarded in Psalm 112 as being reflected in the life of the true believer. Thus, just as the righteousness of God 'endures forever' (עֹמֶדֶת לָעַד, 111:3b), so the righteousness of the upright 'endures forever' (עֹמֶדֶת לָעַד, 112:3, 9); just as God is 'gracious and merciful' (חַנּוּן וְרַחוּם, 111:4b), so the pious is 'gracious, merciful and righteous' (חַנּוּן וְרַחוּם וְצַדִּיק, 112:4b); just as God 'gives' (נָתַן) food for those who worship him (111:5), so the godly exhibit a similar generosity by 'giving' (נָתַן) freely of their possessions to those in need (112:9); just as God acts with 'justice' (מִשְׁפָּט) towards his people (1117a), so the pious will act 'with justice' (בְּמִשְׁפָּט) towards each other and just as the works of God will always be remembered (זֵכֶר עָשָׂה לְנִפְלְאֹתָיו, 111:4a), so the righteous will never be forgotten (לְזֵכֶר עוֹלָם יִהְיֶה צַדִּיק, 112:6b). In fact, Psalm 112 may be understood as an elaborate way of saying that the characteristics of the pious mirror those of God himself, and that an element of conformity exists between the acts of the faithful and those of the God whom they worship.[93]

This example demonstrates the kind of evidence that exists for imitation of God in the OT. God's people will have lives patterned after God's action in the

---

[91] Barton, "Imitation of God," 44–45.

[92] Ibid., 46.

[93] Davies, "Walking in God's Ways," 107.

world. At this point, I am not concerned with the prominent question asked within the discipline of OT ethics, namely whether or not the motivation for divine imitation is ultimately divine command. Rather, I am interested in the implications of imitation texts for human identity as humanity stands in relation to God through covenant history. *Imitatio Dei* is the privilege of humanity, and the theological rationale for human imitation of God is to be found in the kind of creature humanity is—humanity is the creature made in God's image as God's earthly representative.[94]

G. K. Beale's recent study of idolatry lends credence to this way of understanding the imitation of God.[95] Beale focuses attention upon a series of texts suggesting that humans become like what they worship. Beale begins his study with an analysis of Isaiah 6, attending specifically to God's message of judgment for the people of Israel:

> [9]And he said, "Go and say to this people:
>     'Keep listening, but do not comprehend;
>     keep looking, but do not understand.'
> [10]Make the mind of this people dull,
>     and stop their ears,
>     and shut their eyes,
>     so that they may not look with their eyes,
>     and listen with their ears,
>     and comprehend with their minds,
>     and turn and be healed."

Beale argues persuasively that this kind of judgment is regularly brought upon the idolater: they become like their gods. Among the many texts marshaled in support of this thesis is Ps 115:4–8:

> [4]Their idols are silver and gold,
>     the work of human hands.
> [5]They have mouths, but do not speak;
>     eyes, but do not see.
> [6]They have ears, but do not hear;
>     noses, but do not smell.
> [7]They have hands, but do not feel;
>     feet, but do not walk;
>     they make no sound in their throats.
> [8]Those who make them are like them;
>     so are all who trust in them.

Here the Psalmist deprecates both the pagan idols and those who make and worship them, concluding that "those who make them [idols] are like them." From these and other examples, Beale draws a general inference that he then

---

[94] If there is an appropriate place for seeking anthropological insight by comparing the human creature to other earthly creatures, it is here. For instance, God does not invite, command, or expect squirrels to imitate him.

[95] G. K. Beale, *We Become What We Worship: A Biblical Theology of Idolatry* (Downers Grove, Ill.: IVP Academic, 2008).

traces through the various layers of the OT, intertestamental, and NT litera-ture. "The principle for them and for us is: *we resemble what we revere, either for ruin or restoration.*"[96] If it is indeed the case that humans are the creatures that become what they worship, then the language of imitation is not surprising. A human takes on forms of being in the world that are similar to the ways of being exemplified by that which is worshipped. In other words, over time humans come to imitate God or their idols.

While primarily a study of idolatry and its results, Beale also draws impli-cations concerning the transformative results of worshipping the true God of the gospel. Beale takes special note of Rom 8:29: "ὅτι οὓς προέγνω, καὶ προώρισεν συμμόρφους τῆς εἰκόνος τοῦ υἱοῦ αὐτοῦ, εἰς τὸ εἶναι αὐτὸν πρωτότοκον ἐν πολλοῖς ἀδελφοῖς." Jesus Christ is the firstborn Son to whose image many others will be conformed.[97] Theologically, this is fitting since Jesus is the perfect image of God. Jesus is the fulfillment of human identity, and as people are progressively conformed to the image of Christ their human identi-ties are also realized in him. Beale also considers OT promises about the resto-ration of God's people. Beale concludes, "[W]hereas Israel formed their idols and worshiped them and came to resemble their spiritually deaf and blind image, God, the true image-maker (cf. Gen 1:26–27), could reverse this condi-tion and form them to reflect his image, so that they would be able spiritually to see and hear."[98] Beale's study is a boon to my thesis since he has demon-strated (1) that Scripture presents humanity as a creature that becomes simi-lar to what it worships, and (2) despite the fact that God's people have failed to walk in God's ways, it is a consistent expectation in Scripture that God's people should reflect God's character in the world. The weakness persisting through-out Beale's discussion is that he does not give an account of how humans re-main the image of God even when their way of being reflects their idols.[99] Un-derstanding the *imago Dei* as human identity is useful here. The underlying reason "we resemble what we revere" is that it is a condition of possibility for the realization of humanity's identity as *imago Dei* that humans are the kind of creatures who are conformed to the image of what or whom they worship. This provides the necessary rationale for explaining how a particular human being may have the identity "made in God's image" and still exhibit the char-acteristics of their idols.

Before concluding this section, it is important to differentiate my under-standing of the relationship between the *imago Dei* and *imitatio Dei* from the

---

[96] Ibid., 49 (emphasis original). Another significant passage for Beale's thesis is Rom 1:20–28 where God's punishment for idolatry is that the unnatural and disordered rela-tionship idolaters have with God is then reflected by the unnatural and disordered rela-tionships they have with others (204).

[97] Ibid., 219.

[98] Ibid., 273.

[99] This is a weakness with respect to interpreting the *imago Dei*. But it should be noted that Beale is not primarily interested in providing a systematic treatment of the *imago Dei*.

account given by William Power, since he has attempted a conceptual analysis of this relationship and arrived at very different conclusions.[100] In his article, Power attempts to trace the conceptual rationale for connecting *imago Dei* and *imitatio Dei* in Christian theologies. Power argues from Anselm's notion that God is that being than which none greater can be conceived toward the conclusion that "the metaphysical and necessary identity of God provides the invariant structure for God's variable and contingent interaction with this cosmos."[101] Human beings, who are made in the image of God, may have relative perfections that can be interpreted and assessed against the standard of God's perfect being. For this assessment to be effective, Power argues, there must be literal cataphatic understanding of God's being.[102] Power provides a series of what he takes as positive descriptions of God's being: God is omnipotent, omniscient, omnibenevolent, omniproductive, and omnipassible.

According to Power, God's attributes compel God's action. For example, Power states, "As that being than which none greater can be conceived, God produced all that is possible and desirable to produce."[103] For Power, the claim that God is omniproductive entails that God must produce all that is possible and desirable to produce in order for God to be God. As mentioned in chapter 3, however, the Christian tradition has emphasized that God is free since God has no attributes that are not fulfilled by the intra-Trinitarian relations. Creation is God's free decision because God is fulfilled in himself. Therefore, Power's account of the divine attributes is problematic since it impinges upon God's freedom.

Another problem that arises from Power's account is the order he gives to theological knowledge. Power intends to draw his knowledge of God from his concept of perfection. But why should one suppose that one's particular concept of perfection is correct? It appears that Power's method is again misguided because it is insufficiently Trinitarian. The triune God of the gospel is known through his self-revelation through Jesus Christ and in the Holy Spirit. God's economy occurs through time. It is not the case that God can be known strictly through contemplation of God's perfections, for God's perfections are not merely quantitatively different from the relative perfections encountered

---

[100] William Power, "*Imago Dei—Imitatio Dei,*" *Int J Philos Relig* 42 (1997): 131–41.

[101] Ibid., 140.

[102] Power argues that cataphatic metaphorical language is "parasitic upon the cataphatic way of literal use and interpretation." He does not discuss analogical language, but it appears that he would consider analogical language to be indistinguishable from metaphor since one of his objections to metaphorical language is that "we have no basis for ruling out dissimilarities between the analogates being compared" (134). He suggests, for example, that without literal cataphatic understanding of God's character there would be no way to know whether or not Psalm 23 suggests that God will lead all his people to slaughter since that, like caring for the sheep, is an action of a shepherd. It is important to note that Power believes that literal language must have at least partial univocal meaning (140).

[103] Ibid., 137.

in creation. God's perfections are also qualitatively different from those encountered in creation, and they are known only through God's unfolding relationship with creation. In other words, God the Father is not known prior to his self-revelation through the Son and in the Spirit; rather, God is known precisely on the basis of his self-revelation through the Son and in the Spirit. This evaluation is based upon the doctrine of revelation considered in the second part of this chapter. From a Christian perspective, the *imitatio Dei* can only be imitation of the God known through the Son in the Spirit. The imitation of God is fitting because humans are the creatures intended by God to know God and pattern their lives after God's way of being in the world.

## 3. Conclusions

In this chapter, I examined the doctrine of revelation and its implications for human identity. First, on the basis of the doctrine of revelation, I concluded that God is known through God's triune action in the world, including divine speech-acts. Reception of God's revelation is dependent upon God's own action and God's creational intention for humanity as knowing creatures. Scripture, through its unique testimony, serves the church toward the end of knowing God. Second, I dispelled a number of criticisms leveled against the possibility of interpreting OT texts as affirmations of the imitation of God. I argued that imitation of God formally entails God's creation of humanity as God's image—not because it was intrinsically necessary that God create humanity as God's image, but rather because imitation of God serves as partial realization of God's image in the world. Humans are the creatures that become like what they worship, and this was God's intention for humanity from the beginning—to become like God through knowing God.

Ultimately, the virtues of the identity interpretation need to be demonstrated through exegesis, for which the path has now been cleared. In chapter 5, I will provide such analyses of several OT and NT texts that demonstrate the unfolding character of the *imago Dei*, which is ultimately fulfilled by Jesus Christ.

# Chapter 5

# The Canonical Unfolding Of
# The *Imago Dei*

In chapter 4 I briefly described G. K. Beale's study *We Become What We Worship*. He states that his method in the book could be considered "canonical, genetic-progressive (or organically developmental), and intertextual."[1] In this chapter I take a similar approach for interpreting the *imago Dei* through the biblical canon. Selection of texts is representative rather than comprehensive, and the readings are preeminently theological rather than critical. Because my method is intentionally canonical and theological, it is most helpful to begin with a study of the relevant NT texts on the *imago Dei*. The reason for this is two-fold. As I mentioned in chapter 1, theologians have typically either focused their study of the image of God on Genesis 1 or the NT texts to the exclusion of the other. The conclusions drawn about the meaning of the image of God have differed strongly from one another depending upon which texts were incorporated into the study. In this chapter, the "identity" focus of my argument is used to demonstrate that there is theological continuity between references to the *imago Dei* in Genesis and the NT. I will show how this is the case by drawing a theological line through the relevant OT and NT texts. It is helpful, first, to consider the beginning and end points the line will connect. Chapter 3 provided a theological exegesis of Genesis 1 as the starting point; here, therefore, I will begin by describing the biblical context for understanding the endpoint of the line. After establishing the beginning and ending points, I will indicate how the line should be drawn through various other OT and NT texts. Proceding in this way will demonstrate how the material content of the *imago Dei* develops in relation to the historical unfolding of divine revelation in the context of God's relationship with his people.

---

[1] Beale, *We Become What We Worship*, 34.

# 1. New Testament Texts

Three questions will be answered in this first section on the NT texts. (1) What is the dogmatic relationship between the image of God and the image of Christ? (2) What are the eschatological implications of the image? (3) How can we characterize the differences and similarities between the implications of the image in Genesis 1 and in the NT?

There is some debate concerning which NT texts directly refer to Gen 1:26–28. For example, Bray analyzes eight NT texts (Matt 22:20 and parallels Mark 12:16 and Luke 20:24; Jas 3:9; Rom 1:23; 1 Cor 11:7; 2 Cor 4:4; Col 1:15; Col 3:9–10; 2 Cor 3:18) and concludes that "[t]he image of God in man, understood as something implanted in Adam at his creation, is mentioned only twice in the New Testament, in 1 Corinthians 11:7 and James 3:9."[2] Bray also allows that Col 3:10 alludes to Gen 1:27. These texts refer specifically to the image of God in Genesis 1. Additionally, there are a number of NT texts which refer to the image of Christ, the imitation of God, and the imitation of Christ. Many scholars have found these texts to be important for discerning the material shape of the image of God. The first question that must be answered, therefore, is whether the image of Christ, and therefore the imitation of Christ, relates integrally to the image of God.

## 1.1. 1 John 3:2

It is helpful to begin with 1 John 3:2, a text unexamined by Bray. There are three reasons for this choice. First, it refers directly to the realization of human identity—what humanity will be. If the *imago Dei* is human identity, then the realization of human identity will have some relation to the *imago Dei* interpreted canonically, whether or not the term εἰκών is used. Second, 1 John 3:2 indicates that full transformation into the likeness of God will take place when God or Christ is fully revealed to humanity through his presence. There is a connection of identity to divine revelation. Third, the ambiguity of 1 John 3:2 regarding the one into whose likeness God's people will be changed, whether the Father or the Son, is instructive about the relation between the Father, the Son, and God's adopted children. This ambiguity sheds light on the connection of human identity in Genesis 1 to its development in the NT.

1 John 3:2 reads: "ἀγαπητοί, νῦν τέκνα θεοῦ ἐσμεν, καὶ οὔπω ἐφανερώθη τί ἐσόμεθα. οἴδαμεν ὅτι ἐὰν φανερωθῇ, ὅμοιοι αὐτῷ ἐσόμεθα, ὅτι ὀψόμεθα αὐτὸν καθώς ἐστιν." God's children will be like "him" when "he" appears. As of yet, however, we do not know all that this entails. But we know that when "he" is revealed to us we will be like him because we will see him just as he is. I. Howard Marshall states, "The thought is that the effect of seeing Jesus is to make us like him, just as a mirror reflects the image of the person in front of it."[3] For

---

[2] Bray, "The Significance of God's Image in Man," 222.
[3] I. Howard Marshall, *The Epistles of John* (NICNT; Grand Rapids: Eerdmans, 1978), 173.

Marshall, this is suggestive of 2 Cor 3:18: "And all of us, with unveiled faces, seeing the glory of the Lord as though reflected in a mirror, are being transformed into the same image from one degree of glory to another; for this comes from the Lord, the Spirit." ὅμοιοι in 1 John 3:2 overlaps conceptually with εἰκόνα in 2 Cor 3:18 since both refer to the transformation of God's people into a state which better reflects God and his glory.

Marshall notes that it is ambiguous whether ὅτι ὀψόμεθα depends on ἐσόμεθα or οἴδαμεν. If the former, then "seeing Jesus produces likeness to him." If the latter, then the implication may be either that "[l]ikeness to Jesus results from the fact that, as we know, we shall see him" or that "[t]he fact that we are to see him means that we shall be like him, since being like him is the condition for seeing him."[4] Marshall rightly concludes that the final possibility is highly unlikely since "it depends on the unexpressed premise that we must be like him in order to see him."[5] Therefore, the most likely interpretation, whether ὅτι ὀψόμεθα depends on ἐσόμεθα or οἴδαμεν, is that Christ-likeness or God-likeness results from seeing Jesus or the Father as he is. So Judith Lieu comments, "It is sight that will lead to transformation, likeness to the one seen."[6]

It is linguistically unclear whether it is Jesus or the Father who will appear and be seen by God's children. In another Johannine text, John 17:25, Jesus prays for his disciples acknowledging that the world does not know the Father but that Jesus himself knows the Father and the disciples have believed that the Father has sent him. In John 17:25, then, Jesus mediates the knowledge of the Father to his disciples.[7] Lieu argues that 1 John differs from John 17:25 at this point, since "the transformation that 1 John anticipates may be likeness to God."[8] Stephen Smalley argues that the "αὐτόν" at the end of 1 John 3:1 probably refers to the Father. Nevertheless, he allows that a secondary reference to Jesus may be included. Smalley suggests that the logic of 1 John 3:1; 13 is parallel to Jesus's teaching that the world hates his disciples because the world first hated Jesus (John 15:18–19).[9] While a difference can be discerned between the fact that the world does not know God and the fact that the world hates Jesus, there is a theological link between the world's lack of knowledge and the world's lack of proper loves. It is probable, in my view, that the "αὐτόν" in 3:2 has the same referent as "αὐτῷ" in 2:28 since this also is the one who will appear. In 2:28, the author's use of παρουσία suggests that Jesus is in view. Moreover, the fact that Jesus is spoken of in 3:5 as the one who "was revealed" (ἐφανερώθη) further suggests that likeness to Jesus is discussed in

[4] Ibid., 173 n. 30.
[5] Ibid., 173 n. 30.
[6] Judith Lieu, *I, II, & III John: A Commentary* (NTL; Louisville: Westminster John Knox, 2008), 125.
[7] Ibid., 124 n. 61.
[8] Ibid., 125.
[9] Stephen Smalley, *1, 2, 3 John* (WBC 51; Waco: Word, 1984), 142–43.

3:2. Taking a clue from 2:23, however, it may very well be the case that the author has no interest in separating likeness to the Father and likeness to the Son. "No one who denies the Son has the Father; everyone who confesses the Son has the Father also." The author binds the Son to the Father and the Father to the Son. So, likeness to the Son implies likeness to the Father as God's people are also included as children of God.

The material shape of 1 John 3:2 is similar to Gen 1:26–28. The subject of both texts is human identity in relation to God and, specifically, to God's self-revelation. In Genesis 1, the illustration of the relationship between God and humanity is demonstrated through dominion. God rules all things; God's earthly image rules the earth. The principal teaching is that the image of God will reflect a likeness to God. In 1 John 3:2, this principle is extended eschatologically. Even now, it is not yet known *what* the fullness of human likeness to God will be, but *that* the Christian's participation in likeness to God will be completed upon Jesus's παρουσία is foundational to the Christian hope. In Genesis 1, humanity is tasked to have dominion over the earth because God's dominion over all things had been revealed by the fact that God created them. Likewise, in 1 John 3:2, the fullness of human identity will be known when God in Jesus is seen "καθώς ἐστιν," since knowledge of human identity is dependent upon divine revelation.

It is important to note the *imago Dei* is not Trinitarian in virtue of being one thing with three relations or a union of three things. Rather, the image of God is Trinitarian in virtue of its being fulfilled in Jesus Christ, the Son of God. As the children of God are formed by the Spirit into the likeness of Christ, they are *for that reason* formed in the likeness of God. In order to say that Jesus is the image of God one does not need to identify some way in which Jesus is both three and one; rather, Jesus is the image of God because he is the very Son of God who in relation to the Father is the χαρακτὴρ τῆς ὑποστάσεως αὐτοῦ "exact imprint of God's very being" (Heb 1:3) who πατρὸς ἐκεῖνος ἐξηγήσατο "has made the Father known" (John 1:18). Because of the nature of the relations of the Son to the Father and God's children to the Son, adopted children of God realize the image of God insofar as they are conformed to the image of Christ. For this reason, the biblical texts that refer to the image of Christ are relevant to the NT perspective on the *imago Dei*.

First John 3:2 represents the eschatological hope of the complete realization of the *imago Dei* in God's children in that it points toward the perfection of human identity. If Gen 1:26–28 is the initial canonical indication that human identity is tied to God's self-revelation, 1 John 3:2 indicates that this is permanently the case, even in the future. The material content of these texts is consistent with a progressive understanding of God's revelation and a developmental realization of God's image by his children. Conceptually, these are the beginning and end points of a biblical theology of the *imago Dei*. In between these points, there is a line of theological development.

There are formal indicators that designate the relevant intervening texts. The texts can be identified in one of two ways: (1) the image of God is directly referred to or clearly alluded to; (2) an ethical command is based on and justi-fied by an appeal to God's own character as demonstrated through God's econ-omy. If (1), then further inquiry must be undertaken in order to discern the nature of the reference. If (2), then the rationale is based on the principle of the *imago Dei*—that human identity, and therefore human action, is deter-mined by God's self-revelation. As will be shown, the texts that fall within (2) are the most theologically interesting, with one exception that qualifies under both (1) and (2).

### 1.2. *Colossians 3:9-10*

It is useful to begin with the exception: Col 3:9-10, which reads: "μὴ ψεύδεσθε εἰς ἀλλήλους, ἀπεκδυσάμενοι τὸν παλαιὸν ἄνθρωπον σὺν ταῖς πράξεσιν αὐτοῦ καὶ ἐνδυσάμενοι τὸν νέον τὸν ἀνακαινούμενον εἰς ἐπίγνωσιν κατ᾿ εἰκόνα τοῦ κτίσαντος αὐτόν." That the final words of 3:10, κατ᾿ εἰκόνα τοῦ κτίσαντος αὐτόν, allude to Genesis 1 is widely recognized. So Peter O'Brien asserts, "Even though this phrase is not an explicit Scripture citation one can-not miss the allusion to Gen 1:27, where the first Adam is said to have been created by God 'in his own image' (κατ᾿ εἰκόνα θεοῦ)."[10] Much earlier, Fredrick Westcott had commented, "There can be no question that we have here . . . a double reference to Genesis."[11] In addition to Genesis 1, Westcott connects Col 3:10 to Adam's knowledge of good and evil in Gen 3:22. Likewise, James Dunn argues that the author

> makes . . . explicit use of the motif of Adam and creation, in terms of knowledge and of the image of God. . . . For knowledge was at the heart of humanity's primal failure (Gen. 2:17; 3:5, 7), and human-kind's failure to act in accordance with their knowledge of God by acknowledging him in worship was the central element in Paul's earlier analysis of the human plight, of 'the old self' (Rom. 3:21).[12]

O'Brien argues that "to say that the new man is being renewed 'according to the image of God,' in the light of the hymnic paragraph where Christ is praised as the εἰκὼν ("image") of God (1:15) and Paul's Christological teaching else-where means that God's recreation of man 'is *in the pattern of Christ, who is*

---

[10] Peter O'Brien, *Colossians, Philemon* (WBC 44; Waco: Word, 1982), 191. The latter part of this quotation matches word for word F. F. Bruce, *The Epistles to the Colossians, to Phile-mon, and to the Ephesians* (NICNT; Grand Rapids: Eerdmans, 1984), 147: "In the phrase 'after his Creator's image' it is impossible to miss the allusion to Gen. 1:27, where the first Adam is said to have been created by God 'in his own image'."

[11] Frederick Westcott, *Colossians: A Letter to Asia* (London: Macmillan, 1914; rep. Minne-apolis: Klock & Klock, 1981), 146.

[12] James Dunn, *The Epistles to the Colossians and Philemon* (NIGTC; Grand Rapids: Eerdmans, 1996), 222.

God's Likeness absolutely'."[13] F. F. Bruce concludes, "But the first Adam is now seen as the 'old man' who must be discarded, in order that the believer may put on the new man, the 'last Adam.' . . . The 'last Adam' or 'new man,' that is to say, is effectively Christ."[14]

If it is true that Adam is the "old man" that must be discarded, and Christ is the "new man" that is put on, then it may be difficult to see how this reference to the image of God is a development of the image of God in Genesis 1. It appears that, for Christians, renewal of the image of God requires the rejection of the original "man" which is now corrupted. So the question is pressed by Daniel Fraikin, "image de Dieu retrouvée dans le Christ ou créée?"[15] Bray's overview is instructive here:

> The phrase *kat' eikona tou ktisantos auton* so obviously reflects Genesis 1:26, that commentators have invariably remarked on the relationship. But in modern times at least, they have also agreed that the verse does not speak of a return to the prelapsarian Adamic state, which would go against what Paul says elsewhere about the contrast between Adam and Christ. They correctly point out that the phrase is conditioned by the 'new man', who is a 'new creation' in Christ (2 Cor. 5:17), so that the parallel with Gen 1:26 is one which is also in stark contrast to it.[16]

The "agreement" of modern scholarship, according to Bray, is that the meaning of the image of God in Gen 1:26 is in "stark contrast" to the meaning given it in Col 3:9–10. Fraikin's conclusion is similar, "Il est clair que le premier trait ne s'explique pas à partir d'une simple référence typologique à l'Adam biblique, encore moins la rencontre des deux dans le même sujet. L'origine du premier, en particulier, doit être cherchée ailleurs."[17] On the contrary, howev-

---

[13] O'Brien, *Colossians, Philemon*, 191. The quotation in O'Brien's text is from C. F. D. Moule, *The Epistles of Paul the Apostle to the Colossians and to Philemon* (CGTC; Cambridge University Press, 1957), 120.

[14] Bruce, *Colossians, Philemon, and Ephesians*, 147. Cf. Dunn, *Colossians and Philemon*, 221.

[15] "Image of God recovered in Christ or created?" Fraikin, "Ressemblance et image de Dieu: Nouveau Testament," in *Supplément au dictionnaire de la Bible*, vol. X (ed. Henri Cazelles and André Feuillet; Paris: Letouzey and Ané, 1985), col. 413.

[16] Bray, "The Significance of God's Image in Man," 214.

[17] "It is clear that the first characteristic is not explained by one simple typological reference to the biblical Adam, even less the meeting of the two in the same subject. The origin of the first, in particular, ought to be sought elsewhere." Fraikin, "Ressemblance et Image Dieu: Nouveau Testament," col. 413–14. Fraikin notes that Jacob Jervell's research demonstrates that there was precedence in ancient Judaism for thinking that the image of God had been lost. There is no precedence in ancient Judaism, however, for a Messianic renewal of the image of God as found in the NT. "Der Messias ist niemals als Gottes Bild vorgestellt; auch nicht in den vorchristlichen spätjüdischen Schriften. Er ist nicht der zweite Adam. Nur vereinzelt kann es heißen, daß der Messias die verlorene Urzeitherrlichkeit wiederherstellt." ("The Messiah is never introduced as God's image, not even in pre-Christian, late-Jewish writings. He is not the second Adam. Only in a few instances can it be said that the Messiah restored the lost primeval glory.") (Jacob

er, there is good reason to understand the image of God as portrayed in Gen 1:26 to be continuous with Col 3:10. Continuity between concepts of the image of God can be maintained without sacrificing the distinction made between the "old human(ity)" and the "new human(ity)."[18] In Col 3:9–10, the "old humanity" is taken off and those who have been united to Christ are now clothed with the "new." If it is true that the "old humanity" is shaped by Adam and the "new" by Christ, then the relevant question concerns the nature of the change that occurs. There is now a new "ἄνθρωπον." To what does this refer? Does it refer to a new identity or nature or *telos* or behavior or some combination of these options?

The relationship between the image of God and the human creature described in the third chapter of this study is exegetically useful here: God determined that he would create an image of himself, and humanity is the creature created with this identity. In other words, God created humanity to serve his intention that God's image exist in the world. With this in mind, אָדָם, in Gen 1:26, refers to the creature with the identity "God's image." As argued in chapter 3, the realization of this identity was to take place in the world as humanity came to know God and pattern its life, analogically, in accordance with God's character as expressed in God's action toward the world. In Col 3:9–10 the same is true. The human creature is intended to be "κατ᾽ εἰκόνα τοῦ κτίσαντος αὐτόν." However, the author makes it clear that the "old humanity" cannot realize this identity, since the practices that belong to the "old humanity" are opposed to the Creator. The "new human(ity)"—Christ—must be put on. Once this has occurred, the human creature is once again on a trajectory toward the realization of its true identity in God's image. Knowledge of God is still required for realization of the *imago Dei*, so therefore the "new humanity" is "ἀνακαινούμενον εἰς ἐπίγνωσιν."[19] Colossians 3:9–10 follows that pattern of reflection on the image of God established in Gen 1:26–28 and completed in 1 John 3:2.

The objections to reading Col 3:9–10 as materially continuous with Gen 1:26–28 are: (1) that the "old man" had to be discarded, and the "old man" is the human created in Genesis 1 in God's image; (2) the meaning of the image of God in Genesis 1 is starkly different from its meaning in Colossians 3. These

---

Jervell, *Imago Dei: Gen. 1, 26 f. im Spätjudentum, in der Gnosis und in den paulinischen Briefen* [Göttingen: Vandenhoeck & Ruprecht, 1960], 119).

[18] See Timothy Gombis, "The Triumph of God in Christ: Divine Warfare in the Argument of Ephesians" (Ph.D. diss, University of St. Andrews, 2004), 136–39 for an argument that supports the translation of παλαιὸν ἄνθρωπον and νέον ἄνθρωπον as "old humanity" and "new humanity." Specifically, Gombis's study concerns Eph 4:22–24 where παλαιὸν ἄνθρωπον and καινὸν ἄνθρωπον are used.

[19] Bruce comments, "But what was that new nature? It was the 'new man' who was being continually renewed with a view to their progressive increase in true knowledge—renewed in conformity with the Creator's image" (*Colossians, Philemon, and Ephesians,* 146). Bruce does not describe the manner in which true knowledge is required in order for the new man to be conformed to the Creator's image, however.

objections suffer from a misunderstanding of the relationship between the *imago Dei* and humanity. The *imago Dei* is human identity. Humanity was created in a manner appropriate to the realization of its God-given identity. However, this manner of being was compromised. In fact, the author of Col 3:9–10 suggests that the "old humanity," with its manner of being-in-the-world, no longer retains the possibility of the realization of humanity's identity as God's image. A "new humanity" is required for humanity to fulfill its God-given end. Note that it is never the case that humanity, either "old" or "new," undergoes a change in identity; the identity of humanity, and the *telos* associated with this identity, remain the same through Genesis 1 and Colossians 3. The change occurs in the creature that possesses this permanent identity. Humanity is made new—in Christ. This newness enables the realization of the *imago Dei*, the identity into which God's people are being renewed. In other words, *the creature must be renewed in order to realize its identity; but the identity itself needs no renewal.* Therefore, since the change from "old" to "new" is not a change in human identity but in the realization of human identity, the two objections fail.

Because the human creature cannot be understood without reference to its identity, and because the renewal of the creature was required for the realization of human identity, there is theological warrant for Athanasius's reflection:

> As, then, the creatures whom He had created reasonable, like the Word, were in fact perishing, and such noble works were on the road to ruin, what then was God, being Good, to do? Was He to let corruption and death have their way with them? . . . It was impossible, therefore, that God should leave man to be carried off by corruption, because it would be unfitting and unworthy of Himself. . . . He saw too how unthinkable it would be for the law to be repealed before it was fulfilled. He saw how unseemly it was that the very things of which He Himself was the Artificer should be disappearing. . . . All this He saw and, pitying our race, moved with compassion for our limitation, unable to endure that His creatures should perish and the work of His Father for us men come to nought, He took to Himself a body, a human body even as our own.[20]

God had, from the beginning, determined to establish his image on the earth, and this intention is realized through Jesus Christ.

### 1.3. Ephesians 4:22–24

Ephesians 4:22–24 is parallel to Col 3:9–10. The text reads: "ἀποθέσθαι ὑμᾶς κατὰ τὴν προτέραν ἀναστροφὴν τὸν παλαιὸν ἄνθρωπον τὸν φθειρόμενον κατὰ τὰς ἐπιθυμίας τῆς ἀπάτης, ἀνανεοῦσθαι δὲ τῷ πνεύματι τοῦ νοὸς

---

[20] Athanasius, *On the Incarnation*, §6–8; translation taken from *On the Incarnation: The Treatise* De Incarnatione Verbi Dei (ed. and trans. a religious of C. S. M. V.; Crestwood, NY: St. Vladimir's, 1993), 32–34.

ὑμῶν καὶ ἐνδύσασθαι τὸν καινὸν ἄνθρωπον τὸν κατὰ θεὸν κτισθέντα ἐν δικαιοσύνῃ καὶ ὁσιότητι τῆς ἀληθείας." The concern of this passage is clearly related to Colossians 3 in its parallel claim that the "old humanity" has been stripped off and the "new humanity" put on.[21] In this case, the new humanity is created "κατὰ θεὸν" in righteousness and holiness. The text implies progressive growth in righteousness and holiness according to God since the mind is in the process of being renewed. This righteousness and holiness comes from the truth. As Harold Hoehner comments, "[T]he new person has been identified as one who is characterized by a righteousness that has its source in truth. The new person is directly opposite the old person whose desires and lifestyle have their source in deception."[22]

The phrase "τὸν κατὰ θεὸν κτισθέντα" directs one's thoughts to Genesis 1. Andrew Lincoln describes its meaning in relation to Col 3:10: "The notion of the new creation is explicit in the description of the new person as 'created in God's likeness.' τὸν κατὰ θεὸν κτισθέντα, lit. 'created like God,' is Ephesians' version of Col 3:10, κατ᾿ εἰκόνα τοῦ κτίσαντος, 'according to the image of the one who created it,' with its allusion to the language of Gen 1:26."[23] The righteousness and holiness of the new human is according to God's own righteousness and holiness. "The choice of righteousness and holiness as the ethical qualities that are specified underlines the point that the new humanity has been recreated to be like God, because both are characteristics of God in LXX Ps 144:17 and Deut 32:4 (cf. also Rev 16:5). As the new creation in God's likeness, believers are to be righteous as he is righteous and holy as he is holy."[24] Likewise, Peter O'Brien explains the theological rationale of the text: "God is not only the author of this mighty work; he is also the pattern or model of the new creation. It is made 'in his likeness.'"[25] The new humanity, therefore, is created to be like God and is patterned after God as the spirit of the mind is renewed according to the truth.

---

[21] In Col 3:10, the author uses the word νέος whereas here the word is καινὸς. Bruce notes that in this case "no distinction [in meaning] can be pressed between καινὸς and νέος" (*Colossians, Philemon, and Ephesians,* 358 n. 126).

[22] Harold Hoehner, *Ephesians: An Exegetical Commentary* (Grand Rapids: Baker Academic, 2002), 613.

[23] Andrew Lincoln, *Ephesians,* 287; *contra* Ernest Best, *Ephesians* (ICC; Edinburgh: T&T Clark, 1998), 440.

[24] Ibid., 288. Commenting on meaning of δικαιοσύνῃ καὶ ὁσιότητι, Lincoln persuasively argues, "It is probably best to see the two terms used together as 'a summary of human virtue' (cf. Abbott, 139), as in Wis 9:3 and Luke 1:75 (cf. also the use of the cognate adverbs in 1 Thess 2:10 and adjectives in Titus 1:8). Further support is lent to this interpretation by the fact that most frequently in Plato (*Apology* 35D; *Crito* 54B; *Theatetus* 172B, 176B) and in Philo (*De Sacr.* 57; *De Spec. Leg.* 1.304; 2.180; *De Virt.* 50) both the adjectival and nominal forms of the two terms are employed together to denote virtuous living in general" (*Ephesians,* 288). The in-text citation refers to K. T. Abbott, *A Critical and Exegetical Commentary on the Epistles to the Ephesians and to the Colossians* (ICC; Edinburgh: T&T Clark, 1897).

[25] Peter O'Brien, *The Letter to the Ephesians* (PNTC; Grand Rapids: Eerdmans, 1999), 332.

The theological claims concerning the likeness of God in Eph 4:22–24 mirror those made about the image of God in Col 3:9–10. The new humanity retains its created identity as the image and likeness of God. Therefore, the *telos* of the new humanity is the realization of this identity through participation in, and performance of, righteousness and holiness grounded in the truth. In order for the realization of this identity to occur, the new humanity must be renewed in knowledge of God in the domain of the spirit of the mind. In summary, four observations should be made: the likeness of God is (1) the identity of the new humanity; (2) patterned after God's demonstrated character; (3) dependent upon knowledge of God, which in this case must be renewed; (4) teleological, since the new humanity is in the process of becoming what it is intended to be.

While the theological pattern of reflection represented here is often recognized to be a typical Pauline pattern, what is not recognized is that its logic is derived from Genesis 1, a text to which Pauline literature commonly alludes. It is often assumed that Genesis 1 is used by Paul to support his own unique argument concerning the image of God. My suggestion, however, is that the relationship between Genesis 1 and these Pauline texts is deeper, that the Pauline pattern is dependent upon the theological structure of Genesis 1, and these NT texts represent a faithful interpretation of the OT.

Gregory of Nyssa's interpretation of the creation narrative is, therefore, faithful also to the logic of these Pauline texts: "One who is made in the image of God has the task of becoming who he is."[26] Humanity is made in God's image, and the new humanity has the opportunity to realize this identity through imitation of Jesus Christ, the visible image of the invisible God.

*1.4. 2 Corinthians 3:18*

Second Corinthians 3:18 contains similar material content to Col 3:9–10 and Eph 4:22–24, but special emphasis is placed upon the roles of the Son and the Holy Spirit in relation to the transformation of the new humanity: "ἡμεῖς δὲ πάντες ἀνακεκαλυμμένῳ προσώπῳ τὴν δόξαν κυρίου κατοπτριζόμενοι τὴν αὐτὴν εἰκόνα μεταμορφούμεθα ἀπὸ δόξης εἰς δόξαν καθάπερ ἀπὸ κυρίου πνεύματος." Here it is said that Christians, in freedom (v. 17), behold the Lord's glory and are progressively transformed into God's image by the Holy Spirit.[27]

---

[26] Gregory of Nyssa, *On the Making of Man* (NPNF[2] 5:405), as translated in Andrew Louth, ed., *Genesis 1-11*, Ancient Christian Commentary on Scripture (Downers Grove: IVP, 2001), 35.

[27] While it is possible to interpret τὴν δόξαν κυρίου κατοπτριζόμενοι as "beholding" or "reflecting," "beholding" is preferable since the distinction between Jews and Christians in the immediate context is a difference between those who have a veil covering their hearts and those who have had that veil removed. The removal of the veil allows Christians to "see" the Lord's glory. See Ralph Martin, *2 Corinthians* (WBC 40; Waco: Word, 1986), 71; Murray Harris, *The Second Epistle to the Corinthians* (NIGTC; Grand Rapids: Eerdmans, 2005), 313–14.

Once again, the relationship between seeing God and being transformed into the likeness of God is highlighted. Murray Harris notes the dual implications of having the veil of the old covenant removed: "An unremoved veil prevents recognition of the glory of the new covenant. A removed veil not only guarantees recognition of that glory but also enables participation in that glory."[28] The emphasis on recognition *and* participation is significant; participation in the Lord's glory follows from seeing the Lord's glory by reflection.

According to 2 Cor 4:4–6, the Lord's glory is seen in Christ. Christ is the image of God, the one in whom the glory of God is known. This further informs the meaning of 3:18; the Lord's glory is beheld ἐν προσώπῳ Χριστοῦ. In a manner parallel to 1 John 3:2, it is unclear whether the image into which the Christian is transformed is the image of God or Christ. The resolution of this ambiguity is also the same. The image and glory of Christ *is* the image and glory of God. 2 Cor 3:18 confirms the principles of the Pauline interpretation of the image of God noted above. Progressive realization of human identity as the image of God follows from the knowledge of God gained on the basis of God's action in the world. The further point made in 2 Cor 3:18 is that God's action in the world is known in Jesus Christ, who is the image of God. "Christ both shares and expresses God's nature."[29] While this is a presupposition of all of the Pauline passages included to this point in the chapter, the relationship between Christ as God's image and the realization of God's image in Christians by the work of the Holy Spirit is here made explicit. Christ is the image and glory of God who ultimately establishes the pattern for what it means to realize God's image in the world.

## 1.5. Other Relevant New Testament Texts

If the above interpretations of 1 John 3:2, Col 3:8–9, Eph 4:22–24, and 2 Cor 3:18 are accepted, then a number of other biblical texts can be marshaled as evidence for the identity interpretation of the *imago Dei*. As has been demonstrated, there is no need for each particular text to refer directly to the image of God. Since the image of God is human identity, all that is necessary is that the texts refer to the intended shape or realization of this identity. So, texts such as Rom 8:29, which refers to Christians being predestined to conformation to the image of God's Son, and even Gal 4:19, which expresses Paul's deep desire to see Christ formed in God's people, can be understood as refer-

---

Also, κυρίου πνεύματος most likely refers to the Holy Spirit, especially in light of the reference in v. 17 to "the Spirit of the Lord." Harris summarizes a pneumatological reading of 2 Cor 3:16–18: "The new era of the Spirit, for as a result of conversion to the Spirit (vv. 16, 17a), there is liberation through the Spirit (v. 17b), including the lifting of the veil of spiritual ignorance and hardheartedness, and also transformation by the Spirit (v. 18). The Spirit, his person and his work, is the hallmark of the new covenant" (*The Second Epistle to the Corinthians*, 318).

[28] Harris, *The Second Epistle to the Corinthians*, 313–14.

[29] Ibid., 331.

ences to the realization of the *imago Dei* since conformation to Christ is imaging God.[30]

Take, for example, Eph 4:32–5:2. After describing the *telos* of the new humanity (κατὰ θεὸν; Eph 4:24) and some of the practices that should characterize the life of the new humanity (4:25–31), the exhortation follows: "Be kind to one another, tenderhearted, forgiving one another, as God in Christ has forgiven you. Therefore be imitators of God, as beloved children, and live in love, as Christ loved us and gave himself up for us, a fragrant offering and sacrifice to God." Based on the fact that the new humanity is patterned according to God, it follows that God's people should forgive as God has forgiven them and love as God has loved them in Christ. It should be noted that once again the imitating God takes the form of imitating Christ. Imitation of Christ, therefore, is the means by which the new humanity embodies its likeness to God. It should also be recognized that the new humanity is created to be like God— that is its identity, in continuity with Gen 1:26–28—yet the realization of this identity in the world is known through God's economy and is dependent upon imitation of God.[31]

Imitation of God is logically posterior to the fact that humanity is the creature intended to shape its life according to divine revelation, which in turn is the case because humanity is made in the *imago Dei*. Identity, with its attending *telos*, precedes and supports the actions appropriate to that end and identity; in other words, the fact of the *imago Dei* is the theological basis for the practice of imitating, or imaging, God. In this way, texts such as Luke 6:36, "Be merciful just as your Father is merciful," and the parallel in Matt 5:48, "Be perfect, therefore, as your heavenly Father is perfect" are relevant to the outworking of God's intention for humanity from beginning (Gen 1:26–30) to end (as indicated by 1 John 3:2). The connection between the NT and the OT in this regard is highlighted in 1 Pet 1:15–16: "As he who called you is holy, be holy yourselves in all your conduct, for it is written, 'You shall be holy, for I am holy.'" Ultimately, this presses imitation of God back to the OT, so it will be important to consider some representative OT texts in due course.

At this point, however, a few additional NT texts that are thought to refer directly or allude to Gen 1:26–28 must be addressed. These texts include 1 Cor 11:7, Jas 3:9, and Col 1:15. None of these texts significantly alters what has been

---

[30] See Jervell, *Imago Dei*, esp. 246–48; Berkouwer, *Man: The Image of God*, 101–4.

[31] Clines concludes his brief foray into the NT texts with the following words: "In Christ man sees what manhood was meant to be. In the Old Testament all men are the image of God; in the New, where Christ is the one true image, men are the image of God in so far as they are like Christ. The image is fully realized only through obedience to Christ; this is how man, the image of God, who is already man, already the image of God, can become fully man, fully the image of God" ("The Image of God in Man," 103). Clines comes close to making the distinction between identity and realization for which I have been arguing. Instead, he talks about humanity as the image which can become fully the image in Christ. Conceptually, it is clearer to speak of the permanence of the image of God as human identity and the potential for realization of that identity in Christ.

expressed above, but these texts diversify the contexts in which the image of God is referenced. In 1 Cor 11:7, it is said that "a man ought not to have his head covered, since he is the image and glory of God; but woman is the glory of man." It is not clear that this passage has any bearing upon the current study since it is a claim about the ordering of relationships rather than human identity. It is probably best to concur with Philip Hughes's evaluation that this text is unrelated to a theology of the *imago Dei* as such.[32] Certainly, there is no basis here for arguing that only the man and not the woman is made in God's image.[33]

James 3:9 is an "obvious" reference to Gen 1:26 in its reference to "those who are made in the likeness of God."[34] The author shows the inconsistency of praising God but cursing those made in God's likeness. The continuation of the image of God beyond the fall is confirmed, since it remains a rationale for treating people in an ethical way. Bray convincingly argues,

> [D]espite the fact that James uses *homoiôsis* (the only occurrence of this word in the New Testament), it seems better to relate the verse in the first instance to Genesis 9:6, i.e. to the prohibition against shedding blood. To curse a man is to kill him spiritually in our heart, and it seems probable that James is here alluding to this aspect of Jesus' teaching (cf. Matthew 5:21-2).[35]

As will be shown in the third section of this chapter, Gen 9:6 refers to the extent of human dominion on the earth, and human moral accountability to God. The relation of Gen 9:6 to 1:26-28 will be explored below.

Colossians 1:15 is significant since it directly refers to Christ as the image of God. Hughes and Bray argue that this is a reference to Christ's deity.[36] The context makes this likely since the following verses describe Christ's work of creation. However, the incarnation is also in view, since the reconciliation he affected through the cross is mentioned. Jesus Christ is here portrayed as the fullness of God's image, not merely in his deity but also in his humanity. It is the person of Jesus Christ, and not only his divine or human nature, that is the image of God. This creates the proper context for Col 3:9-10, where the people of God are renewed in knowledge in the image of the Creator since God's people have seen Christ, who is the image of God divinely and humanly.

### 1.6 Conclusions

What I have demonstrated in the first section of this chapter is that the interpretation of the *imago Dei* as human identity helps inform faithful interpretation of the relevant NT texts. In other words, the theological interpretation

---

[32] Philip Edgcumbe Hughes, *The True Image: The Origin and Destiny of Man in Christ* (Grand Rapids: Eerdmans, 1989), 22–24.

[33] Blocher, *In the Beginning*, 92.

[34] Bray, "The Significance of God's Image in Man," 210.

[35] Ibid., 210.

[36] Hughes, *The True Image*, 28–29; Bray, "The Significance of God's Image in Man," 211.

of the *imago Dei* proposed in chapter 3 is a catalyst for better NT exegesis. Not only does the identity interpretation accommodate the NT texts, but it also demonstrates how the authors of the NT were better interpreters of Gen 1:26–28 and its implications than they are usually considered to be.

In summary, three conclusions should be drawn from this study of the NT texts. First, the identity of humanity as the *imago Dei*, with its *telos*, persists in the NT. In all the texts considered, the image of God should be understood as the underlying identity of humanity which shapes humanity's end. Even where this *telos* is currently undefined, it will be determined by likeness to God in Christ. Second, the realization of this identity occurs in the new humanity shaped in likeness to Christ by the Spirit; so, likeness to Christ enables humanity to become what humanity has always been—God's image. Because Christ is the image of God, being transformed into Christ's image is being transformed into God's image. Third, the new humanity is different from the old humanity in that the creature has been so affected that it can now fulfill its original identity, whereas the old humanity could not do so. This transformation comes on the basis of the truth, the knowledge of God which is a necessary prerequisite to realization of God's image.

## 2. *Imago Dei* and Sin

This way of putting the matter does raise another question: What of those who do not realize their identity as *imago Dei*? Is it proper to say that a person has the identity "made in God's image" if they do not realize that identity? To answer these questions, an understanding of the relationship between the image of God and sin is required. If it is true, as I contend, that the *imago Dei* is the permanent identity of humanity, as a whole and individually, then it follows that the entrance of sin does not change this fact. In diverse parts of the biblical canon, Gen 9:6 and Jas 3:9, ethical directives are based on the significance that God made humanity in his image (Gen 9:6) and likeness (Jas 3:9). If the *imago Dei* continues to bear ethical implications after Genesis 3, this is because humanity retains its created status as the creature made in the image and likeness of God. However, after the fall, humanity is a false image; humanity practices a form of life that amounts to a lie about the Creator. Since humanity continues in its vocation as God's image but fails to image God in truthful ways, God establishes the truth by intervening in two ways. First, God determines to establish a truthful image of himself on the earth through his Son. Second, God determines to judge the false, and blasphemous, images of God. The combined effect of these determinations is that humanity, in its relation to God, will be a vehicle for showing forth the God who created humanity in God's image. The truthful image of God is ultimately Christ and his church. The false image is the result of idolatry, so that "those who make them [idols] are like them, so are all who trust in them" (Ps 115:8).[37]

From this perspective, sin is a betrayal of humanity's station, a perversion of humanity's God-given identity and its place in God's ordered creation.[38] Humanity continuously performs its role to make God known on the earth as God's image. However, in sin humans misrepresent God. Humanity is intended to portray truthfully its knowledge of God through godly action in the world. Sin is the portrayal of humanity's knowledge of false gods—idols—and is manifested through ways of action that amount to a lie about the true God. So, for example, whereas God is faithful, humans are unfaithful; whereas God is love, humans are hateful; whereas God is just, humans are unjust.

Humanity is the creature that is intended to have a way of life patterned after God's own character and thus based upon its knowledge of God. When the knowledge of God, in its full relational sense, is lost, however, then the potential for humanity to fulfill God's intention is compromised.[39] Moreover, since humanity is made to be a creature that worships God and patterns its life after God, then when the knowledge and true worship of God are absent, humanity worships and imitates something else. In other words, humanity is prone to idolatry, and when humanity worships idols it becomes like those idols.

As Beale has shown, in the OT, intertestamental Judaism, and the NT, idol worshipers are described in the same terms as their idols. As noted in chapter 4, Beale uses Isa 6:9–13 as a foundational example of God's judgment on idolatry.[40] It is useful here to consider Beale's study in greater detail.

In the context immediately preceding Isa 6:9–13, Isaiah's sins are forgiven by God, and Isaiah volunteers to go to Israel as God's messenger. Beale argues that Isaiah is chosen because *"Isaiah is one who reveres God and, therefore, resembles God's holiness."*[41] This reverence is demonstrated by Isaiah's confession in

---

[37] See Beale, *We Become What We Worship*, 141–60 for a detailed study of Ps 115:4–8 in conversation with other relevant texts.

[38] It is important to note that understanding sin in relation to the *imago Dei* provides one biblical perspective on sin among many. For a careful study of sin and its effects, see Cornelius Plantinga, *Not the Way It's Supposed to Be: A Breviary of Sin* (Grand Rapids: Eerdmans, 1995).

[39] Regarding the fall and its implications for human development and maturity, could it not be said that sin brings about a false or perverted "maturity" of the entire human person, a corruption that holistically caricatures true maturity? Sin corrupts a person spiritually so that they cannot respond properly to God; they are set in their ways—their vices have matured into dispositions leading toward death. So also sin corrupts a person physically so that the apparent maturity of the body digresses from healthy physical development eventually leading toward death. Spiritual and physical resurrection is the only remedy—there is no return to the tree of life apart from resurrection.

[40] Beale, *We Become What We Worship*, 36ff. In the following pages, I rely heavily on Beale's study in order to show how Scripture portrays the imitative relationship that exists between idol worshippers and their idols.

[41] Ibid., 40 (emphasis original).

Isa 6:5, "Woe is me! I am lost, for I am a man of unclean lips, and I live among a people of unclean lips; yet my eyes have seen the King, the Lord of hosts!" God sends Isaiah with a message of judgment. Whereas Isaiah confessed his own inadequacy out of reverence for God's holiness, the people of Israel stand under God's judgment for their unrepentant idolatry. Despite the fact that the terms "idol" or "idolatry" are not used in Isa 6:9–13, Beale shows that the language of sensory organ malfunction, such as the inability to see and hear, is regularly used with reference to idols and idol worship so that the language of organ malfunction should be taken as a sign that idolatry is in view. Specifically, Beale supports this claim with reference to Isaiah 42–44, throughout which sensory organ malfunction, along with the inability of the heart to understand and know God, is related to idolatry and Ps 115:4–8 (= Ps 135:15–18), which notes the inability of idols to speak, see, hear, smell, feel, and walk, ending with the claim that "those who make them [idols] are like them, so are all who trust in them." Beale concludes from these texts that "the principle is this: if we worship idols, we will become like the idols, and that likeness will ruin us."[42] Regarding Isa 6:9–10, Beale argues,

> Here, unbelieving Israel is being given what they want. They are punished by means of their own sin. The idols have physical eyes and ears, but they could not see or hear. But even more, the idols certainly could not see or hear spiritually, though a god was supposed to be behind those idols. And so God commands Israel through Isaiah to become like the idols, and that is their judgment. Thus, in verses 8–10, God is pronouncing through Isaiah that Israel will be judged by being made spiritually insensitive like the idols they worship (Is 6:11–13; Ps 135).[43]

This analysis serves as a paradigmatic illustration of the biblical claim that humanity becomes like what it worships.

Intertestamental literature demonstrates the same conviction, and Beale highlights Philo's reflection on idolatry which is based on his belief that the highest good is to become like God. In *Decalogue* 73, Philo asserts, "the best of prayers and the goal of happiness is to become like God."[44] In *Decalogue* 74, then, Philo argues that the prayer of idol worshippers should be directed toward becoming like their gods, "with eyes that see not, ears that hear not, nostrils which neither breathe nor smell, mouths that never taste nor speak, hands that neither give nor take nor do anything at all, feet that walk not."[45] Philo draws on Psalm 115 in order to describe what an idolater should desire for themselves since becoming like God is intrinsic to the happy life.

Like Philo, the Wisdom of Solomon draws upon Psalm 115 near the end of "the most expanded tirade against idolatry in all of ancient Jewish literature

---

[42] Ibid., 46.
[43] Ibid., 47.
[44] Philo, *On The Decalogue* 73 (LCL 320:43).
[45] Philo, *On The Decalogue* 74 (LCL 320:43).

(see Wis 11:15–20; 12:23–16:1)."⁴⁶ Throughout this passage, idol worshippers are identified with the idols they have made, primarily insofar as they are punished in the same manner. For example, Wisdom 14:8–11 states,

But the idol made with hands is accursed, and so is the one who made it— he for having made it, and the perishable thing because it was named a god. For equally hateful to God are the ungodly and their ungodliness; for what was done will be punished together with the one who did it. Therefore there will be a visitation also upon the heathen idols, because, though part of what God created, they became an abomination, snares for human souls and a trap for the feet of the foolish.

Further, there is a suggestion that idol worshipers somehow "fit" (*axios*) their idols. Wisdom 15:6 states, "Lovers of evil things and fit for such objects of hope are those who either make or desire or worship them." Beale proposes that "fit" should be understood to imply correspondence between an idol worshiper and their idol.⁴⁷ It is difficult to discern the extent of this correspondence. Nevertheless, in the broader context of Wisdom 15:5–17, it is clear that idols are viewed as impotent and, therefore, the idol worshipers have an impotent hope. The people who make idols are greater in their capacities than the idols themselves. The result for idol worshipers, then, is that "[t]heir heart is ashes, their hope is cheaper than dirt, and their lives are of less worth than clay, because they failed to know the one who formed them and inspired them with active souls and breathed a living spirit into them" (Wisdom 15:10–11). Since idol worshipers fail to acknowledge their Creator, they are degraded and only as valuable as the material used to make their idols. So, in Wisdom 15 it is said that there is a correspondence or fittingness of idol worshipers to their idols since both have no hope or ultimate value.

Beale also takes note of interpretive comments added to the biblical text in the targumic literature. A particularly insightful example is found in the rewriting of Deut 32:5 and 32:17–20 in the *Onqelos* targumic tradition.⁴⁸

⁵They have corrupted themselves, the children no longer belong to Him because they worshiped idols, a generation that changed its ways, and in turn were themselves transformed.⁴⁹

The transformation that occurred in these people who corrupted themselves through idol worship is explained in verses 17–20:

---

⁴⁶ Beale, *We Become What We Worship*, 146. Wisdom 15:15 refers to the same sensory organ malfunction described in Ps 115:4–8.
⁴⁷ Ibid., 148.
⁴⁸ Regarding the dating of *Tg. Onq.*, Beale states, "*Tg. Onq.* dates to the third or fourth century A.D., though this Targum itself is likely based on an earlier targumic prototype that goes back perhaps to the first or second century A.D." See Emil Schürer, *History of the Jewish People in the Age of Jesus Christ* (rev. and ed. Geza Vermes, Fergus Millar, and Matthew Black; Edinburgh: T&T Clark, 1973), 101–2.
⁴⁹ *Tg. Onq.* Deut 32:5; as cited by Beale, *We Become What We Worship*, 155.

¹⁷They sacrificed to demons *for whom there is no need*, to deities whom they never
    knew, new ones *who were made only recently . . .*
¹⁸*The worship of the Mighty One* who created you, you did forget; *you have abandoned
    the worship of* the God who *made you.*
¹⁹*Then it was revealed before the Lord and His anger was intensified*, once His sons and
    daughters caused *provocation before him.*
²⁰So He said, "*I will remove My Shekinah* from them; *it is revealed before Me what their
    end will be*; for they are a changed generation, children who have no faith."[50]

The people are envisaged here as those who can no longer remain in God's
presence as God's children because they have no faith. They were once God's
children but are so no longer. Beale argues that "the inevitable conclusion
from this is that they no longer are associated with (or in a position to reflect)
the divine presence and attendant glory, but they are associated with (and
reflect) another reality, a demonic idolatrous reality."[51] Due to their idolatry,
the people are no longer associated with God but with their idols, and they no
longer reflect God but have been corrupted and changed, becoming what they
were not intended to be. The discerning insight of this text is found in its connection of worship to that which shapes and changes a people. When God is
worshiped, a people's ways are shaped by that worship and they stand as God's
children. When idols are worshiped, then a people's ways are shaped by their
idolatry and they cannot stand in God's presence as his children. Concerning
the shape of extracanonical Jewish literature as a whole, Beale argues that "[i]t
is likely that the Jewish view is a development of the Old Testament perspective itself."[52] Philo, Wisdom of Solomon, *Tg. Onq.*, and the other texts discussed
in Beale's study show that the OT texts were understood as portraying an imitative relationship wherein humans become like what they worship.

Building upon the OT texts and their interpretation in Jewish literature,
Beale considers a number of NT texts in relation to this theme. For the purposes of this study it will suffice to focus attention on his interpretation of Rom
1:18–28. The consequences of idolatry are similar to those outlined in the OT.
Idolaters "exchanged the glory of the immortal God for images resembling"
creatures (v 23); "worshiped and served the creature rather than the Creator"
(v 25); "did not see fit to acknowledge God" (v 28); and approved of those who
practice wickedness (v 32). Therefore, God's wrath is poured out on them in
the following ways: God "gave them up in the lusts of their hearts to impurity,
to the degrading of their bodies among themselves" (v 24); "gave them up to
degrading passions" (v 26); and "gave them up to a debased mind and to things
that should not be done" (v 28). God gave them over to disorder, degradation,
and depravity according to their idolatry.

Beale compares Rom 1:18–28 with Rom 12:1–2. In Rom 12:1–2, Paul exhorts
believers to present their bodies as a living sacrifice which is considered a spir-

---

[50] *Tg. Onq.* Deut 32:17–20; as cited by Beale, *We Become What We Worship*, 155.
[51] Beale, *We Become What We Worship*, 156.
[52] Ibid., 155.

itual service of worship. Christians should be no longer conformed to the world but transformed by the renewing of their minds so that they may be able to discern what the will of God is. Romans 12:1–2, then, is a reversal of Rom 1:18–28. Instead of worshiping creation and being conformed to it, Christians should properly worship God and be transformed by their knowledge of God. Then, rather than approving of wickedness, Christians will approve of God's will for human life. This comparison shows the integrative implications of worship for human life, which is continually informed by the knowledge of God or the lack of it.

Romans 8:29 makes it clear that Christians should be conformed to the image of Christ. Beale suggests that "the image of God's Son to which Christians are becoming conformed in Romans 8 is the antithesis of the 'image' that unbelieving humanity had exchanged in place of God's glory in Romans 1."[53] The realization of the image of God in Christ, and in Christians who are conformed to Christ by the Holy Spirit, is a reversal, an undoing, of Romans 1. Moreover, conformation to Christ-likeness surpasses the original state of humanity described in Romans 1 in that it is a fulfillment of God's intention for humanity.

Summarily, then, while Beale's exegesis does at times feel forced, taken as a whole his argument is compelling that according to Scripture humans become like what they worship. This is important support for the interpretation of the *imago Dei* offered in this study since the realization of the *imago Dei* depends upon two anthropological claims that are implied by Beale's study as well. First, humans are intended to be like God, the one they are to worship. Second, humans are transformable. This second claim has happy implications as long as one is growing in knowledge of God and imaginatively patterning one's life after God. But it also implies that one can fail to know God and pattern one's life after something else, thus following the way of idolatry.

Beale does not directly address the question of whether one who is not conformed to the image of Christ remains the *imago Dei*. Based on the logic of his argument one might conclude that humanity under these circumstances is not God's image. But following that path would constitute a failure to appreciate the difference between identity and realization. Surely the punishment for idolatry, including spiritual "organ malfunction," keeps people from realizing their identity as the *imago Dei*. However, this "organ malfunction" in no way implies that they no longer retain their identity. In other words, unbelievers may not be children of God, but this does not mean that they were not created to be God's children. In fact, the permanence of human existence as *imago Dei* provides the context for God's judgment; unbelievers are judged because they have made a mockery of the God in whose image they are created—the unbelieving life is a lie about the God whom the unbeliever continues to represent in the world. So, God's punishment in Isa 6:9–13 is fitting because it is truthful

---

[53] Ibid., 218.

and brings about a truthful state of affairs; those who worship idols are spiritually deaf, blind, and dull. This state is overturned only once the holy seed has borne its fruit and the new shoot has sprung forth from Israel (Isa 11:1)—this new shoot is Jesus Christ.

When humanity lives sinfully, therefore, it fails to realize its identity as God's image. However, since humanity remains in its station as God's earthly representative, human life continues to make claims about God in the world and shapes the world accordingly. This blasphemous proclamation is judged by God as the lie that it is. This implies that the "old humanity," as described in the NT texts, continues to image God but does so as a false (lying) image.

Knowledge of God is the basis for truthful ways of imaging God. Since God has been revealing himself from the beginning, and since the NT texts are dependent upon the theological context of the OT, it is now necessary to consider the relevant OT texts that shape a canonical theology of the *imago Dei* for the people of God.

# 3. Old Testament Texts

In order to give an account of the shape of the OT perspective on the *imago Dei* and the way it is realized in the world, it is necessary to return to Genesis and consider the two explicit references to the image of God outside of Genesis 1. They occur in 5:1–3 and 9:6. I will then summarize the development of the image of God through the OT. A comprehensive study of all the relevant texts is not offered here; rather, representative texts demonstrate the shape of the image of God as it reflects the revelation of God in God's relationship with Israel. These should be taken as keys that unlock a picture of the image of God, which is further developed in the ways taken up by the NT texts already discussed. It is important to keep in mind the intimate connection between the identity "made in God's image" and the realization of that identity through imitation of God.

## 3.1. *Genesis 5:1–3*

The nature of this imitation is expanded in Gen 5:1–3, which reads:

זֶה סֵפֶר תּוֹלְדֹת אָדָם בְּיוֹם בְּרֹא אֱלֹהִים אָדָם בִּדְמוּת אֱלֹהִים עָשָׂה אֹתוֹ׃

זָכָר וּנְקֵבָה בְּרָאָם וַיְבָרֶךְ אֹתָם וַיִּקְרָא אֶת־שְׁמָם אָדָם בְּיוֹם הִבָּרְאָם׃

וַיְחִי אָדָם שְׁלֹשִׁים וּמְאַת שָׁנָה וַיּוֹלֶד בִּדְמוּתוֹ כְּצַלְמוֹ וַיִּקְרָא אֶת־שְׁמוֹ שֵׁת׃

Adam is said to have been created בִּדְמוּת אֱלֹהִים, and Seth is said to be born to Adam בִּדְמוּתוֹ כְּצַלְמוֹ. There are different interpretations of this passage. Either (1) Adam passes his merely human image on to Seth, or (2) Adam passes the image of God on to Seth. Origen emphasizes the first option in his theological treatise, *On First Principles*, where he makes a claim about the nature of sonship: Seth, Adam's son, shared Adam's nature and substance; likewise Jesus, God's

Son, shares God's nature and substance.[54] In Calvin's commentary on Genesis, his interests are more connected to the immediate context of understanding Seth's relation to Adam, but his conclusions are no less theological:

> In saying that Seth begat a son after his own image, he refers in part to the first origin of our nature: at the same time its corruption and pollution is to be noticed, which having been contracted by Adam through the fall, has flowed down to all his posterity. If he had remained upright, he would have transmitted to all his children what he had received: but now we read that Seth, as well as the rest, was defiled; because Adam, who had fallen from his original state, could beget none but such as were like himself.[55]

Calvin sees a contrast between 5:1 wherein Adam is in God's likeness and 5:3 wherein Seth is merely the image and likeness of fallen Adam. Walter Brueggemann has given support to this view recently by claiming that the fact that Seth is not said to be in God's image shows that such a conclusion is "hedged, for the image of God is something less, and marred (cf. Gen. 3)."[56] However, Brueggemann does not interpret this as a clear reference to a sinful image. Rather, Brueggemann sees ambiguity in the text, so that it is unclear whether Seth is God's image or not. "Thus, the text may realistically recognize that Seth and his heirs are a strange, unresolved mixture of the *regal* image of God and the *threatened* image of Adam."[57] Bill Arnold argues for a stronger link between God's image and Adam's image: "[S]ince Seth was made in Adam's image, and Adam was made in God's, the image of God becomes an actuality for all humans."[58] However, in the end Arnold concedes that the image of Adam is a flawed image and concurs with Brueggemann's observation about the ambivalence of humanity's condition.[59] Clines, on the other hand, makes the same interpretive decision without drawing theological implications: "we shall not lay much weight on Genesis 5 as is done by many exegetes, for there we are not dealing with the transmission of the divine image, but with the begetting of a son in Adam's image."[60]

Supporters of (2) interpret 5:1 and 5:3 together, so the reminder that Adam was created in God's image provides the context for understanding what it means for Seth to be Adam's image.[61] For example, Wenham states, "This verse

---

[54] Origen, *On First Principles: Being Koetschau's Text of the* De Principiis *Translated into English, Together with an Introduction and Notes by G. W. Butterworth* (trans. G. W. Butterworth; London: SPCK, 1936; rep. Gloucester, Mass.: Peter Smith, 1973), 19.

[55] John Calvin, *Commentaries on the First Book of Moses called Genesis*, vol. 1 (trans. John King; Grand Rapids: Eerdmans, 1948), 228–29.

[56] Brueggemann, *Genesis*, 68.

[57] Ibid.

[58] Bill Arnold, *Genesis* (NCBC; Cambridge University Press, 2009), 86.

[59] Ibid.

[60] Clines, "The Image of God in Man," 100.

[61] It is tempting to see this as a strictly logical argument: Adam is the image of God; Seth is the image of Adam; therefore, Seth is the image of God. This could be read as a ver-

makes the point that the image and likeness of God which was given to Adam at creation was inherited by his sons. It was not obliterated by the fall."[62] Gerhard von Rad argues along similar lines, concluding that this testimony of the inheritance of the image of God by successive generations was necessary in order for the reader to come to the conclusion that humanity, and not merely one primeval man, is made in God's image.[63]

There are other ways of construing the relationship of Seth to Adam. Benjamin Gladd has recently suggested that the image of God may be constituted by ruling and multiplying, since the command to procreate in Gen 1:28 immediately follows God's act of creation. "Just as God rules over the cosmos, so Adam and Eve are to rule over the earth. Furthermore, just as God created Adam and Eve in his image, so they are to create others in their image, an activity that ultimately reflects the image of God."[64] Strictly speaking, however, God does not multiply himself by creating whereas humans do multiply by procreating. Human reproduction is, therefore, more akin to animal reproduction than divine creation.[65] Yet we can understand the relationship between ruling and multiplying as follows: since two humans cannot rule the entire earth alone, multiplication is necessary for humanity to rule over the earth. So, in Gen 1:28, God tells the human creatures to "fill the earth and subdue it." Filling the earth is required in order to subdue it. Nevertheless, God's blessing in Gen 1:28 may be in the background of 5:1–3. Hamilton explains, "That Adam reproduces himself through Seth, and Seth through Enosh, etc., demonstrates that God's blessing has become effective. They are not only created by God but blessed by God. Such blessing is manifested in multiplication."[66] Of course, the

---

sion of A=B; C=A; therefore, C=B. But this conclusion is not logically necessary for two reasons: (1) Seth may be Adam's image in a different way than Adam is God's image; (2) the form of the argument would only guarantee the conclusion if the words "the image of" were unimportant. In this case the argument would be: Adam is God; Seth is Adam; therefore, Seth is God. But of course, Adam is not God, Seth is not Adam, and Seth is not God. So, the words "the image of" are important to the meaning of the propositions above. Until the nature of the importance of "the image of" is discerned, it is unclear what does or does not follow from these relations.

[62] Wenham, *Genesis 1–15*, 127.

[63] von Rad, *Genesis*, 70–1.

[64] Benjamin Gladd, "The Last Adam as the 'Life-Giving Spirit' Revisited: A Possible Old Testament Background of One of Paul's Most Perplexing Phrases," *WTJ* 71 (2009): 299–300 n. 10; W. Randall Garr, *In His Own Image and Likeness: Humanity, Divinity, and Monotheism* (CHANE 15; Leiden: Brill, 2003), 127–28. See also Hamilton, *Book of Genesis*, 255; Blocher makes a similar suggestion, but leaves the matter undecided (*In the Beginning*, 93).

[65] See Gen 1:22, where God blessed the creatures of the sea and the birds of the air, saying, "Be fruitful and multiply and fill the waters in the seas, and let birds multiply on the earth."

[66] Hamilton, *Book of Genesis*, 255.

account of Cain's line in Gen 4:17–24 also manifests multiplication, so it is unlikely that multiplication *simpliciter* is the point here.[67]

A better approach is to note the connection between "image" and "son" in 5:1–3. By calling Seth the image of Adam, a two-way identification and representation are implied. Seth is identified with Adam and is Adam's representative descendant. Adam is identified with Seth and is represented by Seth. Seth's line is Adam's line.

These observations have important implications for the meaning of the image of God since they reverse the question of how the image of Adam is related to the image of God. Read from this perspective, the text does not explain how the image of God is transmitted to Seth, since all humans are God's image. Rather the text expresses something of the nature of what it means for someone to be another's image. Walton argues,

> 5:1–3 likens the image of God in Adam to the image of Adam in Seth.
> . . . What draws the idol imagery and the child imagery together is
> the concept that the image of God in people provides them the ca-
> pacity not only to serve as God's vice-regents . . ., but also the capac-
> ity to be and act like him. Thus, 5:1–3 is perhaps the most significant
> for determining how we ought to interpret the image of God.[68]

Blocher arrives at a similar conclusion after briefly commenting on Col 1:15: "Nearer the prologue of Genesis, the book of the *tôlᵉdôt* of Adam, having recalled the creation of man 'in the likeness of God' (Gn. 5:1), records that Adam begot his son 'as his own likeness, as his image' (Gn. 5:3). Is that not the obvious key to the language of Genesis 1:26f.?"[69] The father to son relationship is the paradigmatic analogy for understanding what it means for humanity to be

---

[67] Walton offers a promising explanation of the transition from Cain's line to Seth's line: "In these verses (Gen 4:25ff.) we encounter the first example of a literary device that is typical of the narrative style of Genesis. The text has followed the genealogical line of least interest first (here, the line of Cain) and now goes back to pick up the line that is of most significance" (John Walton, *Genesis* [NIVAC; Grand Rapids: Zondervan, 2001], 278–79). Yet, the line of Cain serves as an antitype of Seth's line. Cain's children bear a likeness to him. After killing Abel, Cain was exiled, and God "put a mark on Cain, so that no one who came upon him would kill him." By the end of Cain's genealogy, Lamech is found boasting to his wives about murdering another person. Walton comments, "The text has moved from unrepentant Cain to defiant Lamech. Violence is glorified, and the mark of Cain no longer stands as a stigma of exile but a badge of honor that brings protection . . ." (*Genesis*, 278). Similarly, Hamilton concludes, "Cain's mind-set now surfaces in his great-great-great grandson" (*Book of Genesis*, 241). There is no hope of the realization of the image of God in the line of Cain. Cain's descendants are outside of God's presence and the knowledge of God appears to be lost. However, Adam has another son—Seth. Seth is in Adam's image, and hope is renewed. "At that time people began to invoke the name of the LORD" (Gen 4:26).

[68] Walton, *Genesis*, 131.

[69] Blocher, *In the Beginning*, 89.

made in God's image. This confirms and further strengthens the readings of the NT texts provided above.

In light of this conclusion, both (1), that Adam passes his merely human image on to Seth and (2), that Adam passes the image of God on to Seth, are problematic if they stand alone as explanations of Gen 5:1–3. The first option draws too great a distinction between the image of God and the image of Adam. The image of God is not opposed to the image of Adam. Nor is the image of Adam merely the corruption of the image of God. Rather, they are both descriptive of the identification and representation involved in the relationships referred to: first, the relationship of God with Adam (and all humanity); second, the relationship of Adam to Seth (and all parents with children). There is a positive analogy between these relationships. The second option presses for an unwarranted reference to the transmission of a substance, physical or spiritual, that qualifies Seth as the image of God. This would raise a number of misleading questions, such as whether or not Adam's other children received the substance that makes Adam the image of God. The image of God is analogous to, but not identical to, the image of Adam. Therefore, there is no need to collapse the one image into the other. Rather, the meaning of the image of Adam sheds light on the meaning of the image of God, and, to some extent, *vice versa*. It is best to interpret the use of the "likeness of God" in Gen 5:1 as mutually informative with the "image and likeness of Adam" in Gen 5:3 since both relations are conditioned by צלם and דמות. Identification and representation are the common themes.

## 3.2. Genesis 9:6

Genesis 9:6 contains the third, and final, direct reference to the image of God in the OT. Genesis 9:6–7 states:

שֹׁפֵךְ דַּם הָאָדָם בָּאָדָם דָּמוֹ יִשָּׁפֵךְ כִּי בְּצֶלֶם אֱלֹהִים עָשָׂה אֶת־הָאָדָם:

וְאַתֶּם פְּרוּ וּרְבוּ שִׁרְצוּ בָאָרֶץ וּרְבוּ־בָהּ:

Based on the close relationship that exists between the one imaged and the image, as illustrated in Gen 5:1–3, God has good reason to care about the fate of each human made in his image. As Calvin reasons, "[S]ince they (humans) bear the image of God engraven on them, He deems Himself violated in their person."[70] God is the one imaged, and is therefore the one represented by humanity. So, ultimately, violence is done against God when humans are murdered. In Gen 9:6, there is a limitation of the extent of human dominion. Humans have dominion over the earth. However, it is God who has dominion over human life; humans do not have dominion over each other.[71] It may also be the case

---

[70] Calvin, *Genesis*, 295.

[71] When humans have authority over other humans, such as parental authority over a family or governmental authority over a community, the biblical portrayal is that these authorities are delegated by God. This, in turn, implies that the authorities should exer-

that, after the flood, this limitation of dominion is clarified in consideration of the disastrous consequences of Cain's actions.

The ethical rationale behind Gen 9:6 is similar to that provided by David when explaining his refusal to kill Saul in 1 Sam 26:9–11: "'[W]ho can raise his hand against the LORD's anointed, and be guiltless?' David said, 'As the LORD lives, the LORD will strike him down; or his day will come to die; or he will go down into battle and perish. The LORD forbid that I should raise my hand against the LORD's anointed.'" David, out of reverence for God, would not kill Saul since this would amount to an act of violence against God. Only God has the authority to bring judgment on the one God has chosen to have authority over his people. An act of violence against the LORD's anointed would incur guilt and judgment. Likewise, in Gen 9:6, one should not do violence to God's earthly image. Those who choose to do violence to God's image will stand under like judgment so that their own lives are taken from them.

### 3.3. Other Old Testament Texts

Since Gen 5:1–3 establishes a parallel between the relationship of the one imaged with the one who is the image and the relationship of a father with his son, then there is good reason to think that God's actions toward and expectations of the people of Israel, God's children, will have implications for the material shape of the image of God. This supposition is supported by the parallel ethical reasoning in Gen 9:6 and 1 Sam 26:9–11; since all humanity belongs to God even as God's anointed belongs to God, it is reasonable to expect that those who are chosen out of the world as God's own are intended to live in ways that align with God's purpose for humanity from the beginning.[72] In other words, it is the original fact that humanity is made in God's image that provides the appropriate theological context for God's act of making some humans his adopted children, who then reflect his character in the world; God's decision to make humanity in God's image is the context for God's decision to choose Abraham's descendents as God's children. God's reparation of humanity through the election of a people to whom he would make himself known, and through whom he would provide the new humanity in Christ, is the fulfillment of God's determination that humanity would be his image in the world. God's decision to choose Abraham's descendents is truly the choice to bless the whole of humanity since it is through Abraham that "all the families of the earth shall be blessed" (Gen 12:3) with the realization of human identity in Christ.

---

cise their responsibilities in ways that reflect God's own rule. In this way, human authority over humans is analogous to human dominion over the earth.

[72] It is important to note that God determines what kinds of imitation are appropriate to humanity's identity. Since humans are not God, it cannot be assumed that humanity is to imitate everything God does. On the contrary, humans must be taught what kinds of actions are fitting to their place as God's representatives.

In this context, a number of OT texts become informative of God's intention for humanity expression of the image of God. The texts are discerned through the use of a criterion mentioned for with respect to the relevant NT texts, namely, that an ethical command is based on and justified by an appeal to God's own character as demonstrated through God's economy. The exegetical comments that follow are once again representative. Additional texts could be included. These serve to show how OT texts contribute to the unfolding content of the *imago Dei* as human identity develops in relation to God's self-revelation.

As noted in chapter 4, there is debate about which, if any, OT texts use imitation of God as a basis for ethical action. As I assessed Rodd's criticisms, I argued that they fall short as long as imitation is taken to be analogical rather than univocal. At most, Rodd's analysis showed that if the biblical texts are read independently of human identity as God's image, then the imitation of God should not be treated as a pervasive ethical rationale.[73] However, if God's image is the identity of humanity, then the texts that suggest divine imitation have an ethical rationale that is located dogmatically in the relationship God has with humanity and not merely in the immediate circumstances of the text in question.

Even Rodd concedes that imitation of God may be the ethical rationale for the action described in Deut 10:17–19.[74] Brueggemann has shown that these verses are part of a larger rhetorical movement of Deut 10:12–22:[75]

> [12] So now, O Israel, what does the LORD your God require of you? Only to fear the LORD your God, to walk in all his ways, to love him, to serve the LORD your God with all your heart and with all your soul,
> [13] and to keep the commandments of the LORD your God  and his decrees that I am commanding you today, for your own well-being.
> [14] Although heaven and the heaven of heavens belong to the LORD your God, the earth with all that is in it,
> [15] yet the LORD set his heart in love on your ancestors alone and chose you, their descendants after them, out of all the peoples, as it is today.
> [16] Circumcise, then, the foreskin of your heart, and do not be stubborn any longer.
> [17] For the LORD your God is God of gods and Lord of lords, the great God, mighty and awesome, who is not partial and takes no bribe,
> [18] who executes justice for the orphan and the widow, and who loves the strangers, providing them food and clothing.
> [19] You shall also love the stranger, for you were strangers in the land of Egypt.
> [20] You shall fear the LORD your God; him alone you shall worship; to him you shall hold fast, and by his name you shall swear.

---

[73] Rodd, *Glimpses of a Strange Land*, 65–76.

[74] Ibid., 68.

[75] Walter Brueggemann, *Deuteronomy* (AOTC; Nashville: Abingdon, 2001), 133.

²¹ He is your praise; he is your God, who has done for you these great
   and awesome things that your own eyes have seen.
²² Your ancestors went down to Egypt seventy persons; and now the
   LORD your God has made you as numerous as the stars in heaven.

Brueggemann discovers the following rhetorical structure:

> Four summary imperatives (vv. 12–13)
> A motivation cosmic and concrete (vv. 14–15)
> A particular mandate (v. 16)
> A motivation cosmic and concrete (vv. 17–18)
> A particular mandate (v. 19*a*)
> A particular motivation (v. 19*b*)
> Four summary imperatives (v. 20)
> A motivation rooted in Israel's own life (vv. 21–22)[76]

The particular mandate in verse 19*a* is supported by vv. 17–18 and 19*b*. God's commitment to justice, exemplified by God's just actions on Israel's behalf, provides the motivation for Israel to take just action on behalf of orphans and the widows. This action is part of God's broader concern that Israel be the people he has called them to be. Brueggemann argues:

> The rhythm of imperative and motivation bids for a present-tense
> embrace of identity congruent with the "so now" of verse 12. The
> power of the motivations keeps the imperative from being coercive
> impositions. The motivations intend to dazzle Israel so that Israel
> will gladly and eagerly undertake the obedience that belongs
> properly to its life and identity with YHWH.[77]

Obedience to God takes shape within the relational context that gives Israel its identity. Brueggemann concludes that Deut 10:12–22 presents "an invitation to embrace again identity as YHWH's special people. . . . Such a recovery of identity entails the resituating of self-awareness and imagination in this repository of miracles. . . ."[78] The recovery of Israel's identity is ultimately directed toward the recovery of all peoples in relation to God. So, reflection on this text leads Telford Work to the conclusion that "[a]s God of gods and Lord of lords, YHWH tolerates no petty spiritual or social tyranny as all lesser powers must (cf. 1 Cor. 8:4–6; Rev 19:15–16). Rather, the great God steadfastly pursues a mysterious campaign to end all sin among all peoples through this particular people."[79] God's concern that Israel take on actions analogous to God's own actions, actions which demonstrate God's justice, is tied to Israel's important station as God's son (cf. Exod 4:22–23; Hos 11:1). As suggested above, God's concern for Israel parallels God's concern for all humanity since Israel represents God as God's covenantal people and humanity represents God in the world as

---

[76] Ibid., 133.
[77] Ibid., 133.
[78] Ibid., 134.
[79] Telford Work, *Deuteronomy* (BTCB; Grand Rapids: Brazos, 2009), 130.

his image. Taking on ways of being in the world that reflect God's character and action, therefore, is the embodiment of one's true identity. So, as Duane Christiansen concludes, "The people of Israel were to love others because God has loved them. . . . God loves the stranger, the widow, and the orphan; and therefore his people, if they truly love God, must also be concerned for justice and righteousness in relation to their neighbors."[80] The logic of Deut 10:17–19 points forward to the argument of 1 John 4:9–12:

> God's love was revealed among us in this way: God sent his only Son into the world so that we might live through him. In this is love, not that we loved God but that he loved us and sent his Son to be the atoning sacrifice for our sins. Beloved, since God loved us so much, we also ought to love one another. No one has ever seen God; if we love one another, God lives in us, and his love is perfected in us.

Deuteronomy 10:17–19 is one representative illustration of the ethical implications that arise from one's identity as determined by one's relation to God.

Another important example, over which there has been much debate, is Lev 19:2 (cf. 11:44–45): "Speak to all the congregation of the people of Israel and say to them: You shall be holy, for I the LORD your God am holy." As noted in discussion of the NT texts, 1 Pet 1:14–16 interprets this text ethically: "Like obedient children, do not be conformed to the desires that you formerly had in ignorance. Instead, as he who called you is holy, be holy yourselves in all your conduct; for it is written, 'You shall be holy, for I am holy.'" Rather than being conformed to the evil desires that follow from ignorance, God's children should act in ways that demonstrate that they belong to God. Holy conduct requires knowledge of God and is a witness to God's own holiness.

Some have argued that Lev 19:2 should not be read as a command to imitate God's holiness. On the contrary, the imperative "be holy" is read as a cultic command owing to the fact that God cannot tolerate sin in his presence. But this is not contrary to the implied *imitatio Dei*, as Jacob Milgrom argues, "[T]he *imitatio dei* implied by this verse is that just as God differs from human beings, so Israel should differ from the nations (20:26), a meaning corroborated by the generalization that encloses this chapter (v. 37): Israel is holy only if it observes YHWH's commandments."[81] Here the imitation of God is seen in light of obedience to God's commandments since obedience to God's commandments establishes a different way of being in the world. The Masoretes recognized the difference between divine and human holiness and even reflected it in their pointing of the word in different contexts.[82] Summarizing the implications of the Masoretic pointing, Milgrom states, "Thus the Masoretes, too, imply the doctrine of the *imitatio dei*: observance of the divine commandments

---

[80] Duane Christiansen, *Deuteronomy 1:1–21:9* (rev. ed.; WBC 6a; Nashville: Thomas Nelson, 2001), 206.

[81] Jacob Milgrom, *Leviticus 17–22: A New Translation with Introduction and Commentary* (AB; New York: Doubleday, 2000), 1604.

[82] Ibid., 1606.

leads to God's attribute of holiness, but not to the same degree—not to God, but to godliness." Human holiness, as in all cases of divine imitation, is analogical.

There is no *a priori* theological expectation that humanity should be holy. Holiness indicates the "total otherness of God"[83] observed by God's creatures.[84] However, an *a posteriori* theological rationale can be offered regarding why it is fitting that humanity take on analogous forms of holiness. Humans are made to represent God. Certain human behaviors faithfully represent God's character. Other behaviors are explicitly unfaithful representations of God. With reference to sinful acts, it is not simply the case that certain behaviors are not tolerated in God's presence. Rather, these behaviors are not fitting for humans, given humanity's identity as God's image. For example, animals may be sexually promiscuous without violating God's holy presence. But humanity, because of its identity, is designated for a different way of being in the world, a way that is holy since it is guided by God's character. This way of being is determined by the fact that humans are made in God's image and as such are God's representatives. Commenting on Lev 19:2, John Hartley asserts, "Being Yahweh's representative on earth, Israel is to evidence in her community characteristics that are similar to God's."[85] Perhaps a counterexample will help make the point. When humans commit adultery, they have been unfaithful to their covenantal commitments. But God is always faithful to his covenant commitments. Therefore, they have misrepresented God in the world, which cannot ultimately be tolerated.

Holiness is separation *to* God and *from* sin. There is a weakness in Milgrom's analysis at this point: Israel's holiness is not discovered merely in its being separated from the nations; rather, Israel is holy because it is consecrated and sanctified by God. Holiness can be shared by all humankind. Yet, holiness is always dependent upon God, from whom it is derived.[86] With characteristic insight, John Webster explains:

> And so: as Father, God is the one who wills and purposes from all eternity the separation of humankind as a holy people, destined for fellowship with himself. As Son, God is the one who achieves this separation of humankind by rescuing humanity from its pollution and bondage to unholiness. As Spirit, God is the one who completes or perfects that separation by sanctifying humankind and drawing it into righteous fellowship with the holy God.[87]

With respect to the point that only God brings holiness, Ephraim Radner directs attention to Lev 20:8: "Only God himself *makes holy*, in the sense that it is his own coming that brings close. This is why he says of his law: 'Keep my stat-

---

[83] Ibid., 1606.
[84] Ephraim Radner, *Leviticus* (BTCB; Grand Rapids: Brazos, 2008), 207.
[85] John Hartley, *Leviticus* (WBC 4; Dallas: Word, 1992), 312.
[86] John Webster, *Holiness* (London: SCM, 2003), 77; Radner, *Leviticus*, 207.
[87] Ibid., 98.

utes, and do them; I am the LORD who sanctifies you.'"[88] The sanctifying action of God is the source of human holiness. It is not as though imitation of God is autonomously willed by humans. On the contrary, imitation is the result of God's work of establishing humanity as the creature that it is and perfecting humanity so that it realizes its God-given identity. So, rather than conceiving of these texts as establishing ethical norms of divine imitation outside of any prior context, the *imago Dei* provides an *a posteriori* rationale for these texts without doing violence to their unique situational contexts. Moreover, the identity interpretation can account for the NT interpretations of OT texts such as Lev 19:2 and their ethical implications. With this interpretation, much more of the OT theological context is taken into 1 Pet 1:14–16 than a bare reading of Lev 19:2 or 11:44–45 would otherwise yield.

Further examples of the expectation of divine imitation in the OT could be produced.[89] As noted in chapter 4, the parallels between Psalms 111 and 112 are particularly enlightening.[90] Throughout the prophetic literature, God condemns Israel's failure to embody the righteousness and justice expected in Deut 10:12–22 (e.g., Isa 1:21–31). These passages should be understood in light of the revelation of God's holiness, justice, and mercy. Since Israel, God's people, are unrighteous and unjust, they are under God's judgment.

# 4. Conclusions

In the third section of this chapter, then, I have demonstrated that interpreting the *imago Dei* as human identity can accommodate the relevant OT texts. Moreover, this interpretation also provides an *a posteriori* theological rationale for OT ethical expectations, especially those based on the imitation of God.

Prior to this, I examined a number of NT texts with a similar result. The relevant NT texts can be accommodated by the identity interpretation, and said even more strongly, the identity interpretation provides the context for compelling readings of these NT texts. The second section of this chapter offered a way of understanding the relationship between the identity of humanity as the image of God and the grievousness of sin, which is a violation of that identity. This shows that the *imago Dei* has implications not only for positive realization of God's intention for humanity, but also when there is a failure to realize this identity in accordance with the knowledge of God.

The exegetical studies included in this chapter demonstrate that interpreting the *imago Dei* as human identity is harmonious with a range of careful and faithful interpretations of the relevant OT and NT texts offered by biblical scholars. A further claim can be made. If the biblical interpretations offered in

---

[88] Radner, *Leviticus*, 207.

[89] See Otto, *Theologische Ethik des Alten Testaments*; Davies, "Walking in God's Ways," 99–115.

[90] See Davies, "Walking in God's Ways,"107.

this chapter are compelling, then the identity interpretation should be understood as offering a dogmatic proposal that aids in the task of clarifying exegesis. This makes it preferable to the proposals analyzed in chapters 1 and 2, since a common criticism of those proposals is that they represent dogmatic assertions that misconstrue the relevant texts and so confound careful exegesis.

In chapter six, I will argue that the identity interpretation can also accommodate the best insights of the theological tradition. Most modern scholars have claimed that the greatest Christian theologians failed to understand the *imago Dei*. Yet, while no one theological proposal has been wholly satisfactory, the fundamental insights driving the various other interpretations that have been offered can enrich our understanding of the *imago Dei* interpreted as human identity.

# Chapter 6

# The Identity Interpretation
# and the Christian Tradition

In chapter 5, I demonstrated how the identity interpretation accommodates the NT references to the *imago Dei*. Moreover, I showed how several other biblical texts in the OT and NT can inform the content of the image of God since they refer directly to the appropriate shape of human being-in-the-world. Christian theologians have regularly understood texts that command divine imitation to be related to the *imago Dei*, but the dogmatic relation between the image of God and the imitation of God has most often been left vague. I suggested that the imitation of God is a fitting consequence of human identity as God's earthly image.

In this chapter, I will demonstrate that the identity interpretation can accommodate a number of key theological insights from the Christian tradition regarding the dogmatic context for interpreting the image of God and the implications of this context for theological anthropology more broadly conceived. As noted in chapters 1 and 2, there are various interpretations of the image of God that flow from various theological founts. I have chosen four figures—Irenaeus, Athanasius, Augustine, and Martin Luther—whose interpretations of the image of God have been much maligned in modern scholarship. I will show the theological validity of key insights that led them to interpret the *imago Dei* in the ways they did, and that the identity interpretation provides an exegetically careful alternative that can incorporate these key insights. If this is so, then this provides considerable support for the identity interpretation since the explanatory power of the identity interpretation is broader than its counterparts.

Many recent interpretations eschew the theological tradition. A common criticism of the tradition is that the various theological interpretations offered are dependent upon extrabiblical concepts. For example, Middleton states,

> Although certainly not all proponents of a substantialistic interpretation have been as aware as Augustine was of Middle Platonic and Neoplatonic speculation about the intricacies of *eidōla*, *phantasia*,

144

and psychic self-reflexivity, their dependence on extrabiblical paradigms of philosophical and theological lineage is nevertheless patently obvious.[1]

Middleton does not reserve this criticism for the substantialistic interpretation. "[E]ven granted the New Testament basis of the Reformers' interpretations, they are, like the substantialistic interpreters before them, decisively conditioned by their own historical contexts and theological concerns."[2] Barth's relational interpretation receives the same critique: "Whatever his disclaimers, Barth thus shares with previous interpreters of the image an evident dependence on theological paradigms and agendas derived from outside the Genesis text."[3] In summary, Middleton argues that the traditional interpretations are mistaken since they have been conditioned by factors outside of a careful reading of Genesis 1.[4] It should be noted that the criticisms leveled against the traditional interpretations tend to focus on one or two particular claims concerning the image of God in a theologian's writings rather than on the nature of the investigation as a whole. As will be shown below, this approach misses the thrust of many traditional interpretations. So, when Athanasius identifies the image of God with human reason, he is not reducing the image to the capacity for the practice of Enlightenment rationality. For Athanasius, reason facilitates human existence as the image of God since contemplation of God is the source of a properly ordered human life. While modern criticisms of the identification of the image with reason are appropriate, modern evaluations of the tradition tend to neglect its positive contributions.

Other recent interpretations seek to recover aspects of the tradition. For example, Nonna Verna Harrison argues that there are "patristic concepts that hint at the possibility of a trinitarian anthropology."[5] These hints are intended to support the modern theological claim that the image of God is "essentially communal" and that the intra-Trinitarian relations are the "pattern according to which human relationships and communities can best be structured."[6] However, "the fathers understand the *imago Dei* primarily in christological rather than trinitarian terms" since "in the fourth century the doctrine of the Trinity was itself being articulated definitively for the first time."[7] So the early theologians do not often examine the implications of the intra-Trinitarian relations for human community. Nevertheless, Harrison concludes that these

---

[1] Middleton, *The Liberating Image*, 20.
[2] Ibid., 22.
[3] Ibid., 24. Middleton specifically notes Barth's philosophical and political contexts as the determining factors.
[4] Of course, modern critical interpretations of the *imago Dei* have been very much affected by such factors also, particularly in that they are dependent upon a *modern* critical interpretive methodology.
[5] Nonna Verna Harrison, "Greek Patristic Foundations of Trinitarian Anthropology," *ProEccl* 14 (2005): 400.
[6] Ibid., 399.
[7] Ibid., 400.

hints, and particularly a passage in Gregory of Nazianzus's *First Oration on Peace*, make "a small beginning in articulating a Trinitarian anthropology of the kind theologians find important today."[8]

There are two problems with Harrison's analysis. First, Harrison seems to indicate that the primary value of the patristic contribution to an understanding of the *imago Dei* is that the early theologians almost say what modern theologians are now saying. In this case modern theology is the standard against which the theological tradition is measured. On the contrary, as I will demonstrate below, the early theologians provide dogmatic insights that should inform and chasten contemporary interpretations.

The second problem with Harrison's analysis is theological. Harrison argues that interpreting the image of God Christologically leads to an insufficiently Trinitarian interpretation since Christ is an individual and the Trinity is a divine community. The suggestion that a Christological image of God is in any way contrary to a Trinitarian image of God cannot be maintained. Jesus Christ lived by the power of the Spirit as the perfect image of the Father. In this way, the Christological image of God is established as a Trinitarian image. As shown in chapter five, it is because Jesus is the image of God that transformation into his image is the fulfillment of the image of God for Christians. But perhaps Harrison attempts to make a different distinction. Whereas a Christological conception of the *imago Dei*, as the early theologians espoused it, is the result of reflection on God's economy, Harrison suggests that the image of God is known through reflection on the immanent Trinity and realized through imitation of the intra-Trinitarian relations. Therefore, the conceptual distinction Harrison intends is not between Christological and Trinitarian images; rather, she describes a distinction between the immanent and the economic. Drawing ethical implications from direct contemplation of the immanent Trinity is a common strategy of social Trinitarians since human community is understood to be analogous to divine community. The early church, however, contemplated the Trinity through God's economy, and specifically through careful theological attention to Christology. God's image is revealed through God's action in the world rather than by direct contemplation of the divine essence. With respect to the Trinity, what should be maintained is that direct contemplation of the immanent Trinity would not be *contrary to* or *conceptually distinguishable from* the results of contemplating God's economy.

Problems such as these stem from the effort to find support for modern conceptions of human identity in the early Christian theologians. Instead of following this path, I will bring the different emphases of each theologian's interpretation to light and then direct that light onto the identity interpretation. The light from these theologians' interpretations contributes to the dogmatic shape of the identity interpretation. Seen from another perspective, the identity interpretation provides an interpretive context for their insights that

---

[8] Ibid., 412. Gregory of Nazianzus, *Oration 6* (*De Pace*).

disarms the standard objections to these theologians' interpretations. Of course, the selection of theologians is representative rather than comprehensive, but these have been chosen due to their seminal insights and influence on later interpreters.[9]

# 1. Irenaeus of Lyons

Irenaeus of Lyons is well known for his exegetical decision to interpret εἰκόν as having a different referent than ὁμοίωσις in Gen 1:26. For Irenaeus, all humanity possesses the image (εἰκόν) of God, which is the rational nature that establishes humanity *qua* humanity. The other aspects of human nature are likewise included in the image because human nature as a whole is rational. So, Irenaeus refers to the "admixture of the fleshly nature which was moulded after the image of God."[10] This inclusion of the body in his interpretation of the image of God leads McFarland to call Irenaeus's interpretation "remarkably holistic."[11] On the other hand, for Irenaeus, the likeness (ὁμοίωσις) of God is supernatural conformity to God. Blocher describes the distinction as follows: "From Irenaeus and Clement of Alexandria onwards, many distinguish between the image and the likeness as between the natural and the supernatural; the image is that metaphysical quality which makes mankind distinctively mankind, and the likeness means that growth in conformity to God produced by grace."[12] This exegetical decision is often found wanting. For example, Middleton compares Irenaeus's interpretation to the relational-ethical interpretation: "The Reformed view is thus similar to Irenaeus's proposal centuries earlier that 'image' (*imago*) refers to that which is ontologically constitutive of humanness (for Irenaeus, rationality and freedom), while 'likeness' (*similitudo*) demonstrates the ethical similitude that has been lost by the fall and is restored through Christ."[13] Middleton concludes that while there is some NT

---

[9] Other theologians, such as Gregory of Nyssa or Maximus the Confessor, could have been engaged here. These four studies are intended to be representative of the ways in which the identity interpretation provides an appropriate context for recovering the church's longstanding reflection on the *imago Dei*.

[10] Irenaeus of Lyons, *Against Heresies* (hereafter *AH*), V.6.1.

[11] McFarland, *The Divine Image*, 1.

[12] Blocher, *In the Beginning*, 80.

[13] Middleton, *The Liberating Image*, 21. Cf. David Cairns, *The Image of God in Man* (rev. ed.; London: Collins, 1973), 80; Anthony Hoekema, *Created in God's Image* (Grand Rapids: Eerdmans, 1986), 34; F. LeRon Shults, (*Reforming Theological Anthropology: After the Philosophical Turn to Relationality* [Grand Rapids: Eerdmans, 2003], 221), who comments, "How then can we speak of the image of God as having to do with *both* human reason and human righteousness? One popular approach, which may be traced from Irenaeus through the Protestant Scholastics, is to distinguish between the 'image,' which is essential to human nature (and could not be lost), and the 'likeness' to God, which is merely accidental to human nature (and was lost)." Shults acknowledges that Irenaeus

support for this view, it "does not do full justice to Gen 1:26–27."[14] Charles Sherlock calls the distinction "unsustainable exegetically."[15]

### 1.1. Description of Irenaeus's Interpretation

Because of the exegetical problems involved with the distinction between εἰκόν and ὁμοίωσις, very little serious attention is paid to the precise nature of Irenaeus's distinction. Contrary to Middleton, Irenaeus's claim is not that Adam's likeness to God was gained in creation and lost in Genesis 3 with the fall. Rather, human likeness to God is *never* fully achieved until Christ manifests it. In the original creation, Adam had the "likeness" of God as a potentiality. M. C. Steenberg aptly describes the nature of this potentiality as "possessed-but-not-realized":

> Irenaeus in fact makes extensive use of this possessed-but-not-realized concept in his references to Adam as possessing the image and likeness of God, for he makes clear elsewhere that he does not believe the fullness of the likeness to be attainable before the incarnation of Christ, nor fully manifest until His second coming. The possession may be said, however, to exist in its potential. Adam "possessed" likeness to God, but with respect to the fullness of this likeness he possessed it potentially.[16]

Furthermore, Steenberg argues that potentiality exists even in Irenaeus's explication of the "image." If, as Irenaeus claims, Adam and Eve were created as children (in an immature state), then the human capacity to reason well should also be understood developmentally. For example, Irenaeus states that

> it was necessary, at first, that [the created] nature should be exhibited; then, after that, that what was mortal should be conquered and swallowed up by immortality, and the corruptible by incorruptibility, and that man should be made after the image and likeness of God, having received the knowledge of good and evil.[17]

Here Irenaeus suggests that human growth into the knowledge of good and evil is attached to the image and likeness of God in a sense that opposes the action of Adam (and Eve) in Genesis 3. Adam's immaturity, however, is not initially due to sin. It is due to his created nature.[18] From creation onward, it was necessary for Adam to find fulfillment in Christ.

---

"probably did not intend to separate them," but he introduced the division that became prominent in later Christian literature.

[14] Middleton, *The Liberating Image*, 21.

[15] Charles Sherlock, *The Doctrine of Humanity* (CCT; Downers Grove, Ill.: InterVarsity, 1996), 83.

[16] M. C. Steenberg, "Children in Paradise: Adam and Eve as 'Infants' in Irenaeus of Lyons," *JECS* 12 (2004): 14.

[17] Irenaeus, *AH*, IV.38.4.

[18] Steenberg, "Children in Paradise," 17.

In fact, it does not appear to be the case that Irenaeus makes his distinction between image and likeness because of his reading of Genesis 1. Rather, the impetus for this distinction is his theological interpretation of Christ as the image and likeness of God who enables the image and likeness to reach their fulfillment in God's children. The Genesis text provides the vehicle for an explication of his Christological insight since the text uses two complementary but not identical words.

Irenaeus describes Adam as the real image and likeness of God, but the mature fulfillment of God's intention for Adam is only partially realized at creation. Therefore, the distinction between "image" and "likeness" for Irenaeus is not merely a distinction between a permanent image and a conditional likeness; rather, the image and likeness are two different aspects of human nature that need to be perfected.

When Irenaeus does make his distinction between image and likeness, potentiality is no longer his primary category. Rather, the division arises in his discussion of the three parts of a human person. The entire human, argues Irenaeus, is the likeness of God, including soul, spirit and body. If one speaks of humanity, then one must speak of all the parts; the subtraction of any of them deems the object somehow less than human. It happens that the physical part of humanity appears to mature much more concretely than the spiritual part. But this appearance is only nominal; development is required of the entire human person.[19]

In this way, Irenaeus's interpretation is teleological. Irenaeus assumes that, due to immaturity, the limitations of human nature would have been evident in our first parents. However, God intended them to mature and come to the knowledge of good and evil. Therefore, God's plan always included time for humanity to receive God's self-revelation and be transformed into God's likeness. Both the culmination of divine revelation and the fulfillment of God's intention for humanity arrive with the incarnation. So Irenaeus argues,

> And then, again, this Word was manifested when the Word of God was made man, assimilating himself to man and man to himself, that by means of his resemblance to the Son, man might become precious to the Father. For in times long past, it was *said* that man was created after the image of God, but it was not yet *shown*; for the Word was as yet invisible, after whose image man was created. Wherefore also he did easily lose the similitude. When, however, the Word of God became flesh, he confirmed both of these: for he both showed forth the image truly, since he became himself what was his image; and he re-established the similitude after a sure manner, by assimilating man to the invisible Father through means of the visible Word.[20]

---

[19] Irenaeus, *AH*, V.6.1.
[20] Ibid., V.16.2.

Hoekema takes "he did easily lose the similitude" to mean that humanity "lost the similitude or likeness to God in the Fall."[21] However, Irenaeus's comment that "in times long past, it was *said* that man was created after the image of God, but it was not yet *shown*" leads one to question Hoekema's conclusion. It is better to read the loss of likeness to God as a loss of the potential for a likeness to God. For Irenaeus, humanity had not shown or realized its likeness to God prior to the fall. The fall negated the possibility of humanity realizing this likeness apart from God's reparative intervention since humanity's proper relationship with God had been compromised. So, Christ "re-established the similitude after a sure manner, by assimilating man to the invisible Father through means of the visible Word." Humanity has been reunited to God in Christ, and this re-establishes the potential for individual humans to realize a likeness to God. Since only some individual humans will realize this likeness, the fact that Christ "re-established the similitude after a sure manner" should not be understood to mean that all humans will realize this likeness but that the potential for realization for this likeness is re-established. Christ himself realized the likeness and showed it forth, but individual humans must be reconciled to the Father through Christ in order to join in its realization.

The church participates in the fulfillment of human nature by being conformed to the image of God's Son. The perfection intended as part of God's plan still lies in the future when humanity will be brought to maturity and allowed "to see and comprehend God."[22] Irenaeus continues with an affirmation of human participation in the divine nature:

> For after His great kindness He graciously conferred good [upon us], and made men like to Himself, [that is] in their own power; while at the same time by His prescience He knew the infirmity of human beings, and the consequences which would flow from it; but through [His] love and [His] power, He shall overcome the substance of created nature.[23]

The infirmity of the created nature of humanity is overcome in the resurrection. The whole human person, image and likeness, awaits the resurrection, which marks the fulfilled intention of the Father. So, Irenaeus's interpretation is directed eschatologically toward the way of being that is already established by Jesus Christ's resurrection; the Son's human way of being will be shared by all of God's children (cf. 1 Cor 15:48–49).[24]

---

[21] Hoekema, *Created in God's Image*, 34.

[22] Irenaeus, *AH*, IV.37.7.

[23] Ibid., IV.38.4.

[24] It should be noted that Irenaeus strongly affirms the Creator/creature distinction in all of his uses of the *imago Dei*. This is true even when he argues that those made after the likeness of God are drawn into intimate communion with God and participation in the divine nature. *Theosis* does not compromise the distinction. See Julie Canlis, "Being made human: the significance of creation for Irenaeus' doctrine of participation," *SJT* 58 [2005]: 434–54, esp. 436.

## 1.2. Accommodation of Irenaeus's Interpretation

Hughes notes a strength of Irenaeus's interpretation: "the theology inherent in his [Irenaeus's] interpretation is governed by a sound scriptural instinct. We refer especially to his perception that man as created was not what he finally would be, that his destiny was to advance from glory to glory, and that, even if there had been no fall, the end was designed to be even more splendid than the beginning."[25] The suggestion that Adam and Eve were created immature, as children, has important implications. First, at the point of creation it is already the case that humanity is called the image and likeness of God. But humanity does not inhabit the world in ways that fully embody this image and likeness. The implication is that humanity was directed toward a particular way of being in the world at creation, but that this way of being had not yet been fully actualized. Therefore, one must distinguish between the lofty status given to humanity and its fulfillment. For Irenaeus, it is unclear just how Adam should be considered the image and likeness of God while immature; immaturity may compromise the reality of Adam's likeness to God.[26] So, Steenberg argues that, for Irenaeus, Adam possessed a likeness to God potentially.[27] The problem, here, is that Gen 1:27 speaks as though humanity is, in fact, God's image and not merely potentially so. Moreover, as demonstrated in chapter 5, even after the fall humanity is still referred to as God's image (Gen 9:6; 1 Cor 11:7) and likeness (Jas 3:9).

The identity interpretation can incorporate Irenaeus's insight regarding the developmental nature of the human creature, even in Eden, without compromising the claim made in Gen 1:27 that humanity was made in God's image or the later biblical claims that this image and likeness remains after the fall. Moreover, the identity interpretation is not forced to follow Irenaeus's unlikely interpretation of the meaning of "image" and "likeness" in Genesis 1. It is important to note that "potentiality" does not do full justice to the claims made in these texts. The image is not so much a possession as a state of existence. God made humanity in his image; this is a permanent reality. "Image of God" names the relation between God and the human creature that determines the nature of human existence; it is a fact that humanity is God's image. As I argued in chapter 5, human identity within creation is unchanging.

---

[25] Hughes, *The True Image*, 9.

[26] Irenaeus's difficulties in this regard are exacerbated by the entrance of sin. So, and this is where his exegesis of Gen 1:26 lets him down, Irenaeus argues that the human person who is without the Spirit is imperfect. Irenaeus states that even though "in his formation he has the image of God, he has not yet received the likeness which is given by the Spirit." This state of imperfection is contrasted with the one who is "made perfect and spiritual by reason of the outpouring of the Spirit" (*AH*, V.6.1). It should be noted that Irenaeus is distinguishing here between Christians and non-Christians rather than between pre-fall and post-fall humanity. This is important so that Irenaeus's comments do not lead one to think that, for Irenaeus, Adam "possessed" the image perfectly but the likeness only potentially.

[27] Steenberg, "Children in Paradise," 14.

Because of its identity, humanity is intended to realize ways of being that are appropriate to the creature made in God's image and likeness. The realization of this identity in the world is developmental, as Irenaeus rightly notes. Yet, it is not as though the existence of human identity is dependent upon the realization of this identity. Rather, realization is dependent upon identity.[28] This reorientation of the dogmatic language surrounding the image of God can then accommodate Irenaeus's profound theological insights.

One insight of particular importance has to do with the necessity of the knowledge of God for the realization of likeness to God. It is useful to return to Irenaeus's comments:

> For in times long past, it was *said* that man was created after the image of God, but it was not yet *shown*; for the Word was as yet invisible, after whose image man was created. . . . When, however, the Word of God became flesh, he confirmed both of these: for he both showed forth the image truly, since he became himself what was his image; and he re-established the similitude after a sure manner, by assimilating man to the invisible Father through means of the visible Word.[29]

Prior to the incarnation, when the Word was invisible, humanity did not have a clear vision of what it meant to be God's image. With the incarnation, humanity is drawn again into relationship with God and shown what it means to be God's image. Knowledge of God and the appropriate human relationship to God are provided through the Word incarnate.

Irenaeus does not comment about the developmental nature of God's relationship to humanity from the fall to the incarnation. In chapters 4 and 5 I argued that the OT canonical development is important to understanding the *imago Dei* references in the NT. Still, certainly, the incarnation is the culmination of God's revelation and the realization of human identity in the world. This focus on the incarnation demonstrates that Irenaeus's interpretation is based on a faithful biblical reading of the implications that the Word made flesh has for human existence in relation to God.

## 2. Athanasius of Alexandria

Athanasius of Alexandria's *De Incarnatione* (hereafter, *DI*) is even more directly focused on the incarnation. However, Barth summarizes Athanasius's interpretation of the *imago Dei* in the context of what he considers to be the

---

[28] Humanity's particular identity is necessary for realization of that identity, but merely having this identity is not a sufficient condition for its realization either. More is needed; for example, the realization of human identity is also dependent upon divine revelation, as argued in chapter 4.

[29] Irenaeus, *AH*, V.16.2. It is interesting to note that the theological shape of this passage in Irenaeus's *AH* is parallel to Heb 1:1–3.

fallacious readings of Genesis 1 found in the early church and the ways the exegesis of the early church was taken up by later interpreters:

> The exegesis of the Early Church (cf. Ambrose, *Hexaem.*, VI, 7) maintained at once that since the divine likeness is not to be found directly in the body of the man it is identified with the soul. It can thus be found either with reference to the divine Logos in the intellect (Athanasius, *De incarn.*, 3), with reference to the Trinity in the three spiritual powers of *memoria, intellectus* and *amor* (so St. Augustine and his followers), or with reference to the Law of God (the view of the Reformers), in the moral integrity, purity, justice and holiness which were originally proper to man, correspond to the law, and as Luther saw it were linked with definite physical characteristics.[30]

Barth describes Athanasius's view as problematic because Athanasius seems to define the image as intellect. As with Irenaeus, such contemporary understandings of Athanasius's interpretation do not often take the overall context of Athanasius's theology into consideration; rather, they depend on various isolated statements. For example, Athanasius states that the human creature received a unique grace, having received "a share in the power of [God's] own Word," with the result that humanity would express "rationality" and live "the true life in paradise, which is really that of the saints."[31] To understand properly this dual blessing of rationality and immortality, one must situate these comments in his broader theological argument.

### 2.1. Description of Athanasius's Interpretation

*DI* contains the most systematic presentation of Athanasius's theology, and therefore it will serve as the primary source for this description of Athanasius's interpretation and its place in his theology.[32] In *DI*, Athanasius focuses upon the relationship between the ontological reality of the incarnation and its economic implications. The *imago Dei* plays an important role in Athanasius's development of this model.

Strictly speaking, Athanasius only refers to the second person of the Trinity as the image of God. Only the Word is the image of God who shares the same substance and nature with God the Father and is eternally begotten by him.[33] Humankind was originally created "in" the image of God. Because humanity

---

[30] Barth, *CD* III/1, 192. As noted in the introduction to this chapter, the next three sections will include studies of Athanasius, Augustine, and Luther—three culprits named specifically by Barth.

[31] Athanasius, *DI*, 3.3.

[32] Vincent Twomey, *Apostolikos Thronos: The Primacy of Rome as Reflected in the Church History of Eusebius and the Historico-Apologetic Writings of Saint Athanasius the Great* (MBT 49; Münster Westphalen: Aschendorffsche Buchdruckerei, 1982), 266.

[33] Athanasius, *DI*, 20.1.

was created *ex nihilo*, its natural substance is nothingness.[34] However, since the Word created humanity in his image, God's immortality is communicated to humanity as humanity participates in God.[35] So Athanasius asserts, "[S]eeing that by definition of [the human race's] own existence it would be unable to persist for ever, [God] gave it an added grace, not simply creating men like all irrational animals on the earth, but making them in his own image and giving them also a share in his own Word."[36] In the creation of humanity, therefore, God intended humanity to share in a relationship with God and benefit from it by sharing also in some of the divine attributes that properly belong to God's nature alone.

These benefits were available to humanity, therefore, as long as humanity continued to participate in the Word, in correspondence with God.[37] The human creature is rational, which makes it a creaturely reflection of the Word. The reason imparted by the Word leads to the truly human life lived in the image of God and in relationship with God the Father through the Word. This is "the true life in paradise, which is really that of the saints."[38]

Since the doctrine of creation provides the theological context for the *imago Dei*, further elaboration of Athanasius's view of the relation of God to creation is warranted. Two theological claims hold Athanasius's doctrine of creation together.[39] First, the ultimate transcendence of God establishes an inviolable distinction between Creator and creation. The properties natural to the Creator are properly his alone. The Creator is immortal, incorruptible, omnipotent, omniscient, and omnipresent, whereas the *ex nihilo* creation is mortal and corruptible according to its own nature.[40] Apart from participation in the Word, creation would cease to have being.[41] A similar dualism is found in the Hellenistic philosophy of Athanasius's contemporaries. However, it should be noted that the distinction made by Middle Platonists was between

---

[34] For the details of this claim, see Khaled Anatolios, *Athanasius: The Coherence of His Thought* (RECM; London: Routledge, 1998), 36.

[35] Athanasius, *DI*, 4–5.

[36] Ibid., 3.3.

[37] Ibid., 5.

[38] Ibid., 3.3. Throughout *DI* participation in the Word is said to result in humanity becoming divine. This should not be understood as a substantial development of humanity into deity. Instead, after attributing incorruption and immortality to one who participates in the *imago Dei*, Athanasius explains as follows: "For man is by nature mortal. . . . But because of his likeness to [God] who exists . . . he would have blunted his natural corruption and would have remained incorruptible. . . . [B]eing incorrupt, he would thenceforth have lived as God, as also somewhere the Divine Scripture declares, saying: 'I said that you are gods and all sons of the Highest: but you die like men and fall as one of the princes'" (*DI*, 4.6). Athanasius is careful to note that this incorruption does not belong to humanity by nature; it is a gift through participation in the likeness of the Word.

[39] Anatolios, *Athanasius*, 41.

[40] Athanasius, *DI*, 4.4–6.

[41] Ibid., 4.4–6.

soul/spirit and physical matter, whereas, for Athanasius, the dualism is located in the distinction between Creator and created. So Alvyn Pettersen argues, "The doctrine of *creatio ex nihilo* is then seen to imply that the most fundamental ontological distinction is not that between the spiritual and the material, but that between God and the created order, to which latter both (human) soul and body belong."[42]

Nevertheless, there has been much debate about the sources of Athanasius's cosmology. As E. P. Meiring points out, there are clear connections to Platonism, both in the terms used by Athanasius and in his concept of substances and nature.[43] Lyman states that he "shared the contemporary Christian modification of Middle Platonic participation language" and that he interpreted the Scripture in light of these assumptions.[44] Athanasius's use of the terms that Lyman refers to, however, can be interpreted in several ways. By sharing the contemporary theological language of his era, he may have been utilizing Platonic terminology to explain his understanding of the Christian tradition rather than submitting blindly to Platonism. Furthermore, these terms were common in the writings of other church fathers and he may have employed them to draw theological connections to tradition. Pettersen, in fact, understands this as one way that Athanasius and Origen agree.

> Like his predecessor Origen, Athanasius studied *as a Christian*. Not being a convert to Christianity like Justin Martyr or Clement of Alexandria, Athanasius' attitude towards the intellectual climate was not one of uncritical welcome, but of usefully employing it for the profounder exposition of what he believed to be the Church's thinking.[45]

Some have referred to Origen as the fount of Athanasius's theology, primarily because of his presence in Alexandria. The common location of Origen and Athanasius may be their greatest link, however; their theological orientations are quite different. Others have traced his thought to Irenaeus. Robert Case states, "I would maintain that the 'non-Origenist element' present from the first can, in fact, be traced back to Irenaeus and the second-century Christians. Further, I would maintain that the 'non-Origenist element' comprises the basis for the theology of the *Incarnation*."[46] Case convincingly quotes parallel

---

[42] Alvyn Pettersen, *Athanasius and the Human Body* (Bristol Classical Press: Bristol, 1990), 21.

[43] E. P. Meiring, *Orthodoxy and Platonism in Athanasius: Synthesis or Antithesis?* (Leiden: Brill, 1968).

[44] J. Rebecca Lyman, *Christology and Cosmology: Models in Divine Activity in Origen, Eusebius, and Athanasius* (OTM; Oxford University Press, 1993), 135–36.

[45] Alvyn Pettersen, *Athanasius* (London: Geoffrey Chapman, 1995), 4.

[46] Robert Case, "Will the Real Athanasius Please Stand Up?" in *JETS* 19 (1976): 283.

formulations in Irenaeus and Athanasius, and he also demonstrates the presence of Irenaeus's writings in Alexandria at the time of Athanasius.[47]

In *DI*, Athanasius does not claim novelty, but presents his case as an articulation of established church doctrine. Athanasius drew upon Christian tradition, and probably Irenaeus in particular, for biblical interpretation. Likewise, Athanasius used the well-known philosophical concepts available in Alexandria to articulate some of the ideas inherent in the biblical language. But Athanasius repeatedly turns to the Scriptures themselves as the primary theological authority and the source of a true historical account of God's relation to the world.[48] Obviously, this does not negate the impact that the Christian tradition and Middle Platonism may have had upon Athanasius's theology, but it does provide structure for understanding the authoritative primacy of these sources in his theology.[49] Athanasius's conviction concerning Scripture as the primary basis for knowledge of God had far-reaching implications. For Athanasius, the Scriptures do not simply concern what God has done. What God has done is a demonstration of who God is. God's economy reveals God's very being.[50]

Divine immanence is the second strand which ties Athanasius's doctrine of creation together. Although God is utterly distinct in substance from his creation, God has chosen to dwell immanently within creation. The Word acts as the Creator of the universe, but also as the one who gives it life and sustains its existence. Therefore, God has an intimate connection with all that exists. This balance is demonstrated in Athanasius's discussion of the Word indwelling both a human body and the universe simultaneously.

> [N]or, while present in the body was He absent elsewhere; nor, while He moved the body, was the universe left void of His working and Providence; but, thing most marvellous, Word as He was, so far from being contained by anything, He rather contained all things Himself; and just as while present in the whole of Creation, He is at once distinct in being from the universe, and present in all things by His own power . . . for He was not bound to His body, but rather was Himself wielding it, so that He was not like that (unable to influence the universe while in the body); for He was actually in eve-

---

[47] A similar interpretation is given by Anatolios who states that Athanasius' theological model could be classified as "Irenaean" (*Athanasius*, 206).

[48] Lyman, *Christology and Cosmology*, 129.

[49] Trevor Hart comes to a similar conclusion concerning Harnack's claims about the Greek philosophico-religious terminology used by Irenaeus. Many of his thoughts would apply directly to Athanasius. Trevor Hart, "Irenaeus, Recapitulation, and Physical Redemption," in *Christ in our Place: The Humanity of God in Christ for the Reconciliation of the World: Essays Presented to Professor James Torrance* (ed. Trevor Hart and Daniel Thimell; PTM 25; Exeter: Paternoster, 1989), 155–61.

[50] Twomey, *Apostolikos Thronos*, 266.

rything, and while external to the universe, abode in His Father alone.[51]

Certainly, the indwelling which took place in the incarnation is different in kind from the indwelling of the rest of creation. However, the immanence of the Creator in his creation is demonstrated by his presence in all of creation and, thus, it is not unthinkable that the Word would become human.[52] Athanasius's Christology is often criticized for being very near to Apollinarianism. For example, Aloys Grillmeier analyzes Athanasius's *"Logos-sarx"* Christology, and concludes that Athanasius implicitly ignores the human soul of Christ (without explicitly denying it).[53] However, Pettersen maintains that Athanasius's anthropology necessitates the physical body and the soul. And Christ is fully human.[54] Athanasius's emphasis is upon the fact that humanity is bound to the physical world as a part of creation. Pettersen states, "Indeed, for Athanasius, without that substantival nature of the body, a person's way of being ceases."[55] Therefore, regarding the incarnation, Athanasius states that by taking a body the Word has entered the human "way of being," which implies the physical and non-physical aspects of human nature. This doctrine is important for Athanasius's view of the *imago Dei* as it breaks radically from Middle Platonism and from the Christian Platonism associated with Origen. Jesus Christ reunites the entirety of humanity to the Word of the Father.

The *imago Dei*, for Athanasius, is definitive of humanity's existence in the world. True humanity is discovered as one participates in the likeness of the Son, the perfect image of God. This includes living in the knowledge of God with a correspondence to him in one's being and, therefore, also in one's experience. The result is a relationship with God through the Word who, being perfect in divinity and humanity, enables humankind to be what it was created to be as his image.

---

[51] Athanasius, *DI*, 17.1, 4.

[52] For Athanasius, God's immanence explains how creation as a whole shares in divine blessings. For example, even though life is a necessary property of God's essence alone, God's immanent presence in creation provides life to creatures. Further, it gives reason as to how that life is sustained and fostered. The existence of life in the universe is derived from participation in *the* Life, as the Word quickens all that exists.

[53] Aloys Grillmeier, *Christ in Christian Tradition*, vol. 1: *From the Apostolic Age to Chalcedon* (trans. J. S. Bowden; London: A. R. Mowbray, 1965), 193–219.

[54] Anatolios, for example, notes several passages in Athanasius's writings that would imply that he did see Christ as perfectly and fully human (*Athanasius*). The disagreement, it seems, is concerned with what it means to be fully human rather than whether or not Athanasius claimed that Jesus was fully human. Grillmeier admits that Athanasius never denied the existence of a human soul in Christ. See Grillmeier, *Christ in Christian Tradition*, 1:193–219.

[55] Pettersen, *Athanasius and the Human Body*, 78.

## 2.2. Accommodation of Athanasius's Interpretation

Unlike Irenaeus, Athanasius does not interpret the *imago Dei* as something that develops progressively as humans mature. Rather, for Athanasius, sinful humanity experiences a progressive movement away from God and, therefore, also from God's benefits. Athanasius's interpretation centers on the human relation to God established in creation, broken by sin, and restored in the incarnation. This relation is articulated in terms of participation with and in God. *DI* is focused on the theological rationale of the incarnation, and God's creative determination that humanity be made in God's image and likeness is paramount. Athanasius explains God's response to humanity's sin and its consequences as follows:

> [M]an who was rational and who had been made in the image was being obliterated; and the work created by God was perishing. For indeed . . . by the law death thenceforth prevailed over us. And it was impossible to flee the law, since this had been established by God because of the transgression. And these events were truly at once absurd and improper. For it was absurd that, having spoken, God should lie, in that he had established a law that man would die by death if he were to transgress the commandment, and man did not die after he had transgressed, but God's word was made void. For God would not have been truthful, if after he had said we would die, man had not died. And furthermore, it would have been improper that what had once been created rational and had partaken of his Word, should perish and return again to non-existence through corruption. . . . So it was not right that he should permit men to be destroyed by corruption, because this is neither proper nor fitting for the goodness of God.[56]

Athanasius, therefore, finds the *imago Dei* to have permanent implications for humanity in that it is humanity's relation to God that determines the shape of God's salvific actions towards humanity in Jesus Christ. The nature of the God-human relation makes it unfitting for humanity simply to return to nothingness. Athanasius's *a posteriori* rationale for the incarnation, then, leads him to conclude that only the Word, who created all things, could recreate humanity in God's image, "for it was his task both to bring what was corruptible back to incorruption, and to save what was above all fitting for the Father."[57] This theological rationale of the incarnation can only be investigated *a posteriori*, since God was not forced to send his Son. However, the logic of the incarnation has important implications for what can only be understood as God's final determination that humanity would be the creature he made it to be. Humanity's identity would be fulfilled. In this way, the image of God takes the shape of a covenant promise to the human creature.

---

[56] Athanasius, *DI*, 6.
[57] Athanasius, *DI*, 7.5.

Like Irenaeus, Athanasius considered knowledge of the Father through the Word necessary for the fulfillment of human identity, which in turn leads to the blessed and happy life.[58] The Word instructs humanity in this knowledge of God, and even when humanity turned away from God, the Word incarnate teaches humanity once again to know the Father.[59] The incarnation, therefore, serves also to teach humanity who God is. God's economy is the source of the knowledge of God. The identity interpretation, as noted above, can accommodate this emphasis upon the knowledge of God for the realization of the *imago Dei*. It is important to note that the emphasis on the knowledge of God in the NT and in early Christian theology is not due to the Hellenized reading of Jewish literature.[60] Rather, it is a theological emphasis seen across the literary strata of the canon of Scripture. For example, Genesis 3–11 puts as much emphasis on the loss of the knowledge of God as Rom 1:18–32. Human wickedness is very much the result of a loss of knowing and fearing God. As Prov 1:7 states, however, "the fear of the LORD is the beginning of knowledge."[61] Knowledge and fear of God are foundational for the shaping of appropriate human actions in the world.

As it is related to human knowledge of God, a final point that comes to prominence in Athanasius's interpretation of the *imago Dei* is the nature of the distinction between the Creator and the human creature. Humanity participates in the divine, but always as a creature. The incarnation serves a mediatorial role such that in Jesus Christ God makes himself known since Jesus corresponds fully to the Father. In his humanity, Jesus makes God known analogically. Anatolios argues that the denial of any creaturely analogy to the divine is one reason Athanasius believes Arianism to be contrary to the gospel; that is, Arianism disallows real knowledge (even analogical knowledge) of God in Christ. Anatolios insightfully expresses Athanasius's conviction that "the Arians cannot 'prove' their Word by his works because they do not conceive of the world (the works) as affording any analogical demonstration of God. Since

---

[58] Ibid., 11.3.

[59] Ibid., 14.8.

[60] *Contra* dismissive comments such as Middleton's claim that the "notion of a rational, substantial soul mirroring its divine archetype . . . is part of the pervasive influence of Platonism on Christian theology . . ." (*The Liberating Image*, 19). There are a number of problematic methodological assumptions underlying this claim. First, scholars often assume that the use of philosophical vocabulary inhibits faithful biblical interpretation. However, philosophical vocabulary can often be used to articulate clearly the relevant biblical concepts and so aid the clarifying task of exegesis. Second, in biblical studies literature, serious consideration of a theological claim is often avoided by labeling it as "influenced by Platonism." However, it is not at all clear that claims "influenced by Platonism" are necessarily unbiblical. The suggestion that Platonism is necessarily contrary to Scripture appears to be the product of the genetic fallacy.

[61] "Beginning" here refers not merely to a starting point for knowledge; the fear of the Lord is the ongoing first principle of knowledge. See Henri Blocher, "The Fear of the Lord as the 'Principle' of Wisdom," *TynBul* 28 (1977): 3–28.

they posit an ontological hiatus between the Word 'through whom' creation came to be and the Word who is an immanent power in God, the analogical link between God's external work and his inner being is thus lost."[62] The identity interpretation is informed by Athanasius's concern for maintaining the appropriate distinction between Creator and creation because, as noted in chapter 2, it is God's transcendence that enables God's economy to show forth God *in se* without reducing God to his *ad extra* activity.

Yet, the identity interpretation also makes an improvement on Athanasius's interpretation. Athanasius has no trouble affirming that Adam was rightly considered to be created fully in God's image. However, Athanasius does speak of the image having been lost in the fall. He views the fall as the loss of the image since humanity turns its gaze away from God and down to the earth; knowledge of God is compromised, and reason is darkened. In light of Gen 9:6 and Jas 3:9, however, Athanasius's view is exegetically unwarranted. As I argued in chapter 4, it is better to take knowledge of God and enlightened reason to be conditions of the possibility of the realization of the image of God in the world rather than identifying this knowledge and reason as the image. By making the distinction between the content of the image and the conditions of its possibility, one is able to affirm that the image is a permanent identity of humanity, as fitting these biblical passages, while affirming, with Athanasius, that the realization of the image of God in the world is compromised when knowledge of God and enlightened reason are not present.

## 3. Augustine of Hippo

Augustine's interpretation of the *imago Dei* has been maligned, often because the purpose of his reflections in *De Trinitate* has been misunderstood. Therefore, this section on Augustine's *De Trinitate* will take a slightly different shape than the other studies in this chapter. First, I will consider the purpose of Augustine's interpretation of the *imago Dei* within *De Trinitate*. Second, I will explain how the theological insights accompanying Augustine's reflections can inform and be accommodated by the identity interpretation. I will not explicate Augustine's interpretation in detail, for two reasons. First, much of Thomas Aquinas's experimental interpretation is based upon Augustine's, and Thomas's interpretation was described and evaluated in detail in chapter 2. Second, it is my conviction that the most useful parts of *De Trinitate* are not specifically related to the details of Augustine's effort to discern "trinities" in the human mind and soul. Augustine's own aims for these reflections show why this is the case.

---

[62] Anatolios, *Athanasius*, 116.

*3.1. Augustine's Purpose for Reflecting on the Imago Dei in De Trinitate*

A typical criticism of Augustine's interpretation of the *imago Dei* is that Augustine's method is internal and subjective.[63] John Cavadini notes two kinds of complaints in particular. First, *De Trinitate* is often "held responsible for having hopelessly interiorized the Christian doctrine of God . . . and thus for having set the doctrine of God adrift from any meaningful understanding of human community."[64] Second, some commentators find it "so hopelessly speculative that it has appeared impossible to locate within any social or polemical context that might somehow mitigate its difficulty by affording some sense of what was at stake in its composition."[65]

Michel René Barnes places the blame for insufficient interpretations of Augustine's Trinitarian theology on systematic theologians especially. The reason for these poor interpretations is that "modern appropriations of Augustine . . . depend upon broad, general characterizations of Augustine's theology; these broad general characterizations depend upon turn-of-the-century continental histories of dogma" which skew patristic interpretation through the use of an artificial paradigm.[66] Barnes mentions two problematic disciplinary presuppositions underlying this paradigm, and, therefore, the interpretations of Augustine based upon it. First, characterizations are produced through the positing of supposed polar contrasts, "such as the oppositions between 'Greek' and 'Latin,' or between 'economic' and 'immanent,' or, in more general applications, 'Jewish' versus 'Hellenistic,'" and the details of Augustine's thought are then judged by these characterizations.[67] "In practice," theologians use these oppositions to "describe movement from one doctrinal form to another, whether it is progressive or regressive movement."[68] Second, "presenting doctrines in terms of oppositions yields a synthesizing account of the development of doctrine."[69] The problem, here, is that artificial ideological categories are foisted upon Augustine. Barnes probably generalizes too strongly regarding the disciplinary presuppositions of systematic theologians as a

---

[63] See, e.g., Gunton, *The Promise of Trinitarian Theology*, 45; Tom Smail, *Like Father, Like Son: The Trinity Imaged in Our Humanity* (Grand Rapids: Eerdmans, 2005), 82–83. Gunton's article, "Augustine, the Trinity and the Theological Crisis of the West," *SJT* 43 (1990): 33–58, has led to a flurry of scholarly activity both condemning and defending Augustine.

[64] John Cavadini, "The Quest for Truth in Augustine's *De Trinitate*," *TS* 58 (1997): 429–30. Elsewhere Cavadini argues that *De Trinitate* was intended to "argue against such an interiorized view of the individual's relation to God" (430). See John Cavadini, "The Structure and Intention of Augustine's *De trinitate*," *AugStud* 23 (1992): 103–23.

[65] Ibid., 429.

[66] Barnes, "Augustine in Contemporary Trinitarian Theology," *TS* 56 (1995): 237–50, 239. Barnes considers this dependence upon "turn-of-the-century histories of dogma," such as de Régnon's, very problematic.

[67] Ibid., 239 n. 15.

[68] Ibid., 239 n. 16.

[69] Ibid., 239.

whole, but the examples he uses are convincing enough to make his critique weighty.[70] Cavadini's and Barnes's observations show that there is, in the theological literature, want for a generous interpretation of Augustine's purpose in *De Trinitate*.

Cavadini seeks to moderate these complaints by contextualizing Augustine's *De Trinitate*. He notes a formal aspect of Augustine's writing that hints at his purpose: there is a "deliberate and repeated invocation of the reader as partner in the quest of tracking down truth."[71] The spirit of this work is "undogmatic, open-ended and experimental" and it constantly proclaims this to be the case.[72] Rather than being a medieval or modern study of doctrine for the sake of the doctrine itself, Cavadini argues that "it is self-consciously an example of the deployment of a new kind of 'teaching' or *doctrina* in which 'seeing truth' is coincident with understanding the scriptural text, and all the arts and philosophy are drawn into that exercise."[73] This implies that Augustine's reflection on and analysis of the structures of his mind forms a learning and teaching exercise rather than an articulation of established dogma.[74]

Edmund Hill, in his introduction to *De Trinitate*, summarizes Augustine's purpose as follows: "Augustine is proposing the quest for, or the exploration of, the mystery of the Trinity as a complete program for the Christian spiritual life, a program of conversion and renewal and discovery of self in God and God in self."[75] C. C. Pecknold concurs, and supports the claim that Augustine uses the Trinity "for the purposes of spiritual transformation."[76] Pecknold argues that

> What Augustine is trying to draw the reader into is "the supreme act of contemplative wisdom" that transforms the image of God by a process of introspection that leads to Self-Transcendence and communion with the Other. In this way we can understand the movement from Book X where the inner self is remembering itself, understanding itself, and willing itself to Book XIV where the inner

---

[70] See Barnes's examples illustrating dependence on Théodore de Régnon's studies on the Trinity (*Études de théologie positive sur la Sainte Trinité* [Paris: Victor Retaux, 1892/1898]). Barnes specifically refers to Bertrand de Margerie, *La Trinité chrétienne dans l'histoire* (TH 31; Paris: Beauchesne, 1975), 227; Catherine Mowry LaCugna, *God for Us* (San Francisco: Harper, 1991) 96; David Brown, *The Divine Trinity* (La Salle: Open Court, 1985).

[71] Cavadini, "The Quest for Truth in Augustine's *De Trinitate*," 431.

[72] Ibid., 432.

[73] Ibid., 432–33.

[74] For a useful description of the rhetorical context of *De Trinitate* and the nature of Augustine's anthropological and epistemological concerns, see Lewis Ayres, "Between Athens and Jerusalem: Prolegomena to Anthropology in *De Trinitate*," *ModTheo* 8 (1992): 53–73.

[75] Edmund Hill, "Introduction," in *The Trinity* (De Trinitate) (trans. Edmund Hill; Hyde Park, NY: New City, 1991), 19.

[76] C. C. Pecknold, "How Augustine Used the Trinity: Functionalism and the Development of Doctrine," *ATR* 85 (2003): 139.

self is remembering God, understanding God, and willing or loving God. Instead of seeing the analogies as these admirable but naive attempts to grasp God's Trinity, we really must understand the analogies as tools that perform upon the reader a process of spiritual conversion.[77]

Pecknold highlights Augustine's use of *frui* and *uti* to refer to the Trinity as both epistemological center and eschatological goal. "In terms of *frui* and *uti*, this means that Augustine's epistemological starting point is God's Trinity enjoyed (*in frui*), and that the use of God's Trinity (*in uti*) is intended to return us to the eschatological goal of God's Trinity more deeply enjoyed (*in frui*). For the triune God is not just the goal (*frui*) but also the way (*uti*)."[78] Therefore, it is best to understand *De Trinitate* as a spiritual exercise of attending to the triune God for the purpose of more rightly seeing God and being personally transformed by this vision. Accommodation of Augustine's insights, therefore, will primarily focus on the contemplation of God and personal transformation into godliness.

### 3.2. Accommodation of Augustine's Interpretation

For Augustine, humanity cannot be understood without reference to God. The very designation of humanity as "image of God" makes this point. Image and likeness must be "of" something; to understand an image one must understand who or what is imaged. Therefore, Augustine seeks to understand God, and to understand himself in light of God.[79] By deeply contemplating the human image of God, Augustine also hopes to see God, even if the image is only an enigma.[80]

Augustine takes humans to be flexible creatures, shaped by their loves. The relation between God and humanity in which humans are made in God's image and likeness, implies that each individual human is intended to be a proximal image and likeness of God. The intention is fulfilled as a person loves God above all, and, therefore, becomes like God. However, sinful humanity loves created things more than the Creator. Thus, in sin, humanity becomes like the world and their ability to be like God is lost.[81] Even in this case, however, some remnant of the image remains in the individual.

For the one who stays upon God through contemplation and loves God most of all, the actualization of the image of God grows progressively. The more one knows and loves the Creator, the more one becomes like God. Augustine refers to several biblical texts to confirm this point. In Books XIV and XV, Augustine draws especially on Col 3:10, 1 Cor 13:12, and 1 John 3:2 to argue for the progressive nature of being the image of God, the movement from "the

---

[77] Ibid., 139.
[78] Ibid., 138.
[79] Augustine, *De Trinitate*, IX.1.
[80] Ibid., XV.14, 16.
[81] Ibid., X.7.

glory by which we are sons of God to the glory by which we shall be like him, because we shall see him as he is." Progress in the image and likeness of God proceeds beyond the confines of this world until the believer sees God and is like God.

Because the human image of God is creaturely, it is limited, and because it is not yet perfected, it is uneven. Augustine compares the human image to the Son who knows the Father (and everything else) perfectly in himself, and notes that human knowledge "is vastly dissimilar to this knowledge."[82] Human knowledge can be gained or lost; one can know or not know, and be wise or unwise. Because knowledge is accidental to human existence, any image of the Trinity that can be discerned in the human mind will be a disparate image.[83] Therefore, the Trinitarian analogies Augustine seeks in the human mind are always considered inadequate. These analogies can draw one closer to knowledge of God, and, therefore, toward spiritual transformation, but since knowledge of God the Father, and the Son and the Holy Spirit is much higher than human knowledge can reach, they cannot deliver metaphysical knowledge of God. Augustine's constant anticipation is the fuller knowledge that will be had when one sees God "face to face."

Augustine's interpretation of the image of God is multifaceted. The image of God in humanity refers humanity to God for the shape of its own existence. Because humanity is a creature, the image is limited qualitatively and quantitatively. Augustine's contention that the perfected image is vastly unequal to the Trinity displays a clear grasp of the human creature's relation to its Creator. Even so, humans are created with a relative likeness to the Trinity, and have the potential to grow in approximation to the Trinity progressively through the renewal of their minds.[84] This renewal is ultimately the first movement of spiritual transformation, humanly considered.[85]

There is a convergence between Augustine's interpretation and the identity interpretation in that both recognize the dependence of the image of God on God. Human identity has no definition of its own; humanity can only be defined in relationship to God. The various ways of describing humanity apart from speaking of this dependence, such as the ontological and relational as-

---

[82] Ibid., XV.22.

[83] Ibid., IX.2. For a useful discussion of this point, see Lewis Ayres, "The Fundamental Grammar of Augustine's Trinitarian Theology," in *Augustine and His Critics* (ed. Robert Dodaro and George Lawless; CO; London: Routledge, 2000), 68.

[84] So Ayres states, "Augustine calls for us to learn a new language, one which will reform the memory. He calls in effect for new patterns, for the recognition that it is through the structures of rhetorical patterning that the mind functions." Ayres, "Between Athens and Jerusalem," 68.

[85] The potential for transformation requires that humans are malleable, changeable. As demonstrated in chapter 5 of this study, one becomes like that which one loves; one is shaped by and conformed to one's loves. The Holy Spirit leads one to love God. "The Holy Spirit is the gift of God, in that he is given to those who love God through him" (Augustine, *De Trinitate*, XV.35).

pects of human nature, are properly understood as conditions for the possibility of being the image of God rather than aspects of the image of God itself. Even these conditions can only be understood fully in God's light. But in order to be spoken of at all, the image of God itself requires knowledge of God.

Another convergence is the developmental nature of the image of God. This God-given and God-determined identity develops in a person as one draws nearer to God. By knowing God in greater ways and by gaining wisdom from this knowledge, one is transformed into a closer likeness to God.

Furthermore, this progress ultimately achieves its proper end when perfect knowledge, wisdom, and transformation are realized. Yet, the limitation of humans as creatures is never denied; humanity will be perfected according to their status as creatures. The fulfillment of the human relationship with God will have reached its *telos*.

As noted throughout this study, but particularly in the evaluation of Thomas Aquinas's interpretation in chapter 2, I find problematic Augustine's way of construing the Trinitarian image of God. In that the image is of God, it is Trinitarian; however, it is the Son who is the perfect image of the Father, and humanity realizes its identity in the Son through the Spirit. Augustine's attempts to discern "trinities" are unhelpful, even for his goals of spiritual formation, because, as Athanasius recognized, Jesus Christ is central to the meaning of the image of God. It is union with Jesus Christ that brings one into proper relationship with God the Father. Moreover, because the Son is the perfect image of the Father, imaging the Son is imaging the Father. The image of God is Trinitarian insofar as it is Christological.

A clarification is necessary regarding Augustine's emphasis upon contemplation of the immanent Trinity as the primary method of spiritual transformation. Augustine's conviction that spiritual transformation occurs through the renewal of one's mind as one rightly contemplates God is an important insight. However, what is often missed is that one must contemplate God *through* the redemptive history in which God is known as God.[86] And it is through the interpretation of this history provided in the Scriptures that God's character is explicated and faithful ways of imaging God are discovered. This practice is exemplified in *De Trinitate* as Augustine devotes the first half of his work to biblical study. From the perspective of the identity interpretation,

---

[86] Ayres describes Augustine's method as follows: "Understanding Christ *in forma servi* is not sufficient, we must understand Christ both *in forma servi* and *in forma dei*. . . . Love that loves love can only be fulfilled in the threefold exchange of love in the life of the Trinity. A person is in continual, often hidden relationship to his or her Creator, and it is only over time taken in this relationship that definition can be offered, becoming more complex and more accurate as the relationship grows and deepens." However, it appears that there has not been enough attention focused on God's economy and the implications it has for human identity. Therefore, I have suggested that greater attention be paid to God's *ad extra* activity since it is through the economy that we know the love that loves love.

intentional imaging of God in the world is made possible when God is known through divine revelation.[87]

# 4. Martin Luther

Martin Luther's interpretation takes reflection on God's economy in a different direction. The regular objection to Luther's interpretation of the image of God goes against his assertion that the image of God was lost in the fall. But Luther's reason for believing the image was lost is discovered in what Luther affirms regarding the meaning of the image. Luther interprets the image as Adam's original righteousness. Luther, in Augustinian fashion, viewed Adam as a mature image of God since he embodied God's righteousness. In the fall, humans embodied wickedness rather than righteousness, so the image of God in the world was destroyed. The image is restored in Jesus Christ and in God's people through Jesus Christ. In order to evaluate the contribution of Luther's interpretation and the criticisms leveled against it, it is helpful now to provide a contextual description of his interpretation in his *Lectures on Genesis* and in *The Disputation Concerning Man*.

## 4.1. Description of Martin Luther's Interpretation

Jaroslav Pelikan summarizes Luther's theology, and Luther's doctrine of justification in particular, as based upon a "vigorous reassertion of Augustinian anthropology."[88] Likewise, Heiko Oberman argues that Luther's break from an assertion of nominalism—that "the man who does what is in him acquires all information necessary for salvation"—marked a turning point early in Luther's life.[89] According to Oberman, this turning point occurred by 1509 at Erfurt and led to Luther's critique of scholasticism as a form of Pelagianism nearly ten years later. Though the sources and consequences of Luther's personal and intellectual development are debated, irrespective of such debates it is undoubtedly the case that Luther's Augustinian anthropology, and his belief that Pelagianism had taken hold of the church, were formative convictions.[90]

---

[87] It is important to note, once again, that God's acts include speech-acts.

[88] Jaroslav Pelikan, *The Christian Tradition: A History of the Development of Doctrine*, vol. 4: *Reformation of Church and Dogma (1300–1700)* (London: University of Chicago Press, 1984), 139.

[89] Heiko Oberman, *The Dawn of the Reformation: Essays in Late Medieval and Early Reformation Thought* (Edinburgh: T&T Clark, 1986), 96. Oberman argues that this is a distinctive turning point for the young Luther in *Luther: Man Between God and the Devil* (trans. Eileen Walliser-Schwartzbart; London: Yale University Press, 1989).

[90] E.g., see the exchange between Ronald Frost and Richard Muller. Ronald Frost, "Aristotle's Ethics: The Real Reason for Luther's Reformation?" *TJ* 18 (1997): 223–41; Richard Muller, "'Scholasticism, reformation, orthodoxy, and the persistence of Christian Aristotelianism'," *TJ* 19 (1998): 81–96; Ronald Frost, "'Scholaticism, Reformation, Orthodoxy, and the Persistence of Christian Aristotelianism': A Brief Rejoinder," *TJ* 19 (1998): 97–101.

Remarkably, however, Luther immediately departs from Augustine's interpretation of the image of God in his "Lectures on Genesis." It appears that he feels free to do so because Augustine retained the basic definition of the human constitution that was provided by Aristotle.[91] Thus, Luther rejects the conception that the image of God consists of mind, memory, and will. After all, he argues, if the image of God is simply mind, memory, and will then Satan was also created in the image of God since Satan also has these. Luther also objects to the implications of the Augustinian view. For example, Augustine's interpretation could lead to the following argument: "God is free, therefore since man is created in the image of God, he also has a free memory, mind, and will."[92] This kind of argument, Luther argues, distorts the image of God and the doctrine of salvation that restores it. Although this kind of argument is common among the fathers, Luther dismisses it as the result of "an emotion and of a particular mood that we do not have and cannot have. . . . If this is true, it follows that by the powers of his nature man can bring about his own salvation."[93] Luther infers that Augustine's own thinking on this point smacks of Pelagianism.

Therefore, the image of God must be something different than Augustine's psychological understanding. However, a full understanding of the image cannot be grasped because the image has been lost through sin. Luther appears to mean that the image cannot be known existentially or observationally, because he proceeds to outline the material content of the image theoretically in the discussion that follows.

According to Luther, there were two unmistakable aspects of the image of God in Adam. The first was that Adam knew God and believed that God was good. The second was that he lived a godly life and desired to love God. There were also two benefits gained from the image. First of all, Luther argues that the image of God provided Adam with the clearest and purest experience of life. This applied to both his spiritual and physical existence. Second, Adam had no fear of death or other anxiety.[94]

After Adam sinned, however, the image was completely lost. Therefore, Adam's faith in God, knowledge of God, godly life, pure experience, and lack of fear and anxiety were all destroyed and replaced by their opposites. This loss of the image of God is passed down as original sin and it characterizes the experience of all humans from birth. Original sin has corrupted humanity and the rest of creation so that nothing is as it was.[95]

---

[91] Martin Luther, "Lectures on Genesis," in *Luther's Works,* American Edition (55 vols.; ed. Jaroslav Pelikan and Helmut T. Lehmann; Philadelphia: Muehlenberg and Fortress, and St. Louis: Concordia, 1955–1986), 1:60.

[92] Ibid., 61.

[93] Ibid., 61. Of course, Luther's interpretation of Augustine on the image of God is more a commentary on his contemporaries' use of Augustine than Augustine himself.

[94] Ibid., 63.

[95] Ibid., 64.

Luther continues with an analysis of how the image is restored through the Gospel. Each of the areas of experience that were lost through the fall are regained in Christ. The fullness of this restoration will surpass the image as it was experienced by Adam and it cannot be fully realized in this life. Yet, by Christ's merit and by the Holy Spirit in the believer, one may begin to experience the restoration of the image of God.[96]

"The Disputation Concerning Man" was originally part of a series of university disputations that took place in 1536. This disputation includes forty theses concerning the nature of humanity plus a fragment of objections and responses to the proposed theses.[97] There are several theses that pertain to Luther's understanding of the image of God.

In the twentieth and twenty-first theses Luther states, "Theology to be sure from the fullness of its wisdom defines man as whole and perfect: Namely, that man is a creature of God consisting of body and a living soul, made in the beginning after the image of God, without sin, so that he should procreate and rule over the created things, and never die."[98] Luther again focuses attention upon the existential qualities of the image of God. The three aspects noted are significant. The fact that humans are directed by God to procreate is a chief facet of Luther's argument for marriage on behalf of the clergy. Humanity's obligation to rule over creation brings fullness to his doctrine of the image of God in respect to Adam's original position among created things. Moreover, an implicit aspect of the image of God is found in the fact that humans are intended to live forever.

In related studies, it has been suggested that Luther's reference to the two distinct aspects of human existence, body and living soul, tends toward a Neoplatonic view of the human person. Stephen Ozment has treated this subject at length in *Homo Spiritualis*.[99] Ozment limits his discussion to the *Dictata super psalterium*, "the first major 'voyage' of the Reformer."[100] In support of the Neoplatonic thesis, there are several passages in the *Dictata* that refer to the works of creation as transitory signifiers of eternal realities. Furthermore, Luther states that the body is a "basket which weighs down the soul" and insists that

---

[96] Ibid., 64–65.

[97] Jaroslav Pelikan, "Introduction," in *Luther's Works*, American Edition (55 vols.; ed. Jaroslav Pelikan and Helmut T. Lehmann; Philadelphia: Muehlenberg and Fortress, and St. Louis: Concordia, 1955–1986), 34:135.

[98] Martin Luther, "The Disputation Concerning Man," in *Luther's Works*, American Edition (55 vols.; ed. Jaroslav Pelikan and Helmut T. Lehmann; Philadelphia: Muehlenberg and Fortress, and St. Louis: Concordia, 1955–1986), 34:138.

[99] Stephen Ozment, *Homo Spiritualis: A Comparative Study of the Anthropology of Johannes Tauler, Jean Gerson and Martin Luther (1509-1516) in the Context of Their Theological Thought* (SMRT 6; Leiden: E. J. Brill, 1969), 87–130.

[100] Ibid., 89.

spiritual things are "the very opposite" of temporal things.[101] Moreover, the soul is a direct creation of God rather than a result of human seed.[102]

Ozment is willing to acknowledge a Neoplatonic influence in these instances, but is unwilling to admit that this implies that Neoplatonism is an adequate interpretive framework for Luther's thought. He argues, "Most of all, it should not be forgotten that the old man is a 'whole man;' divine judgment falls upon the soul as well as upon the flesh . . ." Therefore, Ozment concludes that Luther does not divide the human person into two distinct parts, one fully entrenched in this world and the other limited to a spiritual realm.[103] On the contrary, Luther teaches that the soul exists in every part of the body and directs it. The soul ought to desire heavenly things, and Christ may dwell in the soul through faith. However, the soul is also a place of sins and suffering. It is not naturally inclined to the things of God. Those things can only be had through faith in Christ and the promises of God. This shows that, contrary to Neoplatonic thought, Luther did not imply that the soul is a distinctively good spiritual aspect of humanity.[104] Rather, the soul is the seat of human personhood, where sin is experienced and where the work of God may be done in one's life through faith in Jesus Christ.

The dualism in Luther's anthropology remains to be explained. Ozment continues his analysis of Luther's *Dictata* by exploring another thesis: the existentialist approach. Immediately, Ozment finds the existentialist thesis more appealing.[105] This thesis argues that Luther's dualism lies in a distinction between the interior, hidden person and the exterior, carnal person. The distinction is located in one's lifestyle. Those who live in a godly manner are called "interior" persons.[106] On the other hand, those who live carnally may be described as "exterior" persons.

However, this thesis also has faults, and they may be understated by Ozment. The problem with a strict adherence to the existentialist thesis is that Luther takes one's status as an interior or exterior person to be an objective reality. The interior person lives in a godly way because they have, as a foundation for that way of life, been formed by God in their soul. The exterior person lives carnally because their intellect and affections are grounded in original sin. Therefore, the existentialist thesis falls short of Luther's intention. The dualism does not merely refer to two ways of living.

The dualism presented by Luther is not a simple body/soul distinction; nor is it a carnal life/spiritual life distinction. Instead, Luther's dualism is located in his distinction between the soul that is directed by God and one that is

---

[101] Ibid., 90–92.   The phrase translated "the very opposite" is found in *WA* 4,400.350401.16.

[102] Ibid., 95. This reference is found in *WA* 3,387.27 and 4,290.19f.

[103] Ibid., 92–93.

[104] Ibid., 101.

[105] Ibid.

[106] Ozment, *Homo Spiritualis*, 102–3.

absorbed by carnal desires. The entire person is affected and controlled by the soul, so the person whose soul is directed by God will live a godly life and the person whose soul is directed by Satan will live a carnal life.

Even so, the interior person does not leave the flesh behind. It is in this context that Luther's statements concerning the conflict of the flesh with the soul find their meaning. The soul that is directed by God longs to be godly, but the flesh in which the soul dwells is sinful. This longing, however, is not simply a desire to be free from the physical aspect of human existence, but a desire to be free from the entirety of creation that has been tainted by sin. It is a teleological/soteriological desire to be a part of the new creation and to be re-formed in the image of God.

The significance of this aspect of Luther's anthropology becomes apparent when one considers the effect of Adam's fall upon the image of God. The effect of the fall is apparent in the twenty-second thesis of "The Disputation Concerning Man," "But after the fall of Adam, certainly, he was subject to the power of the devil, sin and death, a twofold evil for his powers, unconquerable and eternal."[107] Although the image of God was lost, humanity did not lose its reason or will. However, reason and will have been tainted by the fall and are subject to Satan. Therefore, it is impossible for humans to create a good will or a right precept within themselves. This buttresses the soteriological aspect of Luther's anthropology. Humanity can look to none other than God for grace and rescue.

Luther is quick to point out that one can be freed from the power of Satan and given eternal life through Jesus Christ by believing in him. This is where Luther's "Disputation" comes to a head. Thesis 32 states, "Paul in Romans 3 [:28], 'We hold that a man is justified by faith apart from works,' briefly sums up the definition of man, saying, 'Man is justified by faith.'" Luther concludes that "man in this life is the simple material of God for the form of his future life."[108] He proceeds to argue that just as the heaven and earth were chaotic prior to their present form, so is humanity in comparison with its future form, "when the image of God has been remolded and perfected."[109] Even though the image of God is now lost, one can regain hope in the future restoration of the image through faith in Jesus Christ and God's promises.

According to Luther, then, Adam experienced a life that was appropriate for one bearing the divine image. It may even be more appropriate to say that Adam experienced the image of God, rather than that he was the image. This experience was evidenced by Adam's lack of fear or anxiety and his complete trust and faith in God. Because of Adam's relationship with God, he enjoyed the full existential blessings that accompany God's promises.

Bernhard Lohse states that the "uniqueness of Luther's exposition of the article on creation consists first in its existential reference, then in its inclu-

---

[107] Luther, "The Disputation Concerning Man," 138.
[108] Ibid., 139.
[109] Ibid., 140.

sion of justification."[110] This also summarizes the contribution of his doctrine of the image of God. In his account, Luther places faith at the very center of human existence and the image of God. It results in a life existentially qualified by faith. The doctrine of the image of God should inspire one toward faith and the hope for salvation. "Instead of condemnation for sin, faith receives the victory of Christ over sin, death, and the wrath of God."[111] Therefore, the image of God is ultimately a promise to the Christian. Through faith in Jesus Christ and God's promises one no longer fears death or God's wrath, but is strengthened in the assurance of salvation and the promise that believers will one day be like Christ and the image of God will be restored.

### 4.2. Appropriation of Luther's Interpretation

In the fragment that follows the forty theses in "The Disputation Concerning Man," Luther was apparently challenged several times concerning the freedom of the reason and the will. Those who challenged Luther argued that the Scriptures call people to master sin and that this implies that it must be possible to do so. Luther's response was simple: "The words of the law say, 'You ought.' They do not say, 'You are able to.' From the 'ought' to the 'able' is not a valid consequence."[112] This exchange illustrates one of Luther's key insights that can be accommodated by the identity interpretation. When the image of God is viewed as a set of powers or abilities, then it appears that the image of God can be realized through the exercise of these powers, whether or not they are directed by God. Luther rightly insisted that the realization of the *imago Dei* was impossible apart from a relationship with God by grace through faith. And, ultimately, this faith is established by, and through, Jesus Christ.

Luther's interest in protecting this insight led him to deny the existence of the image in fallen humanity since its relationship with God was compromised. However, if the image is interpreted as identity, and not as a set of powers or abilities, then one can affirm that humanity remains God's image even though the relationship between God and humanity has been compromised by sin. The result is that humanity stands under God's judgment as a false image. Thus, when God restores the true image of God in Christ, humanity is now able once again to enjoy the existential benefits resulting from a proper relationship with God.

Another of Luther's insights accommodated by the identity interpretation is his understanding that the "oughts" that God intends for humanity do not necessarily imply that humanity, at that moment, is able to do what God intends. The fulfillment of these "oughts" arrives first in Jesus Christ and second in God's people eschatologically. Because the "oughts" are the proper shape of

---

[110] Bernhard Lohse, *Martin Luther's Theology: Its Historical and Systematic Development* (Edinburgh: T&T Clark, 1999), 241.

[111] Randall Zachman, *The Assurance of Faith: Conscience in the Theology of Martin Luther and John Calvin* (Minneapolis: Fortress, 1993), 57.

[112] Luther, "The Disputation Concerning Man," 143.

human life as God's earthly image, they inform the realization of human identity. However, as Luther rightly discerns albeit with different words, the realization of human identity is dependent upon right relationship with God through faith.

## 5. Conclusions

In this chapter, I have demonstrated that the identity interpretation can incorporate several important insights from the Christian theological tradition that get eschewed by other interpretations. Three insights in particular are relevant. First, human identity is dependent upon God, and God's action in the world shapes that identity holistically. In other words, it is not only one aspect of human identity that is shaped by God's identity, such as humanity's rule over the earth; rather, the overall shape of human existence finds its reference point in God. Second, there is a common testimony in the Christian tradition to a progressive and developmental realization of human identity. In different ways, Irenaeus, Athanasius, Augustine, and Luther each discerned in Scripture a growing expression of what humanity was intended to be—even if they emphasized different aspects of that development. The identity interpretation incorporates this teleological and eschatological emphasis, as demonstrated in chapter 5. Third, each of the theologians struggled to affirm how fallen humanity continued to be the image of God even when humanity's relationship with God was compromised by sin. I demonstrated that a major contribution of the identity interpretation is that it maintains the tradition's attentiveness to the devastating effects of sin without having to compromise the necessary claim that God determined, from the moment of creation, that humanity is made in God's image.

# A Brief Conclusion

In this book, I have demonstrated that interpreting the *imago Dei* as human identity is exegetically and theologically preferable to substantialistic, functional, and relational interpretations. The identity interpretation has been shown to be dogmatically coherent and faithful to the range of canonical texts that refer to the image of God.

The argument has proceeded along three lines. First, in chapters 1 and 2, the opportunity for a canonical re-reading of the *imago Dei* was suggested through a survey of several contemporary interpretations of the *imago Dei* and a careful analysis of the classic interpretations offered by Thomas Aquinas and Karl Barth. It was shown that, theologically and exegetically, interpreters have had difficulty incorporating the full range of relevant OT and NT texts and, especially, explicating the dogmatic links between the image of God in creation and the image of God in Christ.

Second, in chapters 3 and 4, a conceptual and exegetical basis for the identity interpretation was established through an analysis of the term "identity," a theological reading of Genesis 1 in its theological and cultural context, and an exploration of the dogmatic relationship between the doctrine of revelation, human identity, and the imitation of God. It was concluded that humans are identified as God's representatives within the creation order and intended to make God known in the world through analogous ways of being-in-the-world. The structures of human existence were determined by God in order to facilitate the realization of human identity, so the particulars details of human ontology and relations are best considered to be conditions of possibility for the realization of the *imago Dei*. Since God reveals himself progressively through the divine economy, human identity in relation to God is also revealed progressively.

Third, in chapters 5 and 6, it was shown that the identity interpretation accommodates the relevant OT and NT texts that refer to the image of God and human identity, on the one hand, and the formative theological insights of the Christian tradition, on the other. Interpreting the image of God as human identity provides the requisite conceptual context for the realization and fulfillment of human identity described in the NT, thus linking the OT development of human identity to its fulfillment in Jesus Christ. Coherence is maintained between the OT and NT references to the image of God. The identity interpretation accommodates the insights of Irenaeus, Athanasius, Augustine, and Martin Luther regarding humanity's dependence upon God for its identity, the developmental realization of the *imago Dei*, and the devastating effects of the fall. The identity interpretation provides a conceptual context for recognizing fully the effects of the fall without compromising the permanence of God's determination that humanity is God's image.

The thesis of this book invites four lines of further research. First, with the identity interpretation under consideration, OT and NT scholars with dogmatic interests in theological anthropology should take up detailed exegesis of the biblical material examined in this study and extend the examination to additional biblical texts. Second, the theological insights of the Christian tradition should be further investigated for the sake of *ressourcement*, either by attending to additional figures from the tradition or by further explicating the accounts of the figures discussed here. Third, the Christological fulfillment of human identity deserves more careful exposition, as does the possibility of others participating in Jesus Christ's fulfillment of the *imago Dei*. I would like to see a book-length study of Jesus Christ's realization of the *imago Dei* in light of the identity interpretation. Fourth, I hope to develop the ethical implications of my thesis for the sake of constructive Christian ethical reflection. In Christian ethics, the *imago Dei* is used to support a variety of principles used for making moral judgments. I believe that there is a need to discipline the use of the doctrine of the *imago Dei* in ethical dialogue through careful theological interpretation of Scripture. Yet, it is clear that the doctrine of the *imago Dei* carries important ethical implications. The next step, then, is to show how interpreting the *imago Dei* as human identity would both discipline and fund constructive work in Christian ethics.

# Works Cited

Abbott, T. K. *A Critical and Exegetical Commentary on the Epistles to the Ephesians and to the Colossians.* International Critical Commentary 36. Edinburgh: T&T Clark, 1897.

Adam, A. K. M., Stephen Fowl, Kevin Vanhoozer, and Francis Watson. *Reading Scripture with the Church: Toward a Hermeneutic for Theological Interpretation.* Grand Rapids: Baker Academic, 2006.

Allen, R. Michael. *The Christ's Faith: A Dogmatic Account.* T&T Clark Studies in Systematic Theology 2. London: T&T Clark, 2009.

Anatolios, Khaled. *Athanasius: The Coherence of His Thought.* Routledge Early Church Monographs. London: Routledge, 1998.

Anselm of Canterbury. *The Major Works.* Oxford World's Classics. Edited by G. R. Evans. Oxford: Oxford University Press, 2008.

Aquinas, Thomas. *Summa Theologiae: Latin text and English translation, Introductions, Notes, Appendices, and Glossaries.* 60 vols. Edited by T. Gilby and T. C. O'Brien. New York: McGraw-Hill, 1963–1976.

Arnold, Bill. *Genesis.* New Cambridge Bible Commentary. Cambridge University Press, 2009.

Athanasius. *contra Gentes—de Incarnatione.* Edited and Translated by Robert Thomson. Oxford: Clarendon, 1971.

_____. *On the Incarnation: The Treatise* De Incarnatione Verbi Dei. Edited and Translated by A Religious of C. S. M. V. New edition. Crestwood, NY: St. Vladimir's, 1993.

Augustine. *The Trinity (De Trinitate).* Edited by John Rotelle. Translated by Edmund Hill. Works of Saint Augustine. Hyde Park, N.Y.: New City, 1991.

Ayres, Lewis. "Between Athens and Jerusalem: Prolegomena to Anthropology in *De Trinitate.*" *Modern Theology* 8 (1992): 53–73.

_____. "The Fundamental Grammar of Augustine's Trinitarian Theology," Pages 51–76 in *Augustine and His Critics.* Edited by Robert Dodaro and George Lawless. Christian Origins. London: Routledge, 2000.

Ball, Edward, ed. *In Search of True Wisdom: Essays in Old Testament Interpretation in Honour of Ronald E. Clements.* Journal for the Study of the Old Testament: Supplement Series 300. Sheffield: Sheffield Academic, 1999.

Barnes, Michel. "Augustine in Contemporary Trinitarian Theology," *Theological Studies* 56 (1995): 237–50.

Barr, James. *Biblical Faith and Natural Theology.* The Gifford Lectures for 1991: Delivered at the University of Edinburgh. Oxford: Clarendon, 1993.

_____. "The Image of God in the Book of Genesis: A Study of Terminology."
        *Bulletin of the John Rylands Library* 51 (1968): 11–26.

Barth, Karl. *Anselm: Fides Quaerens Intellectum: Anselm's Proof of the Existence of
        God in the Context of His Theological Scheme.* Eugene, OR: Pickwick, 2009.

_____. *Church Dogmatics,* I/1–IV/4. Edited by G. W. Bromiley and T. F.
        Torrance. Edinburgh: T&T Clark, 1936–1977.

Barton, John. "Imitation of God in the Old Testament." Pages 35–46 in *The God
        of Israel.* Edited by Robert Gordon. University of Cambridge Oriental
        Publications 64. Cambridge Univeristy Press, 2007.

Bauckham, Richard. *God Crucified: Monotheism and Christology in the New
        Testament.* Grand Rapids: Eerdmans, 1998.

Bavinck, Herman. *Reformed Dogmatics.* 3 vols. Edited by John Bolt. Translated by
        John Vriend. Grand Rapids: Baker Academic, 2003–2006.

Beale, G. K. *We Become What We Worship: A Biblical Theology of Idolatry.* Downers
        Grove, Ill.: IVP Academic, 2008.

Berkouwer, G. C. *Man: The Image of God.* Studies in Dogmatics; Grand Rapids:
        Eerdmans, 1962.

Best, Ernest. *Ephesians.* International Critical Commentary. Edinburgh: T&T
        Clark, 1998.

Bird, Phyllis. "'Male and Female He Created Them': Gen 1:27b in the Context of
        the Priestly Account of Creation." *Harvard Theological Review* 74 (1981):
        129–59.

Blocher, Henri. "The Fear of the Lord as the 'Principle' of Wisdom." *Tyndale
        Bulletin* 28 (1977): 3–28.

_____. *In the Beginning: The Opening Chapters of Genesis.* Translated by David
        G. Preston. Downers Grove, Ill.: IVP, 1984.

_____. "Karl Barth's Anthropology." Pages 96–135 in *Karl Barth and
        Evangelical Theology: Convergences and Divergences.* Edited by Sung Wook
        Chung. Grand Rapids: Baker Academic, 2006.

_____. "Karl Barth's Christocentric Method" Pages 21–54 in *Engaging with
        Barth: Contemporary Evangelical Critiques.* Edited by David Gibson and
        Daniel Strange. Nottingham: Apollos, 2008.

Bonhoeffer, Dietrich. *Creation and Fall: A Theological Interpretation of Genesis 1–3.*
        Translated by John Fletcher. New York: Macmillan, 1959.

Bray, Gerald. "The Significance of God's Image in Man." *Tyndale Bulletin* 42
        (1991): 195–225.

Bromiley, Geoffrey. "Karl Barth." Pages 27–62 in *Creative Minds in Contemporary
        Theology.* 2d rev. ed. Edited by Philip Hughes. Grand Rapids: Eerdmans,
        1969.

Brown, David. *The Divine Trinity.* La Salle: Open Court, 1985.

Brubaker, Rogers, and Frederick Cooper. "Beyond 'identity'." *Theory and Society* 29 (2000): 1–47.

Bruce, F. F. *The Epistles to the Colossians, to Philemon, and to the Ephesians.* New International Commentary on the New Testament. Grand Rapids: Eerdmans, 1984.

Brueggemann, Walter. *Deuteronomy.* Abingdon Old Testament Commentaries. Nashville: Abingdon, 2001.

_____. *Genesis.* Interpretation Bible Commentary. Atlanta, John Knox, 1982.

Brunner, Emil. *Man in Revolt: A Christian Anthropology.* Translated by Olive Wyon. London: Lutterworth, 1939.

Burrell, David. *Analogy and Philosophical Language.* New Haven: Yale University Press, 1973.

_____. "Creator/Creatures Relation: 'The Distinction' vs. 'Onto-Theology.'" *Faith and Philosophy* 25 (2008): 177–89.

_____. *Exercises in Religious Understanding.* Notre Dame: University of Notre Dame Press, 1974.

_____. "Response to Hasker and Cross." *Faith and Philosophy* 25 (2008): 205–12.

Cairns, David. *The Image of God in Man.* Rev. ed. The Fontana Library of Theology and Philosophy. London: Collins, 1973.

Calvin, John. *Commentaries on the First Book of Moses called Genesis.* Vol. 1. Translated by John King. Grand Rapids: Eerdmans, 1948.

_____. *Institutes of the Christian Religion.* 2 vols. Edited by John McNeill. Translated by Ford Lewis Battles. Library of Christian Classics 20–21. Louisville: Westminster John Knox, 1960.

Canlis, Julie. "Being made human: the significance of creation for Irenaeus' doctrine of participation." *Scottish Journal of Theology* 58 (2005): 434–54.

Case, Robert. "Will the Real Athanasius Please Stand Up?" in *Journal of the Evangelical Theological Society* 19 (1976): 283–95.

Cavadini, John. "The Quest for Truth in Augustine's *De Trinitate.*" *Theological Studies* 58 (1997): 429–40.

_____. "The Structure and Intention of Augustine's *De trinitate.*" *Augustinian Studies* 23 (1992): 103–23.

Christensen, Duane. *Deuteronomy 1:1–21:9.* Rev. ed. Word Biblical Commentary 6a. Nashville: Thomas Nelson, 2001.

Chung, Sung Wook, ed. *Karl Barth and Evangelical Theology: Convergences and Divergences.* Grand Rapids: Baker Academic, 2006.

Clines, David J. A. "The Image of God in Man." *Tyndale Bulletin* 19 (1968): 53–103.

Cooper, John. *Body, Soul and Life Everlasting: Biblical Anthropology and the Monism-Dualism Debate.* New ed. Grand Rapids: Eerdmans, 2000.

Cortez, Marc. *Embodied Souls, Ensouled Bodies: An Exercise in Christological Anthropology and Its Significance for the Mind/Body Debate.* T&T Clark Studies in Systematic Theology 1. London: T&T Clark, 2008.

Crisp, Oliver. "Problems with Perichoresis." *Tyndale Bulletin* 56 (2005): 119–40.

Curtis, Edward M. "Man as the Image of God in Genesis in the Light of Ancient Near Eastern Parallels." Ph.D. diss. University of Pennsylvania, 1984.

Davies, Eryl. "Walking in God's Ways: The Concept of *Imitatio Dei* in the Old Testament." Pages 99–115 in *In Search of True Wisdom: Essays in Old Testament Interpretation in Honour of Ronald E. Clements.* Edited by Edward Ball. Journal for the Study of the Old Testament: Supplement Series 300. Sheffield: Sheffield Academic, 1999.

Davis, Ellen and Richard Hays, eds. *The Art of Reading Scripture.* Grand Rapids: Eerdmans, 2003.

de Margerie, Bertrand. *La Trinité chrétienne dans l'histoire.* Theologie historique 31. Paris: Beauchesne, 1975.

de Régnon, Théodore. *Études de théologie positive sur la Sainte Trinité.* Paris: Victor Retaux, 1892/1898.

Dion, Paul E. "Ressemblance et image de Dieu." Columns 365–403 in *Supplément au dictionnaire de la Bible.* Vol. X. Edited by Henri Cazelles and André Feuillet. Paris: Letouzey and Ané, 1985.

Dodaro, Robert, and George Lawless, eds. *Augustine and His Critics.* Christian Origins. London: Routledge, 2000.

Dunn, James. *The Epistles to the Colossians and Philemon.* New International Greek Testament Commentary. Grand Rapids: Eerdmans, 1996.

Eichrodt, Walther. *Theology of the Old Testament.* 2 vols. Translated by J. A. Baker. Old Testament Library. Philadelphia: Westminster, 1961.

Emery, Gilles. *The Trinitarian Theology of Saint Thomas Aquinas.* Translated by Francesca Aran Murphy. Oxford University Press, 2007.

Fackre, Gabriel. *The Doctrine of Revelation: A Narrative Interpretation.* Edinburgh Studies in Constructive Theology. Edinburgh University Press, 1997.

Fermer, Richard. "The Limits of Trinitarian Theology as a Methodological Paradigm." *Neue Zeitschrift für Systematische Theologie* 41 (1999): 158–86.

Fowl, Stephen. *Engaging Scripture: A Model for Theological Interpretation.* Challenges in Contemporary Theology. Oxford: Blackwell, 1998.

_____. "The Role of Authorial Intention in the Theological Interpretation of Scripture." Pages 71–87 in *Between Two Horizons.* Edited by Joel Green and Max Turner. Grand Rapids: Eerdmans, 2000.

Fraikin, Daniel. "Ressemblance et image de Dieu." Columns 403–414 in *Supplément au dictionnaire de la Bible.* Vol. X. Edited by Henri Cazelles and André Feuillet. Paris: Letouzey and Ané, 1985.

Frei, Hans. *The Identity of Jesus Christ.* Eugene, Ore.: Wipf and Stock, 1997.

_____. *The Identity of Jesus Christ: The Hermeneutical Bases of Dogmatic Theology.* Philadelphia: Fortress, 1975.

_____. "Theological Reflections on the Accounts of Jesus' Death and Resurrection," *Christian Scholar* 49 (1966): 263–306.

Fretheim, Terence. "The Book of Genesis: Introduction, Commentary, and Reflections." Pages 319-674 in *The New Interpreter's Bible.* Vol. 1. Edited by Leander Keck et al. Nashville: Abingdon, 1994.

_____. *The Suffering of God: An Old Testament Perspective.* Overtures to Biblical Theology 14. Minneapolis: Fortress, 1984.

Frost, Robert. "Aristotle's Ethics: The Real Reason for Luther's Reformation?" *Trinity Journal* 18 (1997): 223–41.

_____. "'Scholaticism, Reformation, Orthodoxy, and the Persistence of Christian Aristotelianism': A Brief Rejoinder." *Trinity Journal* 19 (1998): 97–101.

Garr, W. Randall. *In His Own Image and Likeness: Humanity, Divinity, and Monotheism.* Culture and History of the Ancient Near East 15. Leiden: Brill, 2003.

Geertz, Clifford. *The Interpretation of Cultures.* Scranton, Penn.: Basic, 1977.

Gibson, David, and Daniel Strange, eds., *Engaging with Barth: Contemporary Evangelical Critiques.* Nottingham: Apollos, 2008.

Gladd, Benjamin. "The Last Adam as the 'Life-Giving Spirit' Revisited: A Possible Old Testament Background of One of Paul's Most Perplexing Phrases," *Westminster Theological Journal* 71 (2009): 297–309.

Gombis, Timothy. "The Triumph of God in Christ: Divine Warfare in the Argument of Ephesians." Ph.D. diss. University of St. Andrews, 2004.

Gordon, Robert. *The God of Israel.* University of Cambridge Oriental Publications. Cambridge University Press, 2007.

Green, Joel and Max Turner, eds. *Between Two Horizons: Spanning New Testament Studies and Systematic Theology.* Grand Rapids: Eerdmans, 2000.

Gregory of Nyssa, *On the Making of Man.* Vol. 5 of *The Nicene and Post-Nicene Fathers,* Series 2. Edited by Philip Schaff. 1886–1888. 14 vols. United States: Christian Literature Publishing Co., 1888. Reprint, Peabody, Mass.: Hendrickson, 1994.

Grenz, Stanley. *The Social God and the Relational Self: A Trinitarian Theology of the Imago Dei.* Louisville: Westminster John Knox, 2001.

Grillmeier, Aloys. *Christ in Christian Tradition.* Vol. 1: *From the Apostolic Age to Chalcedon.* Translated by J. S. Bowden. London: Mowbray, 1965.

Gundry, Robert. *Sōma in Biblical Theology: With Emphasis on Pauline Anthropology.* Society for New Testament Monographs Series 29. Cambridge University Press, 1976.

Gunkel, Hermann. *Genesis: Translated and Interpreted by Hermann Gunkel.* Translated by Mark E. Bibble. Macon, GA: Mercer University Press, 1997.

Gunton, Colin. "Augustine, the Trinity and the Theological Crisis of the West." *Scottish Journal of Theology* 43 (1990): 33–58.

_____. *A Brief Theology of Revelation.* New York: T&T Clark, 1995.

_____. *Christ and Creation.* Carlisle: Paternoster, 1992.

_____. *The Promise of Trinitarian Theology.* Edinburgh: T&T Clark, 1991.

_____. *The Triune Creator: A Historical and Systematic Study.* Edinburgh Studies in Constructive Theology. Grand Rapids: Eerdmans, 1998.

Gunton, Colin, ed. *The Cambridge Companion to Christian Doctrine.* Cambridge Companions to Religion. Cambridge University Press, 1997.

Hall, Douglas. *Imaging God: Dominion as Stewardship.* Grand Rapids: Eerdmans, 1986.

Hamilton, Victor. *The Book of Genesis: Chapters 1-17.* New International Commentary on the Old Testament. Grand Rapids: Eerdmans, 1990.

Harris, Harriet. "Should We Say that Personhood is Relational?" *Scottish Journal of Theology* 51 (1998): 214–34.

Harris, Murray. *The Second Epistle to the Corinthians.* New International Greek Testament Commentary. Grand Rapids: Eerdmans, 2005.

Harrison, Nonna Verna. "Greek Patristic Foundations of Trinitarian Anthropology." *Pro Ecclesia* 14 (2005): 399–412.

Hart, Trevor, and Daniel Thimell, eds. *Christ in our Place: The Humanity of God in Christ for the Reconciliation of the World: Essays Presented to Professor James Torrance.* Princeton Theological Monograph Series 25. Exeter: Paternoster, 1989.

Hart, Trevor. "Irenaeus, Recapitulation, and Physical Redemption." Pages 152–81 in *Christ in our Place: The Humanity of God in Christ for the Reconciliation of the World: Essays Presented to Professor James Torrance.* Princeton Theological Monograph Series 25. Edited by Trevor Hart and Daniel Thimell. Exeter: Paternoster, 1989.

Hartley, John. *Leviticus.* Word Biblical Commentary 4. Dallas: Word, 1992.

Hill, Edmund. "Introduction," Pages 18–59 in *The Trinity* (De Trinitate). Translated Edmund Hill. Works of Saint Augustine. Hyde Park, NY: New City, 1991.

Hodge, Charles. *Systematic Theology.* Vol. 2: *Anthropology.* Grand Rapids: Eerdmans, 1946.

Hoehner, Harold. *Ephesians: An Exegetical Commentary.* Grand Rapids: Baker Academic, 2002.

Hoekema, Anthony. *Created in God's Image.* Grand Rapids: Eerdmans, 1986.

Horton, Michael. *Covenant and Eschatology: The Divine Drama.* Louisville: Westminster John Knox, 2002.

_____. *Lord and Servant: A Covenantal Christology.* Louisville: Westminster John Knox, 2005.

Houston, Walter. "The Character of YHWH and the Ethics of the Old Testament: Is *Imitatio Dei* Appropriate?" *Journal of Theological Studies* 58 (2007): 1–25.

Hughes, Philip Edgcumbe. *The True Image: The Origin and Destiny of Man in Christ.* Grand Rapids: Eerdmans, 1989.

Humbert, Paul. *Etudes sur le récit du Paradis et de la chute dans la Genèse.* Mémoires de l'Université de Neuchâtel 14. Secretariat de l'Université de Neuchâtel, 1940.

Irenaeus of Lyons. *Against Heresies.* Vol. 1 of *The Ante-Nicene Fathers.* Edited by Philip Schaff. 10 vols. United States: Christian Literature Publishing Co., 1888. Reprint, Peabody, Mass.: Hendrickson, 1994.

Jenson, Robert. *The Triune Identity: God According to the Gospel.* Minneapolis: Fortress, 1982.

Jervell, Jacob. *Imago Dei: Gen. 1, 26 f. im Spätjudentum, in der Gnosis und in den paulinischen Briefen.* Göttingen: Vandenhoeck & Ruprecht, 1960.

Jónsson, Gunnlauger A. *The Image of God: Genesis 1:26-28 in a Century of Old Testament Research.* Translated by Lorraine Svendsen. Revised by Michael Cheney. Coniectanea Biblica Old Testament Series 26. Stockholm, Sweden: Almqvist and Wiksell, 1988.

Kelsey, David. *Eccentric Existence: A Theological Anthropology.* 2 vols. Louisville: Westminster John Knox, 2009.

_____. "The Human Creature," Pages 121–39 in *The Oxford Handbook of Systematic Theology.* Edited by John Webster, Kathryn Tanner, and Iain Torrance. Oxford Handbooks in Religion and Theology. Oxford University Press, 2007.

Köhler, Ludwig. *Old Testament Theology.* Translated by A. S. Todd. Library of Theological Translations. Philadelphia: Westminster, 1957.

Krötke, Wolf. "The humanity of the human person in Karl Barth's anthropology." Pages 159–176 in *The Cambridge Companion to Karl Barth.* Edited by John Webster. Cambridge Companions to Religion. Cambridge University Press, 2000.

LaCugna, Catherine Mowry. *God for Us.* San Francisco: Harper, 1991.

Levenson, Jon. "The Temple and the World." *Journal of Religion* 64 (1984): 275–98.

Levering, Matthew. "The *Imago Dei* in David Novak and Thomas Aquinas: A Jewish Christian Dialogue," *The Thomist: A Speculative Quarterly Review* 72 (2008): 259–311.

_____. *Scripture and Metaphysics: Aquinas and the Renewal of Trinitarian Theology*. Challenges in Contemporary Theology. Malden, Mass.: Blackwell, 2004.

Lieu, Judith. *I, II, & III John: A Commentary*. New Testament Library. Louisville: Westminster John Knox, 2008.

Lincoln, Andrew. *Ephesians*. Word Biblical Commentary 42. Waco: Word, 1990.

Lohse, Bernard. *Martin Luther's Theology: Its Historical and Systematic Development*. Edinburgh: T&T Clark, 1999.

Long, D. Stephen. "Moral Theology." Pages 456–75 in *The Oxford Handbook of Systematic Theology*. Edited by John Webster, Kathryn Tanner, and Iain Torrance. Oxford Handbooks in Religion and Theology. Oxford University Press, 2007.

Louth, Andrew, ed. *Genesis 1-11*. Ancient Christian Commentary on Scripture, Old Testament I. Downers Grove, IL: IVP, 2001.

Luther, Martin. *Luther's Works*. American Edition. 55 vols. Edited by Jaroslav Pelikan and Helmut T. Lehmann. Philadelphia: Muehlenberg and Fortress, and St. Louis: Concordia, 1955–1986.

Lyman, J. Rebecca. *Christology and Cosmology: Models in Divine Activity in Origen, Eusebius, and Athanasius*. Oxford Theological Monographs. Oxford University Press, 1993.

MacDonald, Nathan. "The *Imago Dei* and Election: Reading Genesis 1:26–28 and Old Testament Scholarship with Karl Barth." *International Journal of Systematic Theology* 10 (2008): 303–27.

Marshall, I. Howard. *The Epistles of John*. New International Commentary on the New Testament. Grand Rapids: Eerdmans, 1978.

Martin, Ralph. *2 Corinthians*. Word Biblical Commentary 40. Waco: Word, 1986.

McCormack, Bruce. *Karl Barth's Critically Realistic Dialectical Theology: Its Genesis and Development 1909-1936*. Oxford: Clarendon, 1995.

_____. "Seek God where he may be found: a response to Edwin Chr. van Driel." *Scottish Journal of Theology* 60 (2007): 62–79.

McFadyen, Alistair. *The Call to Personhood: A Christian Theory of the Individual in Social Relationships*. Cambridge: Cambridge University Press, 1990.

McFarland, Ian. *Difference and Identity: A Theological Anthropology*. Cleveland: Pilgrim, 2001.

_____. "The Body of Christ: Rethinking a Classic Ecclesiological Model." *International Journal of Systematic Theology* 7 (2005): 225–45.

_____. *The Divine Image: Envisioning the Invisible God*. Minneapolis: Augsburg Fortress, 2005.

Meiring, E. P. *Orthodoxy and Platonism in Athanasius: Synthesis or Antithesis?* Leiden: Brill, 1968.

Merriell, D. Juvenal. *To the Image of the Trinity: A Study in the Development of Aquinas' Teaching.* Studies and Texts 96; Toronto: Pontifical Institute of Medieval Studies, 1990.

Middleton, J. Richard. *The Liberating Image: The* Imago Dei *in Genesis 1.* Grand Rapids: Brazos, 2005.

Milgrom, Jacob. *Leviticus 17-22: A New Translation with Introduction and Commentary.* Anchor Bible. New York: Doubleday, 2000.

Moltmann, Jürgen. *God in Creation: An Ecological Doctrine of Creation.* London: SCM, 1985.

Moule, C. F. D. *The Epistles of Paul the Apostle to the Colossians and to Philemon.* Cambridge Greek Testament Commentary. Cambridge University Press, 1957.

Muller, Richard. "Scholasticism, Reformation, Orthodoxy, and the Persistence of Christian Aristotelianism." *Trinity Journal* 19 (1998): 81–96.

Oberman, Heiko. *The Dawn of the Reformation: Essays in Late Medieval and Early Reformation Thought.* Edinburgh: T&T Clark, 1986.

Oberman, Heiko. *Luther: Man Between God and the Devil.* Translated by Eileen Walliser-Schwartzbart. London: Yale University Press, 1989.

O'Brien, Peter. *Colossians, Philemon.* Word Biblical Commentary 44. Waco: Word, 1982.

_____. *The Letter to the Ephesians.* Pillar New Testament Commentary. Grand Rapids: Eerdmans, 1999.

O'Donovan, Oliver. *Resurrection and Moral Order: An Outline for Evangelical Ethics.* 2d ed. Grand Rapids: Eerdmans, 1994.

Origen, *On First Principles: Being Koetschau's Text of the* De Principiis *Translated into English, Together with an Introduction and Notes by G. W. Butterworth.* Translated by G. W. Butterworth. London: SPCK, 1936. Reprint, Gloucester, Mass.: Peter Smith, 1973.

Otto, Eckart. *Theologische Ethik des Alten Testaments.* Theologische Wissenschaft. Stuttgart: Verlag W. Kohlhammer, 1994.

Ozment, Stephen. *Homo Spiritualis: A Comparative Study of the Anthropology of Johannes Tauler, Jean Gerson and Martin Luther (1509-1516) in the Context of Their Theological Thought.* Studies in Medieval and Reformation Thought 6. Leiden: Brill, 1969.

Pasnau, Robert. *Thomas Aquinas on Human Nature: A Philosophical Study of Summa Theologiae 1a 75-89.* Cambridge University Press, 2002.

Pecknold, C. C. "How Augustine Used the Trinity: Functionalism and the Development of Doctrine." *Anglican Theological Review* 85 (2003): 127–42.

Pelikan, Jaroslav. "Introduction." In Vol. 34 of *Luther's Works*. American Edition. 55 vols. Edited by Jaroslav Pelikan and Helmut T. Lehmann; Philadelphia: Muehlenberg and Fortress, and St. Louis: Concordia, 1955-1986.

_____. *The Christian Tradition: A History of the Development of Doctrine*. 5 vols. London: University of Chicago Press, 1975–1991.

Pettersen, Alvyn. *Athanasius*. London: Geoffrey Chapman, 1995.

Pettersen, Alvyn. *Athanasius and the Human Body*. Bristol: Bristol, 1990.

Philo. *On the Decalogue*. Loeb Classical Library 320. Translated by F. H. Colson. Cambridge, Mass.: Harvard University Press, 1968.

Placher, William. *The Domestication of Transcendence: How Modern Thinking About God Went Wrong*. Louisville: Westminster John Knox, 1996.

Plantinga, Alvin. *Warranted Christian Belief*. New York: Oxford University Press, 2000.

Plantinga, Cornelius. *Not the Way It's Supposed to Be: A Breviary of Sin*. Grand Rapids: Eerdmans, 1995.

Power, William. "*Imago Dei—Imitatio Dei*," *International Journal for Philosophy of Religion* 42 (1997): 131–41.

Procksch, Otto. *Theologie des Alten Testaments*. Gütersloh: C. Bertelsmann, 1950.

Quash, Ben. "Revelation." Pages 325–44 in *The Oxford Handbook of Systematic Theology*. Edited by John Webster, Kathryn Tanner, and Iain Torrance. Oxford Handbooks in Religion and Theology. Oxford University Press, 2007.

Radner, Ephraim. *Leviticus*. Brazos Theological Commentary on the Bible. Grand Rapids: Brazos, 2008.

Ricoeur, Paul. *Oneself as Another*. Translated by Kathleen Blamey. University of Chicago Press, 1992.

Rodd, Cyril. *Glimpses of a Strange Land: Studies in Old Testament Ethics*. Old Testament Studies. Edinburgh: T&T Clark, 2001.

Rowley, Harold Henry. *The Faith of Israel: Aspects of Old Testament Thought: The James Sprunt Lectures Delivered at Union Theological Seminary, Richmond, Virginia, 1955*. London: SCM, 1956.

Schürer, Emil. *History of the Jewish People in the Age of Jesus Christ*. Edited and Revised by Geza Vermes, Fergus Millar, and Matthew Black. Edinburgh: T&T Clark, 1973.

Schwöbel, Christoph, and Colin Gunton, eds. *Persons, Human and Divine: King's College Essays in Theological Anthropology*. Edinburgh: T&T Clark, 1991.

Sherlock, Charles. *The Doctrine of Humanity*. Contours of Christian Theology. Downers Grove, Ill.: IVP, 1996.

Shults, F. LeRon. *Reforming Theological Anthropology: After the Philosophical Turn to Relationality*. Grand Rapids: Eerdmans, 2003.

Smail, Tom. *Like Father, Like Son: The Trinity Imaged in Our Humanity.* Grand Rapids: Eerdmans, 2005.

Smalley, Stephen. *1, 2, 3 John.* Word Biblical Commentary 51. Waco: Word, 1984.

Steenberg, M. C. "Children in Paradise: Adam and Eve as 'Infants' in Irenaeus of Lyons." *Journal of Early Christian Studies* 12 (2004): 1–22.

Tanner, Kathryn. *God and Creation in Christian Theology.* Minneapolis: Fortress, 2005.

Taylor, Charles. *Sources of the Self: The Making of the Modern Identity.* Cambridge, Mass.: Harvard University Press, 1989.

Thiemann, Ronald. *Revelation and Theology: The Gospel as Narrated Promise.* Notre Dame: University of Notre Dame Press, 1985.

Treier, Daniel. *Introducing Theological Interpretation of Scripture: Recovering a Christian Practice.* Grand Rapids: Baker Academic, 2008.

_____. "Proverb 8." Pages 57–72 in *Theological Commentary: Evangelical Perspectives.* Edited by R. Michael Allen. New York: T&T Clark, 2011.

_____. *Virtue and the Voice of God: Toward Theology as Wisdom.* Grand Rapids: Eerdmans, 2006.

Twomey, Vincent. *Apostolikos Thronos: The Primacy of Rome as Reflected in the Church History of Eusebius and the Historico-Apologetic Writings of Saint Athanasius the Great.* Münsterisch Beitrage zur Theologie 49. Münster Westgalen: Ashendorffsche Buchdruckerei, 1982.

van Driel, Edwin Chr. "Karl Barth on the Eternal Existence of Jesus Christ." *Scottish Journal of Theology* 60 (2007): 45–61.

Vanhoozer, Kevin, ed. *Dictionary for Theological Interpretation of the Bible.* Grand Rapids: Baker, 2005.

_____. *The Trinity in a Pluralistic Age: Theological Essays on Culture and Religion.* Grand Rapids: Eerdmans, 1997.

Vanhoozer, Kevin. "Does the Trinity Belong in a Theology of Religions?" Pages 41–71 in *The Trinity in a Pluralistic Age: Theological Essays on Culture and Religion.* Edited by Kevin Vanhoozer. Grand Rapids: Eerdmans, 1997.

_____. *The Drama of Doctrine: A Canonical-Linguistic Approach to Christian Theology.* Louisville: Westminster John Knox, 2005.

_____. "Human Being, Individual and Social." Pages 158-88 in *The Cambridge Companion to Christian Doctrine.* Edited by Colin Gunton. Cambridge Companions to Religion. Cambridge University Press, 1997.

_____. *Is There a Meaning in this Text?: The Bible, the Reader, and the Morality of Literary Knowledge.* Grand Rapids: Zondervan, 1998.

_____. "Pilgrim's Digress: Christian Thinking on and about the Post/Modern Way." Pages 71–104 in *Christianity and the Postmodern Turn.* Edited by Myron Penner. Grand Rapids: Brazos, 2005.

Vischer, Wilhelm. *Das Christuszeugnis des Alten Testaments.* 2 vols. Zürich: Evangelishe Verlag, 1943.

Volf, Miroslav. *After Our Likeness: The Church as the Image of the Trinity.* Sacra Doctrina: Christian Theology for a Postmodern Age. Grand Rapids: Eerdmans, 1997.

von Rad, Gerhard. *Genesis: A Commentary.* Rev. ed. Translated by John Marks. Old Testament Library. Philadelphia: Westminster, 1972.

Vriezen, Theodorus C. *An Outline of Old Testament Theology.* Translated by S. Neuijen. Oxford: Blackwell, 1958.

Walton, John. *Genesis.* NIV Application Commentary. Grand Rapids: Zondervan, 2001.

_____. *Genesis One as Ancient Cosmology.* Forthcoming. Winona Lake, Ind: Eisenbrauns, 2010.

Watson, Francis. *Text and Truth: Redefining Biblical Theology.* Grand Rapids: Eerdmans, 1997.

_____. *Text, Church and World: Biblical Interpretation in Theological Perspective.* Grand Rapids: Eerdmans, 1994.

Webster, John. *Barth.* London: Continuum, 2000.

_____. *Barth's Earlier Theology: Four Studies.* New York: T&T Clark, 2005.

_____. *Barth's Ethics of Reconciliation.* Cambridge University Press, 1995.

_____. *The Domain of the Word: Scripture and Theological Reason.* New York: T&T Clark, 2012.

_____. *Holiness.* London: SCM, 2003.

_____. *Holy Scripture: A Dogmatic Sketch.* Current Issues in Theology. Cambridge University Press, 2003.

_____. "Introducing Barth." Pages 1–16 in *The Cambridge Companion to Karl Barth.* Edited by John Webster. Cambridge Companions to Religion. Cambridge University Press, 2000.

_____. "Principles of Systematic Theology." *International Journal of Systematic Theology* 11 (2009): 56–71.

_____. "Trinity and Creation." *International Journal of Systematic Theology* 12 (2010): 4–19.

Webster, John, ed. *The Cambridge Companion to Karl Barth.* Cambridge Companions to Religion. Cambridge University Press, 2000.

Webster, John, Kathryn Tanner, and Iain Torrance, eds. *The Oxford Handbook of Systematic Theology.* Oxford Handbooks in Religion and Theology. Oxford University Press, 2007.

Wenham, Gordon. *Genesis 1–15.* Word Biblical Commentary 1. Nashville: Thomas Nelson, 1987.

Westcott, Frederick. *Colossians: A Letter to Asia: Being a Paraphrase and Brief Exposition of the Epistle of Paul to the Apostle to the Believers at Colossae.* London: Macmillan, 1914. Reprint, Minneapolis: Klock & Klock, 1981.

Westermann, Claus. *Genesis 1-11: A Commentary.* Translated by John Scullion. London: SPCK, 1984.

Williams, Rowan. *On Christian Theology.* Challenges in Christian Theology. Oxford: Blackwell, 2000.

Wolterstorff, Nicholas. *Justice: Right and Wrongs.* Princeton University Press, 2008.

Work, Telford. *Deuteronomy.* Brazos Theological Commentary on the Bible. Grand Rapids: Brazos, 2009.

Zachman, Randall. *The Assurance of Faith: Conscience in the Theology of Martin Luther and John Calvin.* Minneapolis: Fortress, 1993.

Zizioulas, John. *Being as Communion: Studies in Personhood and the Church.* London: Darton, Longman and Todd, 1985.

# Scripture Index

*Scripture Index*

# Author and Subject Index